Sunset Introduction to
Basic
Gardening

3/'82

By the Editors of Sunset Books and Sunset Magazine

LANE PUBLISHING CO. Menlo Park, California

Many thanks

to the gardeners and "plant people" who helped with this book. A special thank-you to Karla Patterson, who spent many hours researching and checking information.

Other consultants from across the country who assisted us in reviewing plants are John Bracken, C. Sterling Cornelius, Barbara Cunningham, Philip Edinger, Mark M. Holeman, Gene Joyner, and Gil Whitton.

Supervising Editor:
Maureen Williams Zimmerman

Staff Editors:
John R. Dunmire
Associate Editor, *Sunset* Magazine

Dorothy N. Krell

Design:
Roger Flanagan
Paula Schlosser

Illustrations:
Carol Etow, Rik Olson,
Terrence Meagher, Charles Eckart,
Cyndie Clark-Huegel, Richard
Sachs, Dinah James, Mary Davey
Burkhardt

Cover: To brighten a garden corner, sunny marigolds are transplanted from a cell pack into the ground. Chrysanthemums in background will add autumn color. Photographed by Ells Marugg. Cover design by Zan Fox.

Contents

Understanding Your Soil 4

Planting Procedures 15

Fertilizing Techniques 29

Basic Garden Plants 33
    Shrubs, trees, annuals & biennials, perennials,
    bulbs, lawn grasses, ground covers, vines

Watering Your Garden 49

Controlling Weeds 59

Propagating New Plants 64

Summer Heat & Winter Cold 79

Garden Specialties 89
    Vegetables, fruits & berries, herbs, roses,
    succulents & cacti, house plants

Pruning, Pinching & Tying 107

Pests & Diseases 119

Garden Tools & How to Use Them 131

Using Plants Effectively 137
    Hedges, screens, backgrounds, barriers;
    exposures; paved areas & parking strips;
    shade; dramatic foliage; fragrant;
    birds, bees, & butterflies; fall color

Glossary 153

Index 158

Understanding Your Soil

- Solutions for six soil problems: page 5
- How to improve your soil: page 6
- Working the soil: page 8
- Organic soil amendments & conditioners: page 10
- Mixing a batch of potting soil: page 11
- Making compost: page 12
- Using raised beds & retaining walls: page 14

Solutions for six soil problems

If you find that certain plants do poorly regardless of care, or the whole garden grows too slowly, looks stunted, and has a high mortality rate, examine the six soil problems and solutions discussed below.

These soil problems are by no means the only ailments to occur, but they are common ones that home gardeners should be aware of.

Nursery personnel, experienced local gardeners, and agricultural extension agents can be helpful in testing or evaluating your soil. You could also get a detailed analysis from a commercial laboratory or use a do-it-yourself soil testing kit. The kits are widely available and will give you a good idea of the status of your soil.

Acidity

Acid soil is at the other end of the scale from alkaline soil. It is most common in areas of heavy rainfall and is often associated with sandy soil (but ocean beaches are rarely or never acid). Soils high in organic matter tend to be acid rather than alkaline.

Mildly acid soils cause little trouble, and some plants—azaleas, rhododendrons, and camellias, to name a few—prefer soil that is moderately acid. But for most plants an intense acid condition is highly undesirable.

When a test indicates that soil is acid, adding liming materials will help to neutralize it, since all acid soils are low in calcium (lime). Fertilizers can be another very important factor in controlling acidity: some fertilizers can actually increase soil acidity.

Alkalinity

Alkaline soil, common in light-rainfall areas, is soil that is high in calcium carbonate (lime) and certain other minerals. Many plants will grow well in a moderately alkaline soil, though camellias and other acid-loving plants will not.

Gardens in which softened water is used are quite likely to have alkaline soil.

Gypsum may be useful in some alkaline soils; iron and sulfur benefit moderately alkaline soils. Since large-scale chemical treatment of extremely alkaline soils is expensive and complex, it might be easier to plant in improved soil in raised beds and containers.

Chlorosis

Chlorosis is a plant condition frequently caused by the inability of plants to take in iron from the soil through their root systems. If the deficiency is mild, areas of yellow show up between the veins of the leaf; if the deficiency is severe, the entire leaf turns yellow.

Iron deficiency in the plant is only occasionally the result of deficient amounts of iron in the soil; more frequently it is the result of some other substance (principally lime) that renders the iron unavailable. Sometimes chlorosis results from magnesium deficiency, even when iron is present.

Chemical treatment of the soil with chelated iron or iron sulfate can correct chlorosis. You can treat plants with serious iron shortages by spraying foliage with a special iron solution.

Nutrient deficiency

Most soils, left alone, yield the three major plant nutrients—nitrogen, phosphorus, and potassium—very slowly.

Fertilizers, either chemical or organic, are the quickest and easiest answer to a nutrient deficiency. Many complete fertilizers, containing all three major elements, are available (see the chapter on fertilizing techniques beginning on page 29). There are also formulations of nitrogen, phosphorus, or potassium compounds that provide these nutrients separately. Organic amendments and soil conditioners are also beneficial in varying degrees.

Salinity

An excess of salts in the soil is a widespread problem in arid and semiarid regions. It can prevent germination; or if plants are already growing, it stunts them and in advanced cases burns their foliage and finally kills them. Its presence can usually be detected by white deposits of salt on the surface of the soil. Frequent and shallow watering (especially with softened water), as well as use of certain fertilizers, can cause salts to build up. Periodic slow, deep watering will help wash the salts beyond roots (if there's no compacted soil).

Shallow compacted soil

A tight, impervious layer of soil can give trouble if it lies at or near the surface. Such a layer—known as hardpan—can be a natural formation or it can be manmade. Roots cannot penetrate the hard layer, and water cannot drain through it.

If the hardpan layer is thin and if your garden plot is accessible to heavy equipment, you may be able to lessen or eliminate the problem by having the soil plowed to a depth of 12 inches or more. If this is impractical, you can drill through it with a soil auger when planting. If the layer is too thick, you may want to have a landscape architect help you with a drainage system, which might involve sumps (side or bottom) or drain tiles. Or you can switch to raised beds and container gardening.

How to improve your soil

In some gardens the soil is like glue when it's wet and like brick when it's dry. In others you can pour on water until the bill reaches three figures and still find some plants drying up. But even if that first spadeful of soil looks as if it wouldn't grow weeds, there's no reason to be discouraged. With a little time and effort you can improve almost any soil.

Soil types

Soil is a mass of mineral particles mixed with living and dead organic matter, incorporating quantities of air and water. The size and form of the mineral particles chiefly determine the structure of the soil. Clay particles are the smallest, sand particles are the largest, and silt represents the intermediate size. Clay and sand give their names to two soil textures, while a combination of the three particle sizes forms loam soil.

Clay soil. Called either clay or adobe, heavy soil is easy to recognize but hard to work with. When it's wet it sticks to your spade. Squeeze a handful together and you'll get a gummy plastic mass that doesn't break apart even if you tap it with your shovel. When heavy soil dries, it tends to crack, and often becomes hard enough to deflect a pick.

There's little air in soil like this, and drainage is poor. Plant roots will refuse to grow because of the lack of air and often drown because of the lack of drainage.

You can improve heavy soil by adding an organic amendment, such as compost, peat moss, or leaf mold. Mixed in thoroughly, these materials immediately create countless tiny air pockets between the flat plates of clay. As they continue to decay, a material called "humus"

forms, preventing the clay particles from packing down again.

The advantage of heavy soil is that this type of soil tends to retain moisture and fertilizer. And if you improve it by adding an amendment, heavy soil pays you back by making every drop of water and every ounce of fertilizer count.

Sandy soil. At its worst, sandy soil is the exact opposite of clay. No matter how often you wet it, the big rounded particles quickly dry up.

There's plenty of air in soil like this, and roots can go where they like. But water pours right through, taking with it any fertilizer.

Sandy soil can also be improved by the addition of organic amendments. The amendment particles fill the open spaces between sand particles and help to retain water and nutrients. As an amendment decays, however, the resulting humus tends to leach away with each watering. That won't happen right away, but if after a few seasons

you seem to be watering more than usual, give your soil another application of the organic amendment.

Soil amendments

Soil amendments, or conditioners, are of two distinctly different types.

The first type may be almost anything that comes originally from an animal or plant (bone meal, peat moss, or manure). Some organic materials are primarily a source of nutrients and are normally used in small quantities as fertilizer (see page 30). An example is bone meal, which is rich in phosphorus. Others have no nutrients but help fluff up heavy soil and then rot to produce humus (peat moss is of this type). Some contain tiny amounts of plant nutrients (manure is an example) but are used mainly as soil improvers.

The chart on page 10 will help you choose among the many kinds of organic amendments. Even the best soil will benefit from reapplications of an amendment.

The second type of amendment is purely mineral. It comes in small-chunk form. Added to fine, heavy soil, it stays in place more or less permanently. Some examples are sand, perlite, pumice, and vermiculite. Most of these materials are too expensive for large areas but are often used in special soil mixtures for containers.

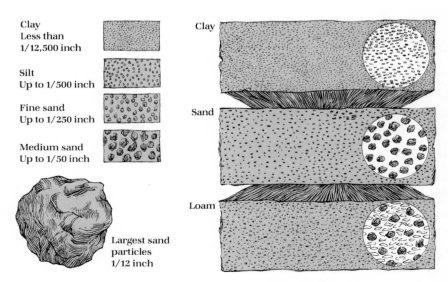

Clay
Less than
1/12,500 inch

Silt
Up to 1/500 inch

Fine sand
Up to 1/250 inch

Medium sand
Up to 1/50 inch

Largest sand
particles
1/12 inch

Clay

Sand

Loam

Soil type *is chiefly the result of the size and form of mineral particles.*

Texture is important. In choosing an amendment, give special consideration to texture. In the chart on page 10, texture is described in the column "Pros & Cons."

If possible, select an amendment that is granular and fine-grained for container mixes (see page 11). Granular materials give an even texture to the potting soil. More variable, coarser-grained amendments are beneficial in providing drainage in the open ground (but don't use extremely large chunks here, either). The variable-size pieces aid in water penetration and improve aeration of the soil.

Check for salt content. If you live in an area with an average amount of rainfall, some salt content in soil amendments will cause little if any trouble. But if you live in a region with low rainfall, the salt content is crucial. Manures often contain quantities of salts. Without heavy rains to wash away these salts, you may find that young or sensitive plants begin to show burned leaf edges.

What about nitrogen? Materials such as sawdust, ground bark, and straw decompose quickly after you mix them with soil. The rotting agents are fungus and bacteria. As they work to break down the amendment, they use up nitrogen. Unless you add nitrogen to the soil along with these amendments, plants will not have enough nitrogen for growth.

You can use either a chemical fertilizer, such as ammonium nitrate, or an organic fertilizer, such as blood meal. Both chemical and organic fertilizers can injure plants if applied too heavily or too frequently, though most organics are safer for plants. Avoid over-fertilizing with any product.

The chart on page 10 gives—in number of actual pounds—the amount of nitrogen you should add to your amendment. If you choose a chemical fertilizer, the package label tells you only the *percentage* of nitrogen it contains, so you'll have to translate the first number on the package of fertilizer into *actual* pounds of nitrogen.

Look for a group of three numbers on the label, something like 10–8–6. From left to right, these numbers give the percentage of nitrogen, phosphorus, and potassium in the material. The hypothetical 10–8–6 fertilizer contains 10 percent nitrogen compounds.

Nitrogen %

Percentage of nitrogen in a given fertilizer is always the first number listed on the package.

If you use raw redwood sawdust, you'll need to add 1/3 pound *actual* nitrogen for each 10 cubic feet of sawdust you add to the soil. If you have a 25-pound bag of fertilizer labeled 10–8–6, you would calculate that 10 percent of 25 pounds is 2.5. That means that the bag of fertilizer contains 2.5 pounds of actual nitrogen. Since you need to add 1/3 pound of nitrogen, you will use roughly 1/7 of the fertilizer. Just approximate what you'll need— you don't have to be exact in measuring.

How much is ash? Also an important consideration in choosing an organic amendment is the quantity of ash (mineral matter) it contains. Ash is of questionable value in improving soil. And the higher the percentage, the less efficient the conditioner.

For example, a truckload of fine sawdust may contain from 1/2 to 3 percent ash. A truckload of poor-quality manure may contain up to 50 percent ash. Almost every grain of the sawdust is useful as a soil improver, while half the manure is composed of salts, stable dust and dirt, gravel scooped up with the manure, or possibly just earth from the pens.

Will it hold fertilizer? The professionals use a complicated term — "cation exchange capacity"—when they are talking about whether the fertilizer you add to amended soil is

going to stay there. Some conditioners will hold to nitrogen and other nutrients; others let them wash away.

Wood products are poor at holding nutrients, but that doesn't matter if the soil is heavy, since it's already a good nutrient holder. Because peat moss does the best job of conserving added nutrients, it is ideal for use in containers and sandy soils. Manure actually supplies nutrients on its own and is also good in sandy soil. Because of its salt content, though, it should not be used in containers.

How much do you add? When you add an amendment, the final soil mixture should contain at least one-quarter amendment and three-quarters soil. But if your soil is almost pure clay or sand, the finished mix should contain about half amendment and half soil.

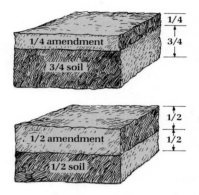

Proportion of amendment to soil varies; use more amendment with soil of mostly clay or sand. Spread amendment layer over soil; mix thoroughly.

If your spade or rotary tiller penetrates 9 inches deep (most do), you should apply a 2 to 3-inch layer of amendment over normal soil before cultivating. For a half-and-half mix, you'll need enough conditioner to make a 4 to 5-inch layer. For instructions on cultivating the soil and working the amendment in evenly, see pages 8 and 9.

Keep in mind that the greater the quantity of amendment you mix in, the more you increase your soil's air and moisture holding capacity—don't skimp.

Working the soil

There's a special language, spoken by gardeners, nursery people, and garden writers, that's a sort of jargon of the trade. It's full of words and expressions that are puzzling to beginners and, quite frequently, not fully understood by more experienced gardeners.

For example, during the spring planting months you find this kind of advice in print almost everywhere: "A week before you plan to plant, cultivate the planting bed deeply and add generous amounts of humus, mixing it thoroughly with the soil. Your purpose is to get a soil that is friable, crumbly, well drained and well aerated."

This is perfectly good garden language, but it's written in shorthand. It attempts to describe the total process of preparing the soil for planting. Analyze that paragraph and you can see that there could be almost as many meanings as there are gardeners. Look at these words and terms: *cultivate, generous, friable, well drained.* What do they mean?

A study of the illustrations here, plus the information on the preceding two pages, will do more than merely clarify these terms; it will give you some basic know-how that can help you in nearly all of your gardening endeavors.

Spade or shovel?

The hard work of turning up the soil will seem a little easier if you use a *spade.* It should be square, sharp, and straight or nearly straight in its shank. When you push it into firm earth with your foot, you want all the force to go straight down the blade. And if you use a file to keep it sharpened, roots and clods of soil won't be major obstacles.

A scoop-shaped *shovel,* with its pointed blade, is the best tool for mixing or turning loose materials. You handle it as if it were a combination of a spade and scoop. The point on the shovel helps you to slide it into the material, and the concave blade keeps the material from sliding off as you lift and turn. A shovel blade is set at an angle to the shaft so it stays flat when you push it horizontally into a pile of material.

Dig with a straight-edged spade, scoop with a curved shovel (right).

In spading up small areas of soil, many gardeners make the mistake of turning each spadeful of earth completely over. If you do this, any weeds, leaves, or other debris in the soil will form a one-spade-deep barrier that cuts off air and water. Instead, you should lay the dirt on its side (against the previous shovelful) so the original surface is vertical to the ground (see sketch).

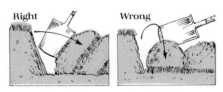

Turn the soil half over, not completely upside down.

Machine power

Using a spade to turn the earth is fine for small areas, but for really big jobs you may want to rent or buy a power tiller. The three drawings at the far right show the basic steps in power tilling.

There is another approach you might consider as well. Because a tiller is adjustable, it can either scratch the surface or dig down several inches. If you want to add amendments to packed soil but find it hard to make the tiller dig deep enough, start tilling at a shallow depth. Go over the area a second time, even a third, with the tiller at a deeper setting each time. (Generally, the larger the tiller and the higher its horsepower, the deeper it can dig into the soil.)

In adding an amendment, you should mix in a quantity that is from a quarter to a half of the finished volume of soil. (For more information on soil amendments, see pages 6–7, 10.) Don't pile up so much amendment that the tiller can't penetrate the soil. To avoid this, start by adding the amendment in 2 or 3-inch layers, tilling in each layer.

If the amendment you choose needs nitrogen, add part of the amount with each amendment layer. Finally, don't till in the same direction each time you add a layer of amendment. For the best mix, the furrows should be at right angles to the furrows you made on your previous run.

When should you cultivate?

Before you turn the first spadeful of earth, ponder this question: How has the weather been? If the soil is gummy wet, wait until it dries out enough to crumble when you try to squeeze it into a handful. If it's brick hard, water deeply and then wait until it dries to the moist but crumbly stage (called "friable"). If your spade slides in easily, it's time to cultivate your garden.

Most gardeners tend to err in the direction of too-moist soil. If the soil is too wet, it is low in oxygen. Until it dries, root development and nutrient absorption are reduced, so plant growth is slowed. Also, harmful organisms proliferate, producing toxic substances. If you try working too-wet soil, you'll be expending extra energy needlessly.

Four notes about soil

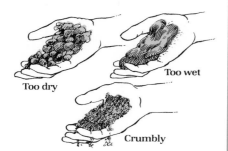
Too dry
Too wet
Crumbly

If compressed soil stays balled, it's too wet to dig. Wait until it's just dry enough to crumble.

Around established plants, cultivate shallowly to avoid cutting or exposing roots near the surface.

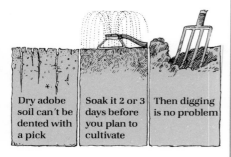
Dry adobe soil can't be dented with a pick

Soak it 2 or 3 days before you plan to cultivate

Then digging is no problem

Heavy clay or adobe soil is difficult to work when it's too dry or wet. Watering ahead helps.

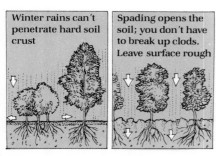
Winter rains can't penetrate hard soil crust

Spading opens the soil; you don't have to break up clods. Leave surface rough

Cultivate crusted soil in fall to reduce surface runoff in winter. Add soil amendments too.

Double-digging

1) Dig a trench 12 to 18 inches wide, 8 to 9 inches deep, running the length of planting bed.

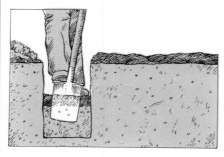

2) Mix compost or other soil amendment into the next level of soil in the trench.

3) Dig an adjoining trench, filling in the first one you dug with a mix of soil and amendment.

4) Continue digging and mixing until the entire planting area has been dug and amendments added.

Using a power tiller

1) Spread a 2 to 4-inch layer of soil amendment over soil with a rake; add nitrogen fertilizer if needed (see chart, page 10). Don't till yet.

2) Scatter superphosphate or bone meal (following package directions). If amendment is sawdust, also add chelated iron.

3) Cultivate in one direction, then at right angles, tilling top 8 or 9 inches of soil. Repeat several times to mix soil evenly with amendment.

Organic soil amendments & conditioners

The materials listed in the chart below are all useful organic amendments with dual use as mulches (see page 52). They can be dug into your soil to improve it at any time of the year.

Because organic material decomposes over a period of time, it's necessary to reapply organic amendments. An easy way to do this is to use an organic mulch, digging it into the soil every year or two and applying a new layer to the soil surface.

Availability of a specific organic amendment varies, depending on where you live. In some areas you can buy organic materials that are by-products of local industries: hops, rice hulls, yucca fiber, ground corncobs, or grape pomace, for example. Some of these you can purchase by the truckful at substantial savings; much of the cost is transportation.

One caution if you use *fresh* ground bark or sawdust: as it breaks down, it draws nitrogen from the soil—nitrogen needed by the plants. To offset this, add 2 or 3 pounds of a high-nitrogen fertilizer to each 1-inch layer of sawdust spread over 100 square feet of ground. Some packagers of these materials now fortify the amendment with nitrogen.

Organic materials that are primarily fertilizers, and are used in small quantities, are discussed under "Fertilizing Techniques" on pages 29–32.

Conditioners	Pros & Cons	Uses	Must You Add Nitrogen?	Ash Content	Nutrient Holding
Compost	Variable material, depending on what you put in. Must be well rotted, screened. May contain disease organisms.	In potting mix, mulch. Conditioner.	No.	Variable 40%	Very good
Mushroom compost	May be free near mushroom grower. Be sure it is well rotted. Moderately saline.	Conditioner.	No.	To 40%	Poor
Dairy manure	In some areas, may be free for the hauling. Moderately saline. Must be thoroughly decomposed. Has strong odor.	Conditioner in sandy soils; mulch.	No. Is a low grade fertilizer.	50%	Good
Steer manure	Sold in trade-name packages. May be very highly saline. Sometimes has strong odor.	Conditioner in sandy soils; mulch.	No. Is a low-grade fertilizer.	To 60%	Good
Stable bedding	May be free from a commercial stable, but must be well composted. Mixture of straw, chips, sawdust, and animal waste.	Conditioner.	No.	Low but variable	Fair
Sphagnum peat moss	Fibrous or powdery. Hard to wet. Do not use dry. Low salinity. Once wet, retains water better than any other amendment.	In container mix; keep damp.	No.	3%	Very good
Hypnum peat moss	Fibrous; texture more variable than sphagnum, but contains more nitrogen. Costs less.	In containers, fern baskets, garden soil.	No.	To 30%	Very good
Sedge peat	Fibrous; texture variable. May be saline. May be cheaper than sphagnum.	In rainy climate, use in garden soil.	No.	30–50%	Good
Bark	Granular. Work in well. Low salinity. Long lasting in soil. Very dense.	In garden soil; in container mix; for orchids.	Fresh bark needs 1 pound actual nitrogen per 10 cubic feet.	3–5%	Poor
Sawdust	Granular. Works in well. Low salinity. Lasts in soil. Raw sawdust may contain chips, shavings.	In garden soil or container mix.	To fresh sawdust add 1/2 pound actual nitrogen per 10 cubic feet.	2%	Poor

Mixing a batch of potting soil

Mixing potting soil is not always the large-scale operation shown here. Many gardeners, when they decide to pot up a plant or two, simply pick up a trowel and mix a small quantity of whatever they need at the moment. Or they buy a sack of ready-to-use mix at the nursery.

But if you do quite a lot of container gardening or if you're putting in some raised beds, a little shovel-and-wheelbarrow work is called for.

Good potting soil should contain sufficient nutrients for plant growth and development; it should be easy to work and easy for roots to penetrate; and it should be sufficiently porous for water to penetrate it thoroughly, yet not so open that water runs through it too rapidly.

A popular basic mixture consists of 2 parts good garden soil, 1 part sand, and 1 part peat moss or the equivalent. (You may also wish to add bone meal or other fertilizer.) This formula is subject to endless variations, depending mainly on two things: 1) the character of the soil, and 2) the kinds of plants you intend to grow.

If you have sandy soil, omit the 1 part sand and use 3 parts sandy soil. Whatever you do, never use clay soil in a container mix.

Certain plants — azaleas, camellias, and rhododendrons, for example—will not do their best unless the mix consists of at least 50 percent organic matter such as finely ground bark, peat moss, or leaf mold.

In the mixes at right, the amount of ingredients listed for a small quantity of basic mix will fill about 18 pots, 12 inches in diameter. The larger quantity of basic mix will give you a cubic yard of potting soil, enough for a raised bed.

At potting time, the mix should be damp but not wet. A good test for dampness is the same as the standard one for soil texture: squeeze a handful hard. If it falls apart quickly when the hand is opened, it's too dry; if any water comes out, it's too wet; if it retains its shape as squeezed and merely cracks slightly, it is damp enough.

BASIC MIX (For a large quantity)

(Suitable for all but acid-soil plants such as azalea, heather, rhododendron.)

2/3 yard	nitrogen-stabilized bark, sawdust, or other organic amendment
1/3 yard	sandy soil or uniform fine sand
6 pounds	0–10–10 or equivalent dry fertilizer
10 pounds	dolomite limestone

BASIC MIX (For a small quantity)

16 gallons	nitrogen-stabilized bark, sawdust, or other organic amendment
8 gallons	sandy soil or uniform fine sand
1 1/3 cups	0–10–10 or equivalent dry fertilizer
1 3/4 cups	dolomite limestone

LIGHTWEIGHT MIX

(Needed for indoor containers, hanging baskets, and outside containers in sheltered areas; may not provide sufficient support for taller plants in windy situations.)

2 parts	basic mix (above)
1 part	perlite or vermiculite

ACID MIX

(For azaleas, rhododendrons, camellias, heather, and other acid-loving plants.)

4 or 5 parts	coarse-textured peat moss
1 part	composted leaf mold

Because these mixes contain no nitrogen, they can be stored for as long as 6 months, possibly longer in a dry spot. When you plant, add nitrogen, either in slow-release capsules or in other forms such as blood meal, to guarantee nourishment for proper plant growth.

1) Prepare soil mix by putting ingredients into a large pile, tossing them into a second pile to mix, and then tossing again if the mix is not blended the first time around.

2) Scatter fertilizer and lime over the blended organic amendment and soil or sand. If you want a lightweight mix, use this stage to spread perlite or vermiculite over basic ingredients.

3) Toss again once or twice to blend ingredients. If you are making only a small quantity of soil mix, use your hands as mixing tools.

Making compost

Well-made compost is a soft, crumbly, brownish or blackish substance resulting from the decomposition of organic material. It has limited value as a nutrient source but great value as an organic soil amendment.

Composting takes time, effort, and space in which to do it. But if you have a ready supply of plant waste or a small garden that could be supplied by a continuously maintained compost pile, the time and effort might be well spent. You'll be improving your garden instead of filling garbage cans, stuffing the kitchen disposer, and hauling yard trimmings to the dump. Remember, though, that a poorly maintained compost pile will be slow to yield its reward and also may breed hordes of flies and give off an odor if animal waste is added.

In its simplest and least efficient form, composting consists of piling up grass clippings, leaves, and other garden debris plus vegetable waste from the kitchen and permitting them to decompose. In 6 weeks to 6 months, depending on temperature, moisture, and size of pieces of material, the compost will have broken down to the point that you can spade it back into your garden soil.

A better system for the average garden is to stack the material for composting to a height of 4 to 6 feet inside an enclosure that has openings in its sides for air to penetrate—a slatted bin or a wire mesh cylinder, for example. Turn the piled-up material once a week or more often to aerate the mass and to relocate pieces in various stages of decomposition (compost decomposes more rapidly in the heat and moisture of the pile's interior than on the outside). Thoroughly moisten the pile as needed; it should be about as wet as a squeezed-out sponge. If you add a few handfuls of complete fertilizer with every sizable load of raw material, the decomposition will proceed more rapidly.

A more sophisticated composting operation will have three receptacles: one for incoming raw

For a better start & finer finish

Compost shredder chops tough material like stems and branches into small pieces that will rot quickly. Wear gloves and protect your eyes when using shredder.

Sift compost through 1-inch wire screen or sieve for general garden use. Half-inch screen is preferable if you want finer-textured compost for potting soil or as lawn dressing.

This compost bin comes apart

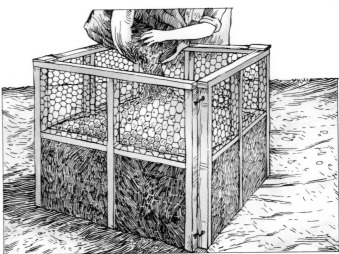

Two L-shaped frames covered with chicken wire form a simple bin. Hook and eye holds corners together. When bin is not in use, detach the two L's and place in a garage corner for space-saving storage. Sections can be any size as long as they are light enough to carry.

Use wire cylinder to try out composting

Welded wire cylinder holds compost; lift bin up and set it aside for easy turning, then fork the mixture back in.

material, one for material in the process of decomposition, and one for the finished product. If receptacles are placed side by side, it will be simple to fork or shovel material from bin to bin.

Composting is much quicker if you add only small bits and pieces of material to the pile. Depending on the size, a whole branch might take months or years to rot away; even a big leaf takes longer to decompose than a few leaf fragments. You can buy machines, both hand-cranked and powered, that will chop big pieces of organic matter into bits. Some models can be rented. And, for the rare occasion when you'll need one, city maintenance departments and tree-trimming firms often have heavy-duty choppers available for rental by the hour.

The organic process that occurs in a compost pile is simple to understand. As the material decays, fungus and bacteria grow. As they "eat" the piled waste, they produce heat, making the center of the pile very hot. Tossing and turning the pile keeps heat down.

When the compost pile has stopped producing heat in the center and the compost looks and even smells ready for use (dark, clean-smelling, earthy), fork it through a frame of fine wire screening to sift out the big pieces. Use only the fine siftings for amending your soil, and pile up the unrotted material for a second go-round.

Separate boxes for easy turning

Compost bin is a collection of bottom-less wooden frames. Treat wood with preservatives or use redwood or cedar in construction. Vary height of bin by removing or replacing box sections; remove one at a time to turn compost. Cover is old window screens.

Classic, but a little more costly

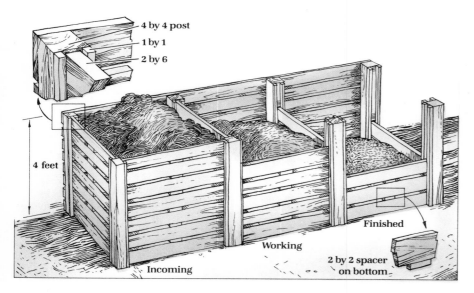

4 by 4 post
1 by 1
2 by 6
4 feet
Incoming
Working
Finished
2 by 2 spacer on bottom

Three-sectioned compost bin is a classic design. First section holds new material, which you fork into second section after it rots. Sift well-rotted material from second section into third section, which acts as storage bin until compost can be used. Front and side boards slide out for easy turning and removal of finished compost.

Using raised beds & retaining walls

Raised bed creates showcase for small tree. This type of bed is easier to reach for weeding and tending than low plantings would be.

Raised beds can be the salvation of the gardener who has perplexing soil problems—particularly if he or she is haunted by the bugaboo of poor drainage. Even if your native soil is excellent, you may want some raised beds to interrupt the monotony of a level garden or paved area.

Many of the methods used for raised beds are followed in building retaining walls as well. If you're planning a wall or a raised bed that's more than 3 feet high, you should check with your local building department about codes.

In either structure, drainage is very important. If a planting bed is open to the ground at the bottom, most excess water will drain out. If it's closed, make drainage (weep) holes on the sides about 2 or 3 inches up from the base. Space them about 2 or 3 feet apart. It's also a good idea to place an 8 to 10-inch layer of crushed rock in the bottom of the bed before you fill it with a loose soil mixture.

The soil mix you use depends on what you're planting (see page 11 for some examples). Before planting, soak the soil so it settles to a natural level. Be sure to keep soil level 3 or 4 inches below the top of the retaining wall or the sides of the raised bed.

Changing driveway grade or other construction grading may leave soil banks that crumble easily, exposing roots of existing trees or shrubs. This retaining wall holds earth, allows drainage; it is slanted into the hillside for extra strength.

Construction materials & methods

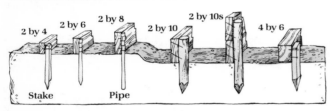

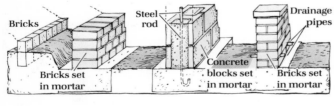

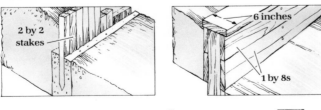

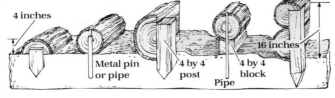

Rough-finish redwood or cedar makes good-looking low wall. It is durable and easy to install, and it weathers well. For best alignment, have one edge and one end of each board surfaced.

Masonry makes strong, enduring wall if footings go down far enough and are heavy enough. To relieve water pressure, provide small holes for drainage through the wall.

Wood stakes in a row can be pounded into ground or embedded in a narrow trench filled with concrete. A facing and cap of lumber will give sleek appearance.

Logs offer variety in shaping a wall. To get them, you might take a truck or trailer to woods and negotiate directly with loggers.

Two ideas for drainage

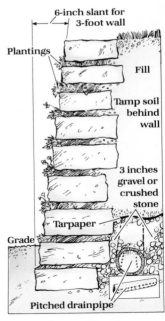

Mortarless wall makes use of two drainage ideas: planted spaces between the stones or masonry blocks and a gravel-and-pipe type of system.

Planting Procedures

- Selecting new plants: page 16
- Planting bare-root shrubs & trees: page 17
- Planting balled & burlapped shrubs & trees: page 18
- Planting from cans & large containers: page 19
- Planting from flats, cell packs, small containers: page 20
- Repotting techniques: page 22
- Planting a lawn: page 24
- Planting bulbs: page 26
- Planting a hedge & other specialties: page 27
- Transplanting a shrub or small tree: page 28

Selecting new plants

Leafy plants, dormant plants, seeds, and bulbs—all of these are ready to plant in your garden. General nurseries, specialty nurseries, garden club and arboretum sales, and mail-order catalogs all offer good stock. Your corner grocery store may have some bedding plants as well as racks of seeds; hardware and variety stores often feature nursery departments.

If you're buying plants on a hot day, don't stop off to shop or visit on the way home, leaving plants in the car—take them home promptly to a cool and protected spot. You can even wait a while to plant if you keep them watered. Most plants should be put in the ground in the relatively cool atmosphere of early evening.

Seeds. Seed racks are usually stocked with everything a given company produces for the year. But just because a package of seeds is there doesn't mean you can run home and plant the seeds. Don't buy anything until you read the directions on the package. Check the suggested planting times. And look for a date stamp. Is the seed meant for the current year?

Bulbs. Be sure to buy bulbs only in the right season. Check the bulb descriptions on pages 44 and 45 for proper planting times; don't buy them in other seasons.

Bedding plants. These are all the flowering plants that you use for a short and brilliant color display. They come in flats, cell packs, and a variety of small containers. Many vegetable plants also come this way.

You should buy young plants that will grow quickly after you plant them. Never choose those that are crowded or straggly: they've been around too long. You want compact plants with good leaf color and vigorous appearance.

Plants in large containers. Plants in 1-gallon and 5-gallon cans or corresponding plastic and pulp containers should be well branched with young and healthy looking bark and foliage. Though it's always a temptation to buy the largest plant you can afford, trees and shrubs often do better if you buy young-looking gallon-sized specimens and let them form their root systems in your garden.

Bare-root plants. These shrubs and trees should have firm, moist stems and roots. If they are shriveled or dry and brittle-looking, avoid the plant. If you can't plant bare-root plants right away, cover the roots with damp sawdust or peat moss or lay the plant in a shallow trench, covering the roots with moist soil.

Balled and burlapped plants. Often referred to simply as B and B, these large shrubs and trees are dug with a ball of soil containing their roots. The soil ball is then wrapped in burlap and tied with twine to keep it intact. Plants sold this way—some deciduous shrubs and trees, evergreen shrubs such as rhododendrons and azaleas, various conifers—have roots that won't survive bare-root transplanting. Planting season varies by locality; appearance of B and B plants at the nursery signifies that planting season has arrived.

Plants at nursery come in these forms: **1)** seeds, **2)** bulbs, **3)** flats, **4)** cell pack, **5)** 6-plant tray, **6)** plastic pots, **7)** fiber pot, **8)** plastic or metal 1-gallon can, **9)** 2-gallon can, **10)** 5-gallon can, **11)** 15-gallon tree-size can, **12)** bare-root, and **13)** balled and burlapped.

Planting bare-root shrubs & trees

Bare-root planting is usually the best method of planting deciduous shrubs and trees (those that lose their leaves in winter, such as roses, apples, or sycamores).

There are two valid reasons for buying and setting out a bare-root plant in winter or early spring rather than waiting until late spring, summer, or fall when you can buy the same plants in containers:

1) You save money. Typically a bare-root plant costs only 40 to 70 percent of what the same container plant will cost later in the year.

2) The manner in which a bare-root plant is put in the ground makes it easier to maintain, often makes it grow faster, and makes it healthier and more vigorous than a container plant would be if set out later in the year.

The bare-root planting season varies, depending on your climate. Mild-climate gardeners plant in winter; in cold-winter regions, the season begins as soon as the ground thaws in the spring. The earlier you plant bare-root shrubs and trees, the better: if you wait until a bare-root plant begins to put on leaves, it may suffer a setback in planting—you might even lose it.

When you set out a bare-root plant, you can refill the planting hole with the native soil you excavated when you dug the hole. If your garden soil generally calls for amendments, be sure to improve the whole area into which the roots of the mature plant will spread (about the same width of soil as the width of the mature top growth).

For bare-root planting to be successful, the roots should be fresh and plump (not dry and withered), and in many cases the roots and tops should be pruned according to the kind of plant.

If you have any doubt about the freshness of the roots, soak them overnight in a bucket of water before planting.

After the initial watering when you plant, water bare-root plantings conservatively until leaves grow.

How to plant a bare-root rose

1) Dig hole to fit roots just before spring growth begins. Form a cone of soil in the bottom.

2) Spread roots evenly over cone-shaped soil at 30° angle. Snip off any broken lengths of root.

3) Use shovel handle to place plant so that first branch is just above ground (or at grade, if the ground freezes).

4) Add soil gradually, firming it around the plant. Straighten the plant as you add each soil layer.

5) Slowly water around plant before you finish filling to ground level, soaking soil deeply. Let water drain.

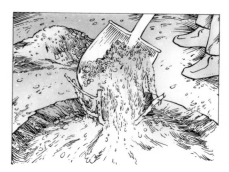

6) Cover plant with loose soil or peat moss until growth begins; at that time, form watering basin and soak deeply.

Planting balled & burlapped shrubs & trees

In fall and early winter, large shrubs and trees are often sold at nurseries with their roots and a ball of soil wrapped in burlap. These B and B (balled and burlapped) plants have a distinct advantage over container plants: they are never rootbound.

As you move a burlap-wrapped plant from the nursery to its planting site in your garden, be careful not to break up the root ball or let it dry out. The best way to carry a small plant is with both hands under the root ball.

If you can't plant right away, put the plant in a shady spot, covering its root ball with moist organic material such as sawdust or peat moss.

Dig a planting hole twice as wide as the root ball and about 6 inches deeper. If your soil is light to medium (and the B and B soil is heavier), incorporate peat moss, ground bark, nitrogen-fortified sawdust, or similar organic amendments (but not animal manures). Add one shovelful of organic amendment to three shovelfuls of the soil you will return to the hole.

It isn't necessary to unwrap the plant entirely (see step 3). The burlap will rot away eventually.

You should normally stake a balled and burlapped plant, because the root area is round and can shift like a ball and socket joint.

During the first couple of years after planting, pay close attention to watering—especially if the root ball soil is heavier than your garden soil. Keep the surrounding garden soil moist, but never continually soggy.

Where there's a great difference between garden soil and root ball soil, you can achieve better water penetration if you carefully punch holes in the root ball with a pointed instrument 1/4 to 1/2 inch wide. Or use a root irrigator.

Also during the first years after planting, check the ties on staked plants at least twice a year to be sure they don't become too tight as the plant grows. Remove the staking as soon as possible (when the plant has its roots firmly established).

Putting a balled & burlapped plant in the ground

1) Ask a friend to help you carry the balled and burlapped plant on a tarp or piece of canvas to the planting site.

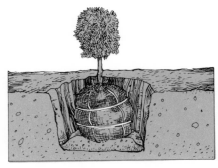

2) Set root ball in a hole that is twice the width of the root ball and 6 inches deeper than its height.

3) Add some soil, cut twine, lay back the burlap. Scrape ball gently if you see a crust. Bury burlap.

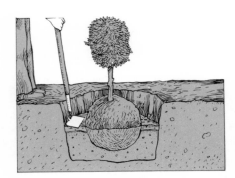

4) Firm soil when hole is half-full so root ball will not settle below ground level after plant has been watered.

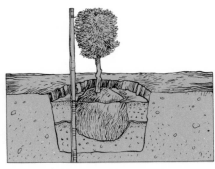

5) Drive stake so that it's anchored in firm soil and rests against (but does not damage) the root ball.

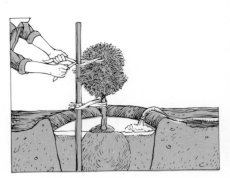

6) Tie trunk securely to stake (not too tightly). Flood the watering basin several times to soak soil very deeply.

Planting from cans & large containers

Most broad-leafed evergreen shrubs and trees are offered only in cans—a circumstance that affects the popularity of plants grown in containers. But container-grown plants are popular for many other reasons: plants in cans are available at all seasons for planting when the gardener is ready to use them; they come in a variety of sizes and prices; they are easy to transport; they do not require immediate planting after purchase; you can buy a container plant in bloom or in fruit and know exactly what color or variety you're getting.

When shopping for container-grown plants, look for plants that have a generally healthy, vigorous appearance and good foliage. The root system should be unencumbered—not tangled or constricted by the plant's own roots. Two signs of a rootbound condition are roots protruding above the soil level and roots growing through the container's drainage holes. Additional indicators of crowded roots are plants that are unusually large for the size of their containers, unusually leggy plants, and dead twigs or branches.

This tree has just been put in nursery can—there is no developed root system to hold the soil ball together. *Better choice* (right) has been in the can long enough to form roots; root ball will hang together when tree is removed from nursery can.

One plant (left) has six buds but looks neglected, is spindly, with poor structure. *No buds* (right), but it's a much better plant—low branching means good form will follow.

The straight-sided metal cans in which some plants are sold must be slit down each side. The best time to cut cans is just before you plant, but you may prefer to have cans cut at the nursery. Handle cut edges with care. If planting is delayed, keep the plants in a cool place and water often enough to keep roots moist (water gently so that you don't wash out soil).

If the plant's roots are crowded or coiled on the surface, straighten, loosen, and cut them.

If you've chosen a container plant from a reputable nursery, it is likely to do well, but remember that the soil is probably a special light mix that is unlike your garden soil. If you simply dig a hole and drop the plant in, it may never root outside the nursery soil mix. The soil difference creates a barrier.

To prevent this, take the following steps: 1) Dig a hole twice as wide as the container and half again as deep (if the removed soil is very dry, soak the hole before planting). 2) Rough up the bottom and sides of the hole, then add a little organic amendment (see page 10) and some superphosphate to the bottom soil (for the amount of superphosphate, follow label directions). 3) Mix the soil you removed with more organic material—2 parts soil to 1 part organic amendment. 4) Use this soil mixture to fill the hole about halfway. Set the plant in and, if needed, add more soil until the top of the root ball is about 1 inch above ground level. 5) Continue adding soil until the hole is filled. 6) Form a watering basin with leftover soil. 7) Water thoroughly.

Corrugated cans and smooth plastic cans need no cutting. Tap the bottom, then pull stem gently. Fiber cans can be torn from root ball.

Cut cans with tin shears or notched screwdriver. Make two cuts, on opposite sides. Be careful of sharp edges.

Roots that encircle the root ball must be pulled loose. Use your fingers, a pointed stick, or a knife to loosen them, but don't break the soil ball.

Planting from flats, cell packs, small containers

The young plants you buy started in flats, cell packs, and other small containers give you a head start. Nurtured through the seedling period by professionals and in ideal growing conditions, they are initially strong enough to withstand transplanting; they grow extremely fast, and usually aren't bothered by pests.

When is it time to plant?

Ideal temperatures at the time you set out plants should be something like this: daytime ground temperatures averaging about 50°F/10°C; daytime air temperatures ranging between 60°F/ 15°C and 80°F/27°C; nighttime air temperatures between 40°F/4°C and 50°F/10°C.

There would be little point in setting out marigolds, for example, early while the weather is still cold; they would simply stand still until activated by favorable temperatures. A sudden freeze could, of course, kill them. The same applies to all summer annuals and warm-weather vegetables.

Weeding, watering, pinching, fertilizing, shading

The drawings here show the planting process only. There are other important preliminary and follow-through steps that can undo all your careful work unless you heed them:

Weeding. Hoe off weeds before you dig. Don't turn them under if you expect to set out plants within a few weeks—it takes a long time for buried weeds to break down.

Watering. Newly set out plants need frequent watering. Once they are well established, let the weather and your soil conditions determine how often to water. Test the soil; when it dries to an inch or two below the surface, water thoroughly.

Pinching. A week or two after setting out transplants, pinch them back to encourage branching and heavier flower production. Annuals such as balsam, dianthus, petunia, and phlox benefit from pinching of the growing tips throughout the summer.

Fertilizing. About a month after setting out plants, boost them by feeding with a complete fertilizer. Continue fertilizing after the plants start to bloom.

Shading. Plants transferred from the nursery's cool lathhouse into full sun need protection in case of a sudden hot spell. If this should occur, shade them with lath frames, shingles, cardboard, newspapers, or plastic shade cloth.

Planting peat pots

If the plant is in a peat pot, you plant it pot and all, and roots will grow through the pot. But make sure that peat pots are moist before you plant them. Several minutes before transplanting, set the peat pots in a shallow container of water. A dry peat pot takes up moisture slowly from the soil, so roots may be slow in breaking through into the soil; this can stunt the plant's growth or cause roots within the peat pot to dry out completely. Also, be sure to cover the top of a peat pot with soil, because exposed peat will act as a wick to draw moisture out. If covering the peat would bury the plant too deeply, break off the top edge of the peat pot down to the plant's soil level or slightly below.

1) Rake surface of prepared (dug and amended) soil, a small section at a time. Level the surface, removing rocks and any clods you can't break up.

2) Remove plants from flats by cutting straight down around each one with putty knife or spatula. Or carefully tear each one out, keeping roots intact.

3) Poke plants out of cell pack by pushing on bottom of individual cell; let gravity help you. If tight, run a knife between side of container and soil.

4) Lightly separate matted roots. If there's a pad of coiled-up white roots at the bottom, cut it off so roots will grow outward into soil.

5) Dig a generous hole deep enough to position the plant at the same level as it was in the nursery flat or container. Fill in soil around plant.

6) Without squeezing roots, form a watering basin around each new plant. Water each one separately, with a gentle flow that won't disturb soil or roots.

7) After watering, spread a mulch of shredded bark, compost, or peat moss to reduce evaporation, insulate roots, and inhibit weed growth.

8) Quickly growing small plants will fill those empty spots between individual plants, so be sure you allow room for spreading as you plant.

Repotting techniques

Sooner or later the roots of a plant in a container fill all available space, and the plant becomes rootbound. Growth slows down or stops completely as the roots become coiled or twined, and even with a stepped-up watering and feeding program the plant will lose vigor and may

Taking plant out of small pot

1) Place one hand on top of pot, with plant stem between index and second finger. Grasp bottom of pot with other hand, then invert pot.

2) Tap rim of pot sharply against edge of potting bench or table. Soil in pot should be moist or root ball may fall to pieces in your hands.

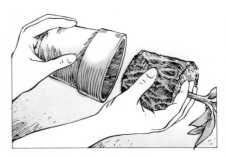

3) Lift pot off, steadying root ball with one hand. If root ball does not come out easily, run a sharp knife around inside edge of pot. Crowded network of roots encircling root ball indicates need for repotting plant.

Moving small plant into larger quarters

1) Choose new pot that's one size larger; for fast growers you can skip a size. Use clean pot and soak it in water first, especially if it is new. Cut off any roots that twine around the root ball.

2) Score root ball with knife, making 1/8 to 1/4-inch-deep cuts. Put broken pottery pieces over drain hole. Put in cushion of new soil to bring top of root ball 1 inch below rim of new pot. Fill in with soil, firm with stick or fingers.

3) Add more soil, then firm around edges with your thumbs or tap pot bottom sharply on work surface to settle soil. Water thoroughly so both new soil and soil in root ball are wet.

Removing plant from

1) If possible, grow large plant in container that can be taken apart easily when it comes time to root-prune or when you want to transplant into a larger container or the ground.

Root-pruning, returning

1) Shave off a few inches of the root ball with a sharp knife (as little as 1 inch on small plants; 4 or 5 inches on large ones). This removes old soil and helps prune roots. Unwind and cut off large roots that encircle outside of root ball. Scoring the root ball with a knife will also cut most of these twining roots.

eventually die. Therefore, if you suspect a rootbound condition, you should remove the plant from its container and have a look at the root ball.

If you have a small plant on which you are trying to speed growth, you should move it into a larger pot, never allowing it to become potbound. But don't use a *much* larger container—the unused soil may become soggy and sour and could kill the plant before it has time to send out enough roots.

In contrast, some fleshy-rooted plants, such as clivia and aga-panthus, bloom better when root-bound.

Repotting sizable shrubs and trees in heavy containers into ever-larger ones may not be practical, but you can rejuvenate the plants by root-pruning and replanting in fresh soil.

large container

2) *One removable side* makes all the difference in plant-moving ease. You can slide the plant onto a dolly without having to lift it. Some containers can be nailed back together and reused.

3) *Or let soil dry out* slightly so ball slides out more easily; lay container on side, tap around rim with mallet or hammer while you (or a helper) pull gently but steadily on the trunk or stem. Protect rim of container with cloth.

4) *Or "float" out root ball* of some plants by forcing water through the drain hole in the bottom. Be sure to hold hose nozzle tightly against hole.

to original container

2) *Cover drainage holes* with fragments of broken pot or pieces of copper window screening. Put in cushion of new soil (usually a little more than was shaved off the bottom). Replace plant. For ease in watering, top of root ball should be 2 inches below rim.

3) *Fill in* around root ball with fresh soil mix. Work it into crevice between root ball and container sides with a stick or a length of metal reinforcing rod. Since containers are heavy, try to replant where the container is to remain. But if you don't, at least move it into location before you water.

4) *The final step* is to soak with water until both the new soil and the root ball are thoroughly saturated. You may have to fill the container to the rim three or four times. Let water run slowly. If there is some settling, add more soil. Repeat entire process when roots once again fill the container.

Planting a lawn

The drawings on the facing page illustrate a step-by-step method for starting a new lawn by sowing grass seed. The soil preparation portion (steps 1–6) also applies to using sod strips, sprigs, stolons, or plugs.

Whether you use seed or something else, water your newly planted lawn gently, keeping it dark with moisture until the grass is established. By following the planting directions carefully, you'll have far less trouble keeping your lawn healthy.

Before you start the job, consider the following points:

1) If your present lawn consists of weeds and crabgrass, the sod should be removed completely. You can rent power cutters that cut sod into strips, or you can use a flat spade to scrape it off. Don't leave any of the sod in your soil.

2) Don't add new topsoil unless you want to raise the level of the lawn. If so, make sure you mix about half of the topsoil into the ground before adding the rest; otherwise the sharp difference in soil quality will create a barrier against water penetration and root growth.

For information on the various kinds of lawn grasses, see page 46. Ground covers—plants to replace lawns—are shown on page 47.

Sod. These strips of lawn are more expensive than seed or stolons but offer quite a saving in labor.

Other advantages of sod include its uniformity and healthiness when you install it (it's been treated to eliminate or prevent weeds, diseases, and insect pests) and its usefulness underneath trees. Because sod roots are already established, the grass prospers where seeds would succumb to tree root competition.

Prepare a seedbed as described in steps 1–6, keeping the surface 3/4 to 1 1/2 inches lower than the surrounding grade. Incorporate the same amount of fertilizer as you'd use on a seeded lawn.

Lay the strips of sod parallel, with ends staggered as in a bricklayer's running-bond pattern. Press each strip snugly against the previous one. Trim with a sharp knife; roll with a half-full roller.

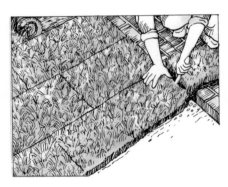

Unroll sod strips in parallel rows with ends staggered as illustrated. Seams between strips should be tight and level—be careful not to overlap edges. Trim away excess sod with sharp knife at corners, edges, along walks. Sod strips usually come from 15 to 18 inches wide, 4 to 5 feet long.

Sprigs and stolons. Certain kinds of grasses, such as hybrid Bermuda grass and some bent grasses, are established by planting sprigs and stolons.

Prepare seedbed as for sowing (steps 1–6). Presoak seedbed so the soil will be damp and of a good working consistency when you plant.

One planting method is to dig a series of parallel trenches 3 inches deep and 10 inches apart. Lay sprigs or stolons (either from plastic bags or freshly torn from flats or sod) in trenches and replace soil.

Another planting method is to scatter stolons evenly over the prepared seedbed at the rate of 3 to 5 bushels per 1,000 square feet. Roll with a half-filled roller (a cleated one if available), then mulch with 1/2 inch of top-grade topsoil, peat moss, sawdust, or ground bark. Roll again and water thoroughly.

Cleated roller turns soil over stolons (pieces of grass stem) after they are broadcast on the seedbed.

Plugs. This method is used for planting dichondra in small areas or to produce an immediate lawn-like effect.

Thoroughly prepare the seedbed (steps 1–6). Turn a flat of dichondra upside down and, using a sharp knife, cut it like a sheet cake into 1 or 2-inch squares. Two-inch squares have less transplanting shock and will give faster coverage. Plant the squares in an offset grid pattern (see drawing below) 6 to 15 inches apart.

Turn flat of dichondra upside down and, using a sharp knife, cut like a sheet cake into 1 or 2-inch squares. Space plugs evenly in prepared ground.

Keep in mind that the closer together plugs are planted, the faster they will grow together. Make sure any runners are set at soil level or just below.

Nine steps to a new lawn

1) Remove old turf with a power sod cutter or a flat spade. Roll up the strips and discard them. Don't dig in any remnants; they'll spoil new lawn.

2) Add soil amendments and fertilizer to improve texture and drainage, supply nutrients. Add any materials to correct acidity, alkalinity problems.

3) Till soil with a rotary tiller, cutting 6 to 9 inches deep and crossing several times at right angles for a thorough and even mix of soil and additives.

4) Install permanent sprinklers at this point, using temporary long risers for heads until the lawn surface has settled and grass is well started.

5) Drag surface with board scraper (any version of the type shown here) to level high spots and fill in depressions. Try attaching a weight.

6) Use light roller to firm and smooth soil. The soil should be dry before rolling, otherwise it compacts, preventing seeds from sprouting.

7) Sow grass seed by hand or with a mechanical seeder. A still, windless day is best for sowing. A mechanical seeder helps distribute seed evenly.

8) Rake surface lightly to even seed, then rake again at right angles. Disperse any dense concentration of seeds with your rake, but don't gouge soil.

9) Scatter organic mulch (1/8-inch layer) over seed or stolons. If you use peat moss, moisten it well before you start or it won't absorb water.

Planting bulbs

Most commonly grown bulbs perform well with a minimum of care. But if you expect maximum performance and beautiful blooms year after year, it is important that bulbs be given a good start.

The first step in planting is to dig the soil at least 12 to 18 inches deep. If you have rich, easily worked soil, nothing need be added except perhaps some bone meal, as shown in the drawing below left.

But if your soil is poor or heavy, add soil amendment such as compost, leaf mold, or peat moss. If you use manure, be sure it is well rotted—*never fresh*—and dig it in well below the depth at which you will set the bulbs, so that it will not come in contact with them.

Dig the planting hole or trench about 3 inches deeper than depth indicated on chart. Mix a tablespoon of bone meal or superphosphate into bottom of hole, then cover with an inch of sand. Set the bulb in the hole, insert a marker next to it, and fill the hole with soil.

Whether you plant one bulb to a hole or several at one time, plant all bulbs at a uniform depth so they'll bloom at the same time.

But if you want to grow gladiolus, for example, for cut flowers, plant them 2 weeks apart. With the staggered plantings you should have a continuous flower supply. Start cutting when the first blooms have opened.

For more information about the many kinds of bulbs and similar plants, see pages 44 and 45.

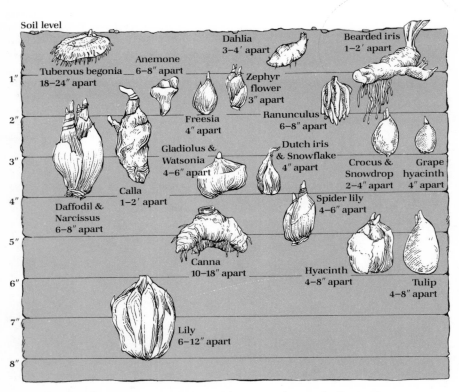

Planting depths and spacings are given for some favorite bulbs. In clay soil, plant less deeply. Bulbs set out later than November should also be planted less deeply. These bulbs are shown on pages 44–45.

Growing bulbs in the ground

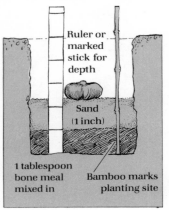

Cover newly planted bulbs with soil, then mulch in cold-winter climates. In mild areas, put bedding plants such as pansies between bulbs or sow seeds of shallow-rooted annuals such as sweet alyssum directly over the bulb bed.

Growing bulbs in containers

To grow bulbs in pots, first cover drainage hole with pieces of broken pot, then add soil mix plus a tablespoon of bone meal. Place bulbs so they almost touch. Cover bulbs so tops are just at soil level; water. Keep in cool, dark place until leaf tips poke through surface (about 8 weeks).

Planting a hedge & other specialties

Be sure to choose just the right plants to create the type of hedge you want (see chart on page 138). Never put in larger plants for quick effect and expect to keep them low by cutting them back—eventually, they'll get away from you.

Planting distance between plants varies by type of plant. As a rule of thumb: If your hedge is to be 6 feet high, space plants 3 feet apart; if you plant low growers and want a 1-foot hedge, space 1 foot apart. Spacing for heights in between should be from 1 to 3 feet.

Informal ones may need only annual trimming, but you'll have to clip frequently if you want to shape the plants formally. Keep hedges wider at the bottom than at the top to permit sunlight to reach the bases of the plants, to encourage vigorous growth, and to keep the lower parts of plants well foliaged.

Special planting situations

Some plants require special care in planting in order to do well. Citrus, for example, is sensitive to moisture and must not be planted too deeply. Acid-loving, shallow-rooted plants such as camellias, azaleas, and rhododendrons require a wide, shallow hole and extra organic material added to the soil.

Two hedge styles

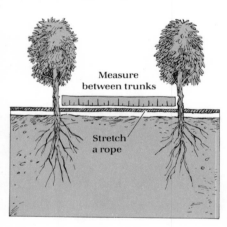

Measure between trunks

Stretch a rope

For a straight hedge, stretch a rope. Measure from trunk to trunk for even spacing. For tall hedges, space plants 36 inches apart; for low border, 12 inches apart is about right.

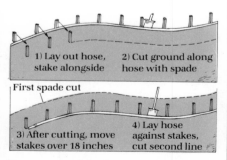

1) Lay out hose, stake alongside
2) Cut ground along hose with spade
First spade cut
3) After cutting, move stakes over 18 inches
4) Lay hose against stakes, cut second line

For a curved hedge, use a hose to form the line, then keep it in place with stakes. Cut alongside hose with spade, move the stakes and hose 18 inches; then dig trench.

How to plant citrus

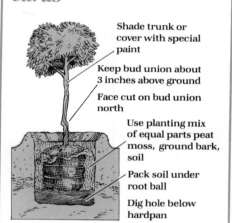

Shade trunk or cover with special paint

Keep bud union about 3 inches above ground

Face cut on bud union north

Use planting mix of equal parts peat moss, ground bark, soil

Pack soil under root ball

Dig hole below hardpan

Most citrus varieties are susceptible to damage from overwatering. Plant away from lawns. If your area is likely to have late frosts, cover trees or shrubs with paper or burlap, or plant under protective overhang.

Camellias, rhododendrons, and azaleas

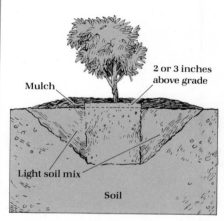

Mulch

2 or 3 inches above grade

Light soil mix

Soil

These acid-loving plants need a planting hole twice the width of root ball; plant slightly high. If soil is heavy clay, plant with half of root ball above soil level and heap mulch around it. Always use light soil mix.

Aquatic plants

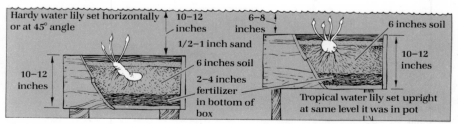

Hardy water lily set horizontally or at 45° angle

10–12 inches

6–8 inches

6 inches soil

1/2–1 inch sand

6 inches soil

2–4 inches fertilizer in bottom of box

10–12 inches

10–12 inches

Tropical water lily set upright at same level it was in pot

Plant water lilies and other aquatic plants in containers that can be submerged and taken out for replanting every 3 years. Put in hardy types in spring. Plant tropicals when the weather and water temperatures warm up.

Transplanting a shrub or small tree

With expert care you can transplant at any time of year, but with most plants you'll be more assured of success if you transplant in cool weather while the plant is dormant or semidormant (tropical plants transplant best after soil has warmed up in spring).

Dormant deciduous plants such as roses can be moved bare-root. Prepare the new planting hole before you dig up the plant to be moved; that way you can accomplish the operation as quickly as possible.

To move evergreen plants (both broad-leafed and conifers) or deciduous ones that are in leaf, dig them with soil around the roots. The bigger the plant, the more difficult and time-consuming transplanting becomes. Prepare a planting hole as described under "Planting balled & burlapped shrubs & trees" (page 18).

Burlap is the traditional material for wrapping a root ball, but chicken wire is easier to use. Use small-mesh wire (1 inch or less) and encircle the root ball tightly, securing the cut ends by wrapping cut wires together or by threading them together with a length of wire.

Replant as described for balled and burlapped plants on page 18.

For small plants with correspondingly small root balls—for example, a plant whose root ball you can carry in a shovel or in both hands—you may be able to eliminate the wrapping or wiring.

Here's how to move a shrub or small tree

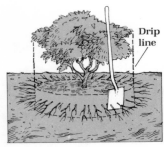

1) Cut outer roots several months to a year before transplanting (this is optional). Plant can adjust to minor shock, will form fresh feeder roots closer to main stem.

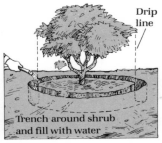

2) Soak roots like this two or three days before moving plant. The water will penetrate into the root area and help hold the soil in a firm ball for easier handling.

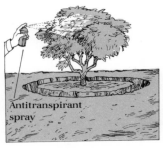

3) Coat foliage with antitranspirant spray to slow down loss of water (this is optional). Spray is available in pressure cans at many nurseries.

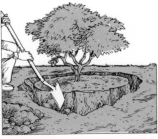

4) Cut down with spade or back of shovel; ideal root ball size is as large as you can manage. Heavy soil will hold together better, allowing larger root ball than sandy soil.

5) Wrap root ball (a foot or more deep) with length of chicken wire, securing the loose ends.

6) Place hay hook or other tool through wire and twist tightly. Do this at four or five places and at different levels.

7) Cut under root ball with mattock or shovel. If earth crumbles, slide chicken wire underneath to keep root ball intact.

8) Position plant in prepared planting hole. Mound a ridge of soil to create a basin that's the same diameter as foliage; water plant well.

Fertilizing Techniques

- Fertilizers &
  how to use them: page 30
- Fertilizing your lawn: page 31
- Fertilizing trees &
  large shrubs: page 32

Fertilizers & how to use them

In nature, whatever comes from the soil usually returns to it. But a gardener normally carries away many nutrients in the form of fruit, flowers, and spent plants. By fertilizing your plants, you make sure they'll always have the various elements they need. By adding organic material to the soil, you provide a healthy environment for the growth of soil organisms that help to keep the natural cycle going.

Buying chemical fertilizer

Many different fertilizers are available in dry, liquid, and tablet form. Those containing all the needed food elements are called complete fertilizers. Others contain a high percentage of only one element such as nitrogen, phosphorus, or potassium. Before you buy a fertilizer, check to see how much of these main elements it contains. Somewhere on the package you'll find three numbers, such as 10–8–6. The first number refers to the percentage of nitrogen, the second phosphorus, and the third potassium. If one of the numbers is zero,

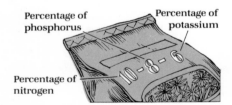

Fertilizer labels show what percentages of the three primary nutrients are inside the package.

then that particular element is not included in the mixture.

You may find that your plants don't always require all three elements. For example, if you see planting instructions that recommend mixing superphosphate or bone meal (an organic fertilizer high in phosphorus) into the planting soil, you are adding phosphorus for strong root growth. Other elements may not be needed at the time of planting.

Special-purpose fertilizers are formulated for certain uses or for certain types of plants, such as "Rhododendron and Azalea Food" or "Citrus Food." Also available are slow-release fertilizers, which are effective longer, and fertilizers combined with insecticides and herbicides.

Buying organic fertilizer

You'll find that organic fertilizers are made of varied materials such as cottonseed meal, blood meal, bone meal, activated sewage sludge, hoof-and-horn meal, or guano (bird or bat droppings). Listed on the package you'll find the percentage of each of the three main elements. Most organic fertilizers are rather slow in giving up their nutrients since bacterial action is required before nutrients can be released.

Some people think that manure and compost are fertilizers. Both may contain tiny amounts of usable nutrients (manure is typically about 1–1–1), but they are best used as soil amendments to improve texture and promote the growth of soil bacteria. The bacteria in turn help your plants to take nourishment from the soil.

Using fertilizers

Labels on packaged fertilizers give instructions for their use. Look for the amounts suggested for an area of square feet, or for the amount to be mixed in a gallon of water.

Most plants should be fertilized in spring when leaf growth begins, and again about 3 months later. If winters are mild, you can also fertilize plants in early fall.

Some plants require special fertilizing schedules. Roses grow so rapidly that you can give them the recommended dose every 6 weeks. Rhododendrons, azaleas, and camellias like nutrients as their blooms fade and again 6 weeks later. Fruit trees benefit from fertilizer about 3 weeks before they bloom. Vegetables need some when their seeds sprout, and again when the plants are established (leaf vegetables require a high-nitrogen food). Container plants and such fast-growing plants as fuchsias and begonias can use a very light fertilizing once a week (about a fourth of what the label recommends).

Most liquid fertilizers must be diluted. For a dry fertilizer to be as effective as possible, you usually dig it into the soil around the root zone. For established plants, work the fertilizer into the upper soil layer, being careful not to damage plant's roots. Water thoroughly after application.

Dry fertilizer. If area is dug but not planted, work fertilizer into future root zone. If young plants are already in, apply in bands on both sides, 4 inches away from roots.

Liquid fertilizer. Young annuals and vegetables like a high-nitrogen feeding. Apply in basins (as shown here) or rows, several inches from base of plants; then reapply when plants are established.

Fertilizing your lawn

No matter what kind of grass seed you use or how carefully you plant it, a lawn must be fertilized regularly if it is to thrive. You can use a slow-acting fertilizer or one of the fast-acting kinds.

Slow-acting fertilizers should be applied only once or twice a year. You can choose from many complete commercial fertilizers, organic types such as activated sewage sludge, synthetic organics plus resins, or stabilized inorganics. Some products combine fertilizer with insecticide and/or weed killer.

Hand application of fertilizer is possible with any product, but it's safer with organic fertilizers than chemical, since organic ones don't burn grass as easily.

Fast-acting fertilizers will begin to turn the grass green in a matter of hours after application, but results are temporary unless you repeat the application every month or so. Many gardeners like to tie in this type of fertilizing with every second or third deep soaking of the lawn, by applying liquid fertilizer with a hose-end applicator just prior to watering.

Other fertilizer application options are a watering can (slow and tedious) or a wheeled hopper. Hopper spreaders must be kept clean and in good condition.

Hopper spreader makes the most uniform pattern. Two strips at each end give you room to shut off spreader, turn, open spreader, and start again. To avoid gap between runs, slightly overlap previous run's wheel track.

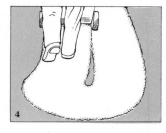

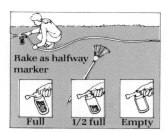

Four common mistakes. **1)** You can't turn an open hopper inside a previous turn and make a uniform pattern. Overlaps burn grass, and grass stays faded in gaps. **2)** In foreground track you see what happens when you stop and start with the hopper open. Walking with an unsteady gait does same thing. Concentrations burn grass or make it lumpy. **3)** Dotted lines trace wheel tracks on grass. If you run inside wheel down the previous run's outside wheel track, you leave an unfed gap. Even a good rain may not merge two swaths. **4)** Turns of 180° cause erratic dispersal.

Hand casting. This works well if you do it in a slow, easy manner. Walk with wedding march cadence, make a semicircular throw with each step.

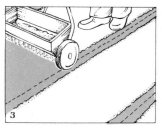

Rake as halfway marker

Full   1/2 full   Empty

Liquid feeding. Use a rake or other object to mark halfway point of area to be covered. Move fast enough to be there when the hose-attachment feeder is half empty, and at the other end when feeder is empty.

Fertilizing trees & large shrubs

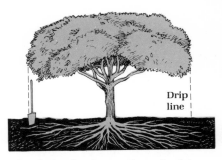

Check for feeder roots at the drip line by slicing out a piece of soil with a sharp spade and crumbling it. If you find a network of fine roots, apply fertilizer at this point. If not, keep searching toward the tree trunk.

Springtime, when soil has warmed up, is a good time for fertilizing trees and large shrubs. The method you use should depend largely on your local climate and the amount of water available to the plant. Be sure to place the fertilizer in the feeder root area, and keep the trees and shrubs well watered throughout the growing season.

Four methods

Any one of the following four fertilizing methods will stimulate new growth.

Root plug fertilizing. This very popular method works best in areas of moderate rainfall and mild climate. Fertilizer placed this way must have sufficient water to make it available to nearby roots, yet not so much as to wash it out of the root area.

Use an auger to drill holes in a circle just inside the drip line. Make holes 18 to 24 inches apart (the sandier the soil, the closer the holes.) Don't drill down too far—just to the surface root zone.

Use a complete fertilizer, carefully following package directions as to the amount to be used and dividing by the number of holes you are going to fill. Before inserting fertilizer in the holes, mix it with an equal amount of sand. Water immediately and thoroughly; otherwise you'll burn the roots.

Liquid fertilizing. This is particularly appropriate in dry soil regions because the nutrients are in a form immediately available to the tree. A follow-up application in 2 months is advisable.

You can use a hollow tube into which are inserted soluble fertilizer pellets or venturi tube attachments for liquid concentrates; both kinds attach to the end of your garden hose (plumbing codes may require antisiphoning devices between hose and water supply). Insert the tube to a depth of about 2 feet; water pressure forces the solution out to the roots. Holes should be about 18 inches apart, just inside the drip line.

Surface fertilizing. This method is popular in heavy rainfall areas. You can apply fertilizer by surface spreading or by creating small depressions at regular intervals and filling with either liquid or dry fertilizer. However, you must water thoroughly when you apply either type (200 gallons of water is not too much). Remember, too, that plants under a tree will absorb some of the nutrient before it can reach the tree-root level.

Foliar fertilizing. Applied with a pressure spray, foliar fertilizer works best in regions of high humidity or as a supplemental source of food where root systems have been damaged. Time foliar fertilizing to take advantage of high humidity; the fertilizer will penetrate the leaves only as long as they are damp. Try to do it in late afternoon, in the evening, or on an overcast day, so midday sun will not dry out the leaves.

Professional help

If you have a number of large trees in your garden or you anticipate special problems with fertilizing, it is best to enlist the services of a tree surgeon. The tree surgeon uses specialized equipment to handle large-scale and problem-tree fertilizing and will set up a program geared to your particular garden.

Root plug fertilizing

Liquid fertilizing

Surface fertilizing

Foliar fertilizing

Basic Garden Plants

- Shrubs, a garden's basic planting: page 34

- Trees elevate the view: page 36

- Annuals & biennials bring almost-instant color: page 38

- Perennials are repeat performers: page 41

- Bulbs, the garden showoffs: page 44

- Lawn grasses...cool to look at, soft underfoot: page 46

- Ground covers for versatility: page 47

- Vines climb, tumble, twine: page 48

Shrubs, a garden's basic planting

Shrubs, along with trees, form the basic framework of a garden. Flowers may come and go, but once you plant shrubs you can look forward to enjoying them for many years.

You'll find shrubs available for almost any use in your garden. Most will do well in sun or part shade, but there is considerable variation depending on climate and variety. Generally speaking, the best shrubs for permanent landscaping are those that grow quite slowly but, once established, maintain their character year after year. Fast growers may overpower the garden unless kept in bounds by constant pruning and attention.

Don't judge a shrub strictly by its flowers, or lack of them. Look for form and foliage. Let perennials, annuals, and bulbs add color to your basic planting scheme where needed.

Some shrubs, of course, are real "show-stoppers." Camellias, rhododendrons, and azaleas are treasured for their magnificence of bloom in temperate regions where they are commonly grown. Like many shrubs, they make handsome container plants.

Wherever winters are fairly mild, shrubs will get a head start if you plant them in autumn. Set the plant out early enough so the soil remains warm while they begin to root. If you're likely to have cold periods or even just a hard frost or two, be sure the plant is one that withstands cold.

The list below includes only a few of the hundreds of excellent shrubs from which you can choose. Evergreen and deciduous types are denoted by "E" or "D" in parentheses.

Abelia   *(Abelia grandiflora)*

Grows to 6' high or more, spreading to 5' or more. Flowers white or tinged pink, June–October. Hardy to 0 to 10°F/−12°C. (E)

Andromeda
(Pieris japonica)

Upright, dense, tiered growth to 9–10'. Many varieties, some grown for flowers. Hardy to 0 to −10°F/−18 to −23°C. (E)

Aucuba   *(Aucuba japonica)*

To 6–15' and almost as wide. Green and variegated varieties. Red berries October–February. Hardy to 0 to 10°F/−18 to −12°C. (E)

Azalea
(Rhododendron)

Many good types; wide range of growth habits, flowers. Most hardy to 0 to 10°F/−18 to −12°C; some tender. (E,D)

Barberry
(Berberis)

Vigorous. Tiny yellow or orange-yellow flowers in spring. Hardy to 10°F/−12°C or lower depending on species. (E,D)

Boxwood
(Buxus)

Many species. Widely used for low or medium hedges, edgings. Hardy to 0°F/−18°C depending on species. (E)

Camellia   *(Camellia)*

Superb blooms, foliage. Wide range of colors, sizes, forms. Outstanding container plants. Hardy to 10 to 20°F/−12 to −7°C. (E)

Cotoneaster   *(Cotoneaster)*

Many species, ranging from ground covers to 20' shrubs. All grow vigorously. Hardy to 0 to −10°F/−18 to −23°C. (E, semi-D, D)

Crape myrtle
(Lagerstroemia indica)

Dwarf, shrubby forms; shrub-tree types 6–30'. Crinkled flowers in clusters. Hardy to 0 to 10°F/−18 to −12°C. (D)

English laurel
(Prunus laurocerasus)

Large shrub or small tree; common as clipped hedge. Hardy to 0 to 10°F/−18 to −12°C. (E)

Euonymus   *(Euonymus)*

Slow to medium growth, 7–10'. Evergreen kinds valued for foliage, texture, form. Hardy to 10 to −10°F/−12 to −23°C. depending on species. (E,D)

Firethorn   *(Pyracantha)*

Fast, vigorous growth. Glossy green leaves, thorny branches, red or orange berries in fall. Most types hardy to 0 to −10°F/−18 to −23°C. (E)

(D) *means deciduous.*
(E) *means evergreen.*

Flowering quince
(Chaenomeles)

Among first shrubs to bloom. Low and tall-growing types; wide color range. Hardy to −10 to −20°F/−23 to −29°C. (D)

Forsythia (Forsythia)

Somewhat fountain-shaped; bare branches covered with yellow flowers February–April. Hardy to 0 to −20°F/−18 to −29°C. (D)

Fuchsia
(Fuchsia)

Hundreds of varieties. Colorful, showy flowers; wide range of colors, sizes, shapes. Erect and trailing forms. Hardy to 30°F/−1°C. (E)

Gardenia
(Gardenia jasminoides)

Vigorous when given warmth, ample water, good drainage, steady feeding. Hardy to 20 to 30°F/−7 to −1°C. (E)

Heavenly bamboo
(Nandina domestica)

Lightly branched, canelike stems; fine-textured foliage. Red berries. Hardy to 0 to 10°F/−18 to −12°C. (E)

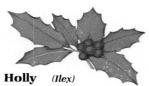

Holly (Ilex)

Many ranging from dwarf to 50′ trees. Male and female plants needed for berries. Hardy to 10 to −10°F/−12 to −23°C (varies). (E, some D)

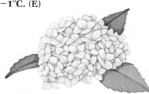

Hydrangea (Hydrangea)

Big leaves; large clusters of long-lasting flowers in white, pink, red, or blue, summer and fall. Most hardy to 0 to −10°F/−18 to −23°C. (D)

India hawthorn
(Raphiolepis indica)

Glossy, leathery leaves. Good background plant, informal hedge. Hardy to 15 to 20°F/−9 to −7°C. (E)

Japanese privet (Ligustrum japonicum)

Dense, compact growth to 10–12′. Excellent for hedges, screens, small standards. Hardy to 0 to 10°F/−18 to −12°C. (E)

Juniper (Juniperus)

Needled evergreen with fleshy, berrylike fruits. Many forms, from shrubs to tall, slender types. Hardy to −10 to −20°F/−23 to −29°C (varies). (E)

Lilac (Syringa)

Best where winter brings definite chill. Can reach 20′. Clustered, fragrant lavender or white flowers in May. Hardy to −10°F/−23°C. (D)

Mock orange
(Philadelphus)

Large, vigorous plant with medium green foliage. White, fragrant flowers. Hardy to 0 to −10°F/−18 to −23°C. (D)

Oleander (Nerium oleander)

Moderate to fast growth, 8–12′; dwarf types. White, salmon, yellow, pink, or red flowers spring–fall. Hardy to 10 to 20°F/−12 to −7°C. (E)

Photinia (Photinia fraseri)

Moderate growth to 10′, spreading wider. White flower clusters in early spring. Heat resistant. Hardy to 10 to 20°F/−12 to −7°C. (E)

Pittosporum
(Pittosporum tobira)

Dense shrub or small tree; can be held to 6′. Creamy white flowers in spring. Hardy to 10 to 20°F/−12 to −7°C. (E)

Rhododendron
(Rhododendron)

Many species and hybrids. Mostly spring-blooming. Most hardy to 0 to 10°F/−18 to −12°C; some tender. (E)

Silverberry
(Elaeagnus pungens)

Rigid, sprawling growth, 6–15′. Grayish-green leaves, some variegated varieties. Hardy to 0 to 10°F/−18 to −12°C. (E)

Spiraea (Spiraea vanhouttei)

Fountain-shaped growth to 6′. Blue-green leaves on arching branches. Showy snow-white flowers in rounded clusters, June–July. Hardy to −10 to −20°F/−23 to −29°C. (D)

Viburnum (Viburnum)

Large group of shrubs. Pink or white flowers in spring (some species in winter). Hardy to 0° to −10°F/−18° to −23°C depending on type. (E, D)

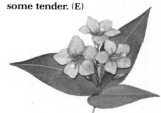

Weigela (Weigela)

Voluminous flower display in late spring. Coarse-leafed, stiff plant; prune to prevent ranginess. Hardy to 0° to −10°F/−18° to −23°C. (D)

Trees elevate the view

Selecting a tree for your garden depends largely on what function you want it to perform. You may want its high, broad branches to form part of a wall, to screen an unwanted view, to cut the force of the wind, or simply to provide shade.

If you want a tree primarily for summer shade, consider one that loses its leaves in winter, letting through sunlight on cold days. If you want a tree for a screen or windbreak, study the various types of evergreens whose foliage will protect you for the entire year.

We show just a few of the many hundreds of trees that can be grown in home gardens. Not all are grown in all sections of the country; but if a tree you like is not available, ask your local nursery personnel to recommend one with similar characteristics.

Small trees

Bottlebrush
Callistemon citrinus
(E); fast;
20–25 feet

Dogwood
Cornus florida
(D); slow to moderate;
to 30 feet

Eastern redbud
Cercis canadensis
(D); moderate;
25–35 feet

Flowering crabapple
Malus 'Katherine'
(D); moderate to fast;
to 20 feet

Flowering plum
Prunus blireiana
(D); moderate;
to 25 feet

Fringe tree
Chionanthus retusus
(D); slow;
to 20 feet

Japanese maple
Acer palmatum
(D); slow to moderate;
to 20 feet

Japanese tree lilac
Syringa reticulata
(D); moderate;
to 25 feet

Loquat
Eriobotrya japonica
(E); moderate;
15–30 feet

Russian olive
Elaeagnus angustifolia
(D); fast;
to 20 feet

Saucer magnolia
Magnolia soulangiana
(D); slow;
to 25 feet

Shadblow
Amelanchier laevis
(D); slow;
30–35 feet

Silver bell
Halesia carolina
(D); moderate;
20–50 feet

Strawberry tree
Arbutus unedo
(E); slow to moderate;
8–35 feet

Washington thorn
Crataegus phaenopyrum
(D); moderate;
to 25 feet

(D) *means deciduous*
(E) *means evergreen*

Medium trees

Bradford pear
Pyrus calleryana 'Bradford'
(D); moderate;
to 30 feet

Chinese pistache
Pistacia chinensis
(D); moderate;
to 60 feet

Flowering cherry
Prunus serrulata
(D); moderate to fast;
to 30 feet

Glossy privet
Ligustrum lucidum
(E); fast;
35–40 feet

Goldenrain
Koelreuteria paniculata
(D); slow to moderate;
to 20–35 feet

Jacaranda
Jacaranda mimosifolia
(D to semi-E); moderate;
25–40 feet

Japanese snowdrop
Styrax japonicus
(D); slow to moderate;
to 30 feet

Katsura
Cercidiphyllum japonicum
(D); slow;
to 40 feet or more

Kentucky coffee tree
Gymnocladus dioica
(D); fast;
to 50 feet

Little-leaf linden
Tilia cordata
(D); slow to moderate;
to 30–50 feet

Mountain ash
Sorbus aucuparia
(D); moderate to fast;
20–30 feet or more

Pagoda tree
Sophora japonica
(D); moderate;
to 40 feet

Persian parrotia
Parrotia persica
(D); slow;
to 30 feet or more

Persimmon
Diospyros kaki
(D); moderate;
to 30 feet or more

Red horsechestnut
Aesculus carnea
(D); moderate;
to 40 feet

Silk tree
Albizia julibrissin
(D); fast;
to 40 feet

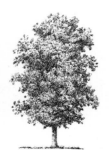

Silver dollar gum
Eucalyptus polyanthemos
(E); fast;
20–60 feet

Sour gum
Nyssa sylvatica
(D); slow to moderate;
30–50 feet

Sweet gum
Liquidambar styraciflua
(D); moderate;
to 60 feet or more

White birch
Betula pendula
(D); fast;
30–40 feet

Annuals & biennials bring almost-instant color

Annuals are fast-growing, temporary plants that bring color to your garden for one season, then die. Biennials complete their life cycle in two years. Also included here are a few tender perennials usually grown as annuals.

Plant spring-blooming annuals in early spring, summer-blooming annuals in spring after the last frost. For winter and early spring bloom in mild-winter areas, set out plants in late summer or autumn while days are still warm enough for good plant growth but nights are lengthening. In hot desert climates, annuals planted in autumn will bloom during winter and spring, then are killed by summer heat.

Whatever the climate, you should plant all annuals in full sun unless you know they will tolerate shade. Newcomers to seed gardening might start with marigolds, nasturtiums, and zinnias—all easy and fast-growing.

Border of mixed annuals—pink cosmos, red nicotiana, pastel annual phlox, white sweet alyssum, blue salvia—provides a vivid splash of color next to garden path.

African daisy
Dimorphotheca
Free-blooming plants unsurpassed for winter, spring color in dry warm-winter areas. Yellow, orange, salmon, white.

Ageratum
Ageratum houstonianum
Tiny lavender-blue, white, or pink flowers in dense clusters. Dwarf varieties make excellent edgings or pattern plantings.

Aster
Callistephus chinensis
Many different flower forms. Plants 1–3' high. Colors range from white to pastel pinks, violet, purple, wine, and scarlet.

Baby's breath
Gypsophila elegans
Much-branched, slender-stemmed plants 1–1 1/2' tall, profusely covered in summer with small white or pink flowers.

Bachelor's button
Centaurea cyanus
Blue, pink, white, or red flowers on 1–2 1/2' stems. Sow seed in late summer or early autumn where winters are mild.

Balsam
Impatiens balsamina
Long, sharply pointed, deeply toothed leaves. White, pink, rose, lilac, or red flowers. Needs ample water.

Calendula
Calendula officinalis
Orange, yellow, cream, apricot daisylike flowers on 1–2' plants. Blooms in winter in warm climates. Effective in masses.

California poppy
Eschscholzia californica
Orange, red, or white flowers on feathery plants. Plant in informal groups. Poppies may reseed themselves in warm areas.

Calliopsis
Coreopsis tinctoria
Yellow, orange, reddish flowers on 1 1/2–3' plants with wiry stems. Much like cosmos in growth habit. Dwarf and double.

Candytuft
Iberis amara, I. umbellata
Free-blooming; white and pastel flowers on 6–15" plants. Good in borders, for cutting, or as cover for bulb beds.

Canterbury bells
Campanula medium
Bell-shaped flowers in blue, purple, pink, white on plants 2 1/2–4' tall. Good cut flowers, container plants.

Chinese forget-me-not
Cynoglossum amabile
Sprays of blue, pink, or white flowers on 1 1/2–2' plants. Biennials; bloom first year from seed sown in autumn or spring.

Chinese pink
Dianthus chinensis
Erect, 6–30" high; stems branching at top; rose-lilac flowers. Compact varieties covered in bright pink, red, white flowers.

Cineraria
Senecio hybridus
Clusters of daisylike flowers in blue, violet, pink, white. Lush foliage. Grows best in cool shade. Will reseed itself.

Clarkia
Clarkia unguiculata
Reddish stems. Rose, purple, or white flowers; double varieties in orange, salmon, crimson, purple, rose, pink, or cream.

Cockscomb
Celosia argentea
Red, yellow, orange plumelike flowers on stems to 3' tall. Dwarfs popular. Grows best in hot-summer climates.

Cosmos
Cosmos bipinnatus
Daisylike flowers in white, lavender, pink, rose, purple, crimson on plants 2 1/2–8" tall. Feathery foliage.

Fairy primrose
Primula malacoides
White, pink, rose, red, lavender in lacy whorls along upright stems. Splendid for winter-spring color; stands light frost.

Forget-me-not
Myosotis sylvatica
Sprays of tiny blue, white-eyed flowers 6–12" tall. Plant in shaded areas—good under flowering shrubs. Reseeds.

Foxglove
Digitalis purpurea
Erect plant to 4' or more with tubular flowers in purple, yellow, white, pastels. Leaves clump at base. Plant in shade.

Gaillardia
Gaillardia pulchella
Red, yellow, gold flowers on stems to 2'. Sun-loving plants thrive in heat. Plant in warm soil after frost danger is past.

Godetia
Clarkia amoena
Pink or lavender flowers; single or double. Grows 1 1/2–2 1/2' tall. Likes light shade or sun. Blooms in spring or summer.

Hollyhock
Alcea rosea
Single or double flowers in rose, red, pinks, yellow, white, apricot. Stems to 9' tall; best used as background plant.

Iceland poppy
Papaver nudicaule
Cup-shaped flowers in many colors on 1–2' stems. In mild climates, set out plants for winter and early spring bloom.

Impatiens
Impatiens wallerana
White, pink, rose, orange, or red flowers on bushy plants to 30" tall. Set out plants after frost in full sun (light shade in heat).

Larkspur
Consolida ambigua
Dense flowers on 1–5' stalks in blues, white, rose, lilac. Good background plant. Best bloom in spring and early summer.

Lobelia
Lobelia erinus
Tiny white or blue flowers on low-growing plants. Compact and trailing types. Good in containers and as borders.

Madagascar periwinkle
Catharanthus roseus
Phloxlike flowers in pure white or white with red, pink, or rose eye. Excellent in hot climates. (Often called *Vinca rosea*.)

Marigold
Tagetes
Yellow, orange, rust single or pompomlike flowers on stems from a few inches to 4' tall. Easy to grow.

Mexican sunflower
Tithonia rotundifolia
Rapid growth to 6'. Spectacular flower heads 3–4" across with orange-scarlet rays, tufted centers. Drought, heat resistant.

Mimulus
Mimulus hybridus
Large yellow flowers to 2 1/2" across spotted with brown, maroon. Needs cool temperatures, shade. Good in pots.

Nasturtium
Tropaeolum majus
Trailing or bushy plants 8–18" tall; can climb to 6'. Maroon, orange, yellow, red flowers. Grows in sun or part shade.

(Continued on next page)

Nemesia
Nemesia strumosa
Flowers in clusters on 3–4"
spikes in many colors, sometimes bicolored. Time plantings
to bloom when cool.

Nicotiana
Nicotiana
Fragrant flowers in white, red,
greenish yellow, mauve on 1–3'
stems. Flowers open at night or
on cloudy days; some stay open.

Pansy
Viola
Two types: Pansies have large
variegated blooms; violas have
smaller solid-colored flowers.
Both prefer semishade.

Petunia
Petunia hybrida
Flowers in many colors; single,
ruffled, or double. Plant in
containers or group together
in beds. Sun, light shade.

Phlox
Phlox drummondii
Numerous, showy bright and
pastel flowers in clusters at tops
of 6–18" stems. Good mass effect in full sun.

Pincushion flower
Scabiosa atropurpurea
Flowers from deep purple to
pink and white on stems to 3'
tall. Good in mixed beds or mass
plantings. Easy to grow.

Portulaca
Portulaca grandiflora
Small, roselike flowers in many
brilliant colors on trailing, succulent stems. Flowers open
fully only in sun.

Salpiglossis
Salpiglossis sinuata
Flowers much like petunias in
shape and size but colors are
shades of mahogany red, reddish orange, yellow, or pink.

Scarlet flax
Linum grandiflorum 'Rubrum'
Brilliant red flowers contrast
with gray-green foliage (also a
rose-colored form). Plants to 18"
tall. Quick, easy color.

Scarlet sage
Salvia splendens
Tall, thin flower spikes (in red,
rose, lavender, or white) 8–30"
on dark green plants. Use as
border or background plant.

Shirley poppy
Papaver rhoeas
Red, pink, orange, white, or
bicolor flowers on 2–5' stems.
Crepe-paperlike petals. Remove
seed pods for longer bloom.

Snapdragon
Antirrhinum majus
Perennial, usually treated as
annual. Many colors, forms.
Among best flowers for sunny
borders and cutting.

Spider flower
Cleome spinosa
Shrubby, branching plant 4–6'
tall with many open clusters
of pink or white flowers. Especially vigorous in warm areas.

Stock
Matthiola incana
Strongly scented flowers in
white, red, pink, cream, laven-
der, or purple on 1–3' plants.
Valued for fragrance.

Strawflower
Helichrysum bracteatum
Flowers with strawlike petals
in orange, red, white, or yellow.
Often grown for use as
dried flowers.

Sunflower
Helianthus annuus
Coarse, sturdy plant with large
yellow flowers. Best-known
form grows to 10'; seeds are
good to eat when roasted.

Sweet alyssum
Lobularia maritima
Masses of tiny flowers in white,
red, or violet. Use for quick
cover in a bulb bed or as a low
border. Reseeds prolifically.

Sweet William
Dianthus barbatus
Dense clusters of white, pink,
rose, red, purplish, or bicol-
ored flowers on 10–20" stems.
Thrives in full sun.

Verbena
Verbena hybrida
Flowers in violet, red, cream, or
pastels in clusters on creeping
stems. Drought resistant; needs
sun and heat to thrive.

Zinnia
Zinnia
Plants come in many sizes,
bright colors. Likes hot summer. Subject to mildew in foggy
areas or when sprinkled.

Perennials are repeat performers

Perennials are long-time favorites of gardeners everywhere. Unlike annuals, they continue to flower year after year, though some go dormant in winter after storing food in their roots for next spring's growth.

As a group, perennials are a hardy lot, even in the coldest climates. Mild-climate gardeners enjoy an added plus: many perennials hold their foliage all year.

Summer is the height of perennial flower season, but some perennials begin blooming in spring; others, such as chrysanthemums, bloom in late summer and autumn.

For many years, perennials were valued chiefly for their effectiveness in border planting. This is still one of their best uses. But today you see perennials used in much the same way as annuals: in mass plantings, in edgings, as bulb covers and ground covers. If you are a container-garden enthusiast, you'll find perennials to be excellent pot subjects for gracing a patio, deck, or terrace.

If you mass perennials, choose them carefully so they will work together in a harmonious pattern of color, form, size, and texture. Don't make the mistake of choosing plants that all bloom at the same time. A carefully planned border or bed will have two crescendos of special glory—early summer and early autumn—but there should be some color at other times (many gardeners include a few bulbs and annuals in the bed).

Plan to divide many perennials in your garden every few years (see pages 68–69). Autumn is a favorite time for dividing and replanting and for planting newly purchased plants. Plant them while the ground is still warm, so roots can get a good start before winter.

Though some require shade, most perennials prefer full sun.

Agapanthus
Agapanthus

Blue or white flower clusters on tall stems; strap-shaped leaves. Blooms in summer. Hardy to about 10°F/−12°C.

Agathaea
Felicia amelloides

Shrubby perennial. Produces sky-blue flowers. Trim severely in late summer. Hardy to about 20°F/−7°C.

Alyssum
Aurinia saxatilis

Tiny, dense golden yellow flowers on 8–12″ gray foliage. Plant as border or bulb cover. Blooms spring, summer.

Aster
Aster frikartii

Lavender-blue flowers on 2′ stalks. Flowers are fragrant single blooms to 2 1/2″ wide. Blooms spring to autumn.

Astilbe
Astilbe

Plumelike flowers in pink, red, or white on stems to 3′ or higher. Leaves serrated. Takes sun, light shade.

Baby's breath
Gypsophila paniculata

Much branched, to 3′ or more. Tiny white flowers, hundreds in a spray. Use in borders. Blooms summer, autumn.

Balloon flower
Platycodon grandiflorus

Balloonlike buds open into star-shaped flowers in blue, white, violet, or pink. Light shade in warm areas.

Bear's breech
Acanthus mollis

Spikes of white, lilac, or rose flowers on 2–3′ stems. Needs shade. Blooms in summer. Hardy to about 10°F/−12°C.

Bergenia
Bergenia

Pink, rose, or white flowers on stalks 12–18″ high; rounded, glossy-leafed foliage. Plant in shade. Blooms early.

Bleeding heart
Dicentra spectabilis

Pink and white heart-shaped flowers hang from 2–3′ arching stems. Best in shade garden. Blooms in spring.

Campanula
Campanula

Blue, white, or pink bell-shaped flowers. Many kinds from a few inches to several feet tall. Blooms in spring and summer.

Candytuft
Iberis sempervirens

White flowers in clusters on spreading plants 4–18″ high. Showy bloom in spring, sporadic bloom where mild.

(Continued on next page)

Carnation
Dianthus caryophyllus

Two types: border carnations 12–14" high, florist carnations 2–3'. Fragrant flowers in wide range of colors, spring to autumn.

Chrysanthemum
Chrysanthemum

Many flower forms. Almost any color except blue on plants 6"–3' tall. Blooms summer to winter.

Columbine
Aquilegia

Spurred flowers in red, yellow, blue, or purple on 1–4' plants. Good in woodland gardens. Blooms early in year.

Coral bells
Heuchera sanguinea

Pink, red, or white flowers on stalks to 2' tall above low rosettes of dark green leaves. Blooms spring, summer.

Coreopsis
Coreopsis

Yellow, orange, maroon, or reddish flowers on long stems. Blooms spring to autumn if faded flowers are removed.

Daylily
Hemerocallis

Many shades of yellow, red, orange, or cream lilylike flowers on stems to 4'. Blooms spring to autumn.

Delphinium
Delphinium

Tall blue, white, lavender, or pink flower spikes reach 6'. Stems need staking. Blooms in summer.

Dianthus
Dianthus plumarius

Single or double rose, pink, or white flowers. Excellent edging for borders. Spicy carnation scent. Blooms summer, autumn.

English daisy
Bellis perennis

White, red, or pink short-stemmed daisies on low rosettes of rounded leaves. Needs shade in hot areas. Blooms early.

False dragonhead
Physostegia virginiana

White, lavender, or rose flowers in dense 10" long spikes on 4' stems. Will take part shade. Blooms in summer.

Fibrous begonia, bedding begonia
Semperflorens begonias

White, pink, or red flowers massed above 4–18" foliage. Needs light shade. Blooms in summer. Sensitive to frost.

Gaillardia
Gaillardia grandiflora

Yellow, bronze, or red daisylike flowers on 2–3-ft. plants. Gray-green foliage. Blooms summer, autumn.

Gazania
Gazania

Yellow, pink, orange, or white daisylike flowers on clumping or trailing gray foliage to 10" tall. Hardy to about 20°F/ −7°C.

Geranium
Pelargonium hortorum

Enormous variety of form and color in flowers and leaves. Blooms summer, autumn. Prefers sun.

Geum
Geum

Double, semidouble, or single flowers in bright orange, yellow, or red. Mounded foliage to 15" high. Hardy to −10°F/ −23°C.

Gloriosa daisy
Rudbeckia hirta

Big yellow, orange, or brownish daisies to 7" across; plants grow to 4' tall. Blooms summer, autumn. Tough, easy plants.

Heliotrope
Heliotropium arborescens

Violet, white, or lavender strongly scented flowers in clusters on shrubby plants to 4' tall. Hardy to about 30°F/ −1°C.

Japanese anemone
Anemone hybrida

Single or semidouble white, pink, or rose flowers; 2–4' tall, dark green foliage. Grows in part shade. Blooms in autumn.

Kniphofia
Kniphofia uvaria

Red, yellow, and white cones of tubular flowers on tall stems. Grows to 8' tall. Hardy to about −10°F/ −23°C.

Lily of the valley
Convallaria majalis

Clusters of tiny, bell-shaped flowers above broad leaves. Needs cold winter. Blooms in spring. Prefers shade.

Lupine
Lupinus hybrids

Great color variety in flowers in dense clusters on 1 1/2–4′ plants. Blooms in summer. Needs cool weather.

Marguerite
Chrysanthemum frutescens

White, yellow, or pink daisylike flowers. Shrubby, rounded plants to 4′ across. Blooms in summer. May freeze.

Meadow rue
Thalictrum

Open, leafy stems 3–6′ high, topped by tiers of small white, lavender, or purple flowers. Blooms in summer.

Michaelmas daisy
Aster novae-angliae, A. novi-belgii

Graceful, branching plants to 4′ tall. Many varieties; flowers in white, pink, rose, red, purple. Long bloom period.

Oriental poppy
Papaver orientale

Brilliant and pastel flowers in reds, pinks, white on showy 4′ plants. Blooms in spring; foliage dies back in summer.

Painted daisy
Chrysanthemum coccineum

Bushy plant to 2–3′ with finely divided, bright green leaves. Daisylike flowers in pink, red, or white. Needs summer heat.

Pelargonium
Pelargonium domesticum

Showy flowers in white and shades of pink, lavender, red. Blooms spring, summer. Hardy to about 15°F/−9°C.

Penstemon
Penstemon

Flowers in shades of red, pink, white, and blue grow on plants that reach 4′ tall. Blooms in spring, summer.

Peony
Paeonia

Spectacular red, white, pink, or cream flowers; plants 2–4′ tall, wider spread; large, handsome leaves. Needs cold, frosty winter.

Phlox
Phlox

Many flower colors; variety of plant types ranging from 6″ to 5′ tall. Uses vary. Blooms in summer.

Plantain lily
Hosta

White or lilac flowers on thin spikes above massed clumps of handsome foliage up to 3′ high. Needs shade. Summer.

Plumbago
Ceratostigma

Deep blue flowers on 6–12″ branches. May freeze in winter; resprouts. Summer, autumn bloom.

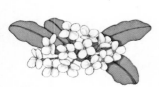

Rockcress
Arabis

White, pink, or rose-purple spring flowers on plants 4–10″ tall. Takes light shade. Hardy to about −30°F/−34°C.

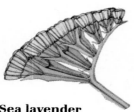

Sea lavender
Limonium

Blue, purple, white, pink two-toned flowers. Coarse foliage to about 1′ tall. Blooms spring, summer. Prefers dry spot.

Sedum
Sedum spectabile

Many varieties with red to pink flowers. Succulent leaves, clumps of erect stems. Blooms summer, autumn.

Shasta daisy
Chrysanthemum maximum

Big, white single or double daisies to 3–4″ wide, 2–4′ tall, above dark, coarse foliage to 18″ high. Blooms in summer.

Tradescantia
Tradescantia andersoniana

Three-petaled blue, lavender, white, or pink flowers open for only a day but are seldom out of bloom in summer.

Transvaal daisy
Gerbera jamesonii

Yellow, orange, coral, flame, or red daisylike flowers on stems to 18″. Blooms summer to late autumn. Hardy to 15°F/−9°C.

Violet
Viola odorata

Small, often fragrant flowers in blue, purple, or white. Leaves to 6″ high. Needs shade. Blooms in spring.

Yarrow
Achillea

Yellow, white, rose, or red flowers in flat clusters on plants from 8″ to several feet tall. Blooms in summer, autumn.

Bulbs, the garden showoffs

The term "bulb" is often loosely applied to a number of unrelated kinds of plants. However, all of these plants share a common characteristic: they store food in swollen underground parts during dormant seasons. When their growth season comes around, roots and leaves sprout from this natural storehouse.

Professional gardeners use several terms when speaking about bulbs, depending on how each plant forms its underground food storehouse. A true bulb (such as a daffodil or a lily) is made up of fleshy underground leaves around a short piece of stem. Bulblike plants with different underground parts are corms, tubers, rhizomes, and tuberous roots.

True bulbs often bloom in spring (tulips, narcissus, and hyacinths, for example), though lilies normally bloom in summer. Tulips and hyacinths grow well for only a season or two after you buy them, since professionals have given them special care (that you cannot duplicate) in order to develop big showy blooms. If you leave them in the ground, the flowers will get smaller (and wilder looking) the second year, then may stop blooming completely.

Tulips and hyacinths require a period of cold weather to send them into complete dormancy before the growing season. Where winters are mild, buy the bulbs in early autumn and store them in the vegetable bin of your refrigerator for a month before you put them in the ground.

Consider the climate requirements of the bulbs you're interested in planting. To gardeners, "hardy" describes a plant's resistance to, or tolerance of, frost or freezing temperatures. The word does not mean tough, pest-resistant, or disease-resistant. A half-hardy plant is hardy in a given situation during normal years, but subject to damage from freezing in the coldest winters.

"Tender" is the opposite of hardy. Plants described as tender are sensitive to cold weather and have low tolerance of freezing temperatures.

Once a bulb has flowered, pick off dead blooms, but wait to cut the foliage. The bulb needs the leaves to make food for the following year's growth and bloom.

Also see pages 26 and 67.

Sure sign of spring, perky yellow daffodils brighten a garden corner beneath birch trees. Massed plantings create an impressive scene, but even a few bulbs placed here and there can be surprisingly effective.

Calla
Zantedeschia

White, gold, red, or pink flowers. Plant in spring or autumn; sun or part shade. Blooms spring, summer. Tender to half-hardy.

Canna
Canna

Many colors (no blues). Plant in May or June; needs sun. Blooms in summer. Half-hardy.

Crocus
Crocus

Yellow, orange, lavender, purple, or white flowers. Plant in autumn; sun, light shade. Needs winter chill.

Daffodil
Narcissus

Yellow, orange, white, or bicolored flowers. Plant in autumn; sun, light shade. Blooms in spring. Hardy.

Dahlia
Dahlia

Many colors (no blue). Plant in spring; sun. Blooms late summer, autumn. Lift tubers in cold-winter areas.

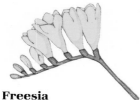

Freesia
Freesia

Many colors. Plant in autumn; sun. Blooms in spring. Killed by freezing temperatures.

Gladiolus
Gladiolus

Many colors and shades. Plant in spring (winter in desert regions); sun. Tender.

Grape hyacinth
Muscari

Blue or white flowers. Plant in autumn; sun, light shade. Blooms in spring. Hardy.

Hyacinth
Hyacinthus

Red, pink, blue, purple, white, or yellow flowers. Plant September–November; sun, light shade. Needs winter chilling.

Iris
Iris

Many colors, species. Plant July–October; sun. Blooms in spring; some varieties repeat bloom. Many species hardy.

Lily
Lilium

Many colors. Plant in autumn; sun or part shade. Blooms in summer. Hardy.

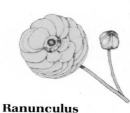

Ranunculus
Ranunculus

Many colors (no blue). Plant in autumn; sun. Blooms in spring. Half-hardy.

Snowdrop
Galanthus

White flowers. Plant in autumn; sun, part shade. Blooms in early spring, even in snow.

Snowflake
Leucojum

White flowers. Plant in autumn; part shade. Blooms in winter, spring. Hardy.

Spider lily
Lycoris

Yellow, pink, rose, or red flowers. Plant in late summer or autumn; sun, part shade. Blooms late. Tender to half-hardy.

Tuberous begonia
Begonia tuberhybrida

Many colors (no blue). Plant in winter, early spring; filtered sun. Blooms summer to fall. Tender; used as bedding, pot plant.

Tulip
Tulipa

Many colors. Plant in autumn; sun, light shade. Blooms in spring. Hardy. Needs winter chilling.

Watsonia
Watsonia

White, pink, lavender, or red flowers. Plant late summer, autumn; sun. Blooms late spring, summer. Half-hardy.

Windflower
Anemone

Blue, red, pink, or white flowers. Plant October–November; sun, light shade. Blooms in spring. Hardy.

Zephyr flower
Zephyranthes

Rose, pink, yellow, or white flowers. Plant in spring (summer, fall in mild areas); sun. Autumn bloom. Half-hardy.

Lawn grasses...cool to look at, soft underfoot

There are more than 40 kinds of grasses for home gardens, but they come under one of two broad classifications: cool-season or warm-season.

If you live in a region where winter brings heavy frosts or snow, you'll have to grow the hardy cool-season types. In mild-winter regions, warm-season grasses thrive with far less care than cool-season.

Cool-season grasses

These are the bents, fescues, bluegrasses, and rye grasses. You can buy a single type or blends.

Bents. Creeping bent (*Agrostis stolonifera, A.s. palustris*), colonial bent (*Agrostis tenuis*), redtop (*Agrostis gigantea*). High maintenance; require careful attention to mowing, fertilizing, watering, disease control. Erect types should be mowed to 3/4 inch to 1 inch; creeping types to 1/2 inch. Avoid shade.

Fescues. Fine fescues (*Festuca*) are found in most fine-leafed lawn mixes. The rolled leaves look like tiny soft needles. Easily grown in most soils; fairly drought resistant. Mow to 1 1/2 to 2 inches. Shade tolerant.

Coarse fescues are rugged; good for athletic fields, children's play yards. Mow to 2 inches. Sun.

Bluegrasses. Kentucky bluegrass (*Poa pratensis*), rough-stalked bluegrass (*Poa trivialis*), annual bluegrass (*Poa annua*). Widely grown. Available in many mixes. Most types do best if mowed to 1 1/2–2 inches. Only one type, *Poa trivialis*, does well in shade.

Rye grasses. Perennial rye (*Lolium perenne*), Italian or annual ryegrass (*Lolium multiflorum*). Both perennial and annual types are fast growers but have bunchy growth habit. Often hard to mow. Keep at 1 1/2 inches.

Warm-season grasses

Unlike cool-season grasses, warm-season grasses grow vigorously during hot weather and go dormant in cool or cold winters.

Zoysia grasses. *Zoysia japonica, Zoysia matrella.* Very slow to establish, but eventually make a strong, dense turf (no weeds, Bermuda, insects, or diseases). Dormant in winter. Quite drought resistant, easy to maintain. Mow to 3/4 inch high. Sun or shade.

Bermuda grasses. Common Bermuda (*Cynodon dactylon*), hybrid Bermudas. Fine-textured. Recent hybrid strains are very popular. For winter green, fertilize in early autumn and remove thatch. Mow to 1/2 inch. Won't take shade.

St. Augustine grass. *Stenotaphrum secundatum.* A coarse, wide-bladed, tough, green grass, extremely easy to maintain. Has short dormancy. You need a power mower for this one; mow to 1 inch in growing season. Takes some shade.

Centipede grass. *Eremochloa ophiuroides.* Grows well in Southeast and Hawaii. Requires less maintenance than other warm-season grasses. Drought resistant, but performs better with regular watering during hot, dry weather. Needs very little fertilizer; too much will kill it. Cut to 1/2 inch.

Bahia grass. *Paspalum notatum.* Common bahia is a pasture grass. Finer-leafed strains, such as Paraguay and Argentine, make good lawn turf in either sun or partial shade. Bahia tends to stay green longer in winter than other warm-season grasses. Two or three applications of fertilizer in early spring and autumn are sufficient. Mow to 1 1/2–3 inches.

Dichondra. A soft, green, ground-hugging, broad-leafed plant that is widely grown as a lawn in mild-winter areas. Can be used as a turf plant in most areas where winter temperatures don't drop below 25°F/−4°C.

Grows low and tight in sunny areas with heavy foot traffic, can reach 6 inches high in shady areas with light foot traffic. Needs regular, thorough waterings, especially during hot weather. Prefers frequent light fertilizing. Mow to 3/4 inch, higher in hot weather.

Green and lush, this well-cared-for lawn complements the house. Yellow marigolds, lavender statice, and a blue house door add just a touch of color. Landscape architect: Mary Gordon.

Ground covers for versatility

Wherever you want a uniform carpet of green but don't want to cope with the difficulties of keeping a lawn healthy, consider ground covers. They usually require far less maintenance, fertilizing, and watering than lawn grasses. Do keep in mind, though, that ground covers aren't suitable in heavy traffic areas.

Ground covers are sold in various forms. For example, junipers may come in gallon-sized metal or plastic containers, dwarf periwinkle may come in a pot, and ajuga in a flat or small plastic container.

Listed here are a few popular ground covers. Your nursery may stock other varieties that will do as well in your region. Some herbs, such as rosemary and thyme, make excellent ground covers (see pages 98–99).

Before you choose a ground cover, consider these points: How much cold will the plant take? How fast will it grow? Does it need sun or shade? How far apart should the plants be spaced?

Tiny white flowers of Scotch moss and large yellow gazania blossoms provide contrast in this combination ground cover planting.

Ajuga
Ajuga reptans

Fast growing; thick carpet of dark green leaves. Blue flowers in spring and early summer. Sun or part shade.

Cotoneaster
Cotoneaster

Several varieties of good, fast-growing ground covers. Deciduous, semideciduous, evergreen varieties. Sun, part shade.

Creeping St. Johnswort
Hypericum calycinum

Evergreen; semideciduous where winters are cold. Short-stalked leaves, bright yellow flowers. Sun or shade.

Dwarf periwinkle
Vinca minor

Trailing stems root as they spread. Lavender-blue flowers; some forms with white, double blue, deeper blue flowers.

Dwarf plumbago
Ceratostigma plumbaginoides

Wiry-stemmed perennial. Bronzy green to dark green leaves. Blue flowers from July until frost. Cut back in winter.

English ivy
Hedera helix

Evergreen, woody ground cover or climbing vine. Dark, dull green leaves with paler veins. Sun or shade in most climates.

Ice plant
Lampranthus

Succulent. Brilliant flowers winter–spring. Full sun; little water. Cut back after bloom. Hardy to 20° to 30°F/−7° to −1°C.

Japanese spurge
Pachysandra terminalis

Rich, dark green leaves. Small, fluffy spikes of white flowers in summer. Plant in shade. Spreads by runners.

Juniper
Juniperus

Ground cover varieties range from a few inches to 2–3′ high. Prostrate and creeping junipers often used in rock gardens.

Mondo grass
Ophiopogon japonicus

Dark green leaves; light lilac flowers in summer. Slow to establish as ground cover. Needs shade in hot, dry areas.

Snow-in-summer
Cerastium tomentosum

Good in mild or cold climates, coastal or desert areas. Silvery gray foliage; masses of white flowers in early summer.

Winter creeper
Euonymus fortunei

Good ground cover where temperatures drop below 0°F/ −18°C. In desert climates, takes full sun better than ivy.

Vines climb, tumble, twine

Before you select a vine for a specific landscape situation, you'll want to know just how it will grow. Will it be dense or rather open and airy? Will it stay within the confines of the area set aside for it? Is it deciduous or evergreen? Does it flower? Is it hardy? Will it be in scale with the rest of the garden?

Some vines produce flowers for cutting or for display. And some have striking foliage. Others bear fruits or berries (see pages 96—97) or vegetables (pages 90—95).

Several of the most popular vines are shown below. But don't forget there are many annual vines that you can easily plant from seed, such as morning glory, sweet pea, black-eyed Susan, scarlet runner bean, and moonflower.

For ways to train and tie vines, see pages 114—115. For vines to grow for specific purposes, see the charts on pages 137—152.

Spring shower of white flower clusters hangs from wisteria vine above deck. Note how blossoms hang in many different levels; branches were trained for upright growth as well as along trellis. Landscape architect: Robert W. Chittock.

Boston ivy
Parthenocissus tricuspidata

Semievergreen in mild-winter areas, deciduous elsewhere. Clings tightly to make fast, dense, even wall cover.

Creeping ñg
Ficus pumila

Evergreen. Attaches securely to wood, masonry, metal. Small, heart-shaped to oval leaves. Hardy to about 15°F/−9°C.

Hall's honeysuckle
Lonicera japonica 'Halliana'

Evergreen; deciduous or semideciduous in cold regions. Rampant grower; good bank or ground cover.

Passion vine
Passiflora

Evergreen, semievergreen, or deciduous. Climbs by tendrils. Vigorous; prune branches annually after second year.

Star jasmine
Trachelospermum jasminoides

Evergreen. Twining vine, or spreading shrub or ground cover. Fragrant, white flowers. Hardy to about 20°F/−7°C.

Trumpet vine
Campsis, Distictis, Clytostoma

Deciduous and evergreen. Strong growing. Scarlet, orange-red, salmon, purple, or white trumpet-shaped flowers.

Virginia creeper
Parthenocissus quinquefolia

Deciduous. Vigorous; clings to or runs over fence, trellis, ground. Good ground cover on slopes. Bright autumn leaves.

Wisteria
Wisteria

Deciduous. Climbing, woody. Prune to control size, shape. Violet, white, purple, or blue flower clusters in spring.

Watering Your Garden

- Watering techniques: page 50
- Mulch saves water & weeding: page 52
- Installing a sprinkler system: page 53
- Garden hoses, sprinklers, & accessories: page 54
- Drip irrigation: page 56
- Watering plants in containers: page 57
- Watering vegetables: page 58

Watering techniques

Most garden plants get their moisture from the soil layers near the surface. Only a few plants—mainly grasses and trees—have roots that can reach down into the deeper layers. But the surface layers of soil are constantly losing water. The plants take it up through their roots and release it through their leaves during the day, particularly in hot weather. Also, as the sun heats the ground, moisture evaporates. Dry winds also cause evaporation. These sources of water loss are at their worst in hot climates with long, dry seasons.

Below and on the following pages are suggestions and techniques for keeping the soil moist. By following these points you'll keep watering to a minimum, and the watering you do will reach the plant roots instead of evaporating.

Soil type is important

When you wet soil, the water penetrates according to the soil type and structure (for description of soil types see pages 6–7).

Soils can take only so much water. Clay or adobe holds moisture like a sponge and can absorb about three times as much water as sand. Therefore, you'll have to water sandy soil more often than clay.

But, heavy clay soil won't accept water as quickly as sandy, porous soil. Copious watering may only create rivers that flow into the gutter and leave much of the soil dry.

Differences in soil structure also affect water penetration. If you lay topsoil on a different kind of native soil, the water is likely to go as far as the boundary line between the types and then just sit or flow away to the side. The same thing can happen when you place a new plant in a hole and put your garden soil back in the hole around the root ball: water outside the root ball won't go in, and water inside won't go out. And since roots only go where there's moisture, they may never grow out of the original nursery soil.

For all these reasons, you should amend the soil as described on pages 8–10. Amendments help to lighten dense soil, hold water in porous soil, and create a transitional zone between the soil types.

Many kinds of amendments can also be used as mulches to help retain water in the soil. A mulch helps keep the ground beneath cool and moist, so mulched plants are able to go longer between waterings than unmulched ones. See page 52 for more information on the benefits of mulching.

Deep soaking for proper root growth

If you water for a brief period each day, you will only wet the upper few inches of soil. This happens because you haven't watered enough to exceed the holding capacity of that layer of soil and force water down. The roots of your plants will stay in the moist upper layer. Because moisture evaporates quickly, you'll waste time and water using this method. And, if you forget to water or there's a hot spell in July, you may lose a lot of plants. Another drawback of frequent watering is that it encourages growth of weed seeds, fungi, and disease organisms.

The best general watering plan is to soak the soil deeply and not water again until the top few inches of soil begin to dry out. Plant roots will extend into deeper soil where they stay cool, and any weeds at the top won't be as likely to grow. If you have dense soil, water slowly so the water has time to penetrate. To be sure it has, wait a day or two, then dig down about 18 inches and see if the subsoil is moist.

Another method of testing water penetration is to use a narrow, pointed probe. You should be able to push the probe as deep as the soil is moist. It won't push easily into dry soil.

To be more scientific, you could use a soil sampler or auger to

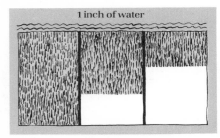

Through sand (left), 1 inch of water penetrates 12 inches. Through average soil (center), 1 inch of water soaks 6–10 inches deep. Through clay (right), 1 inch of water reaches 4–5 inches.

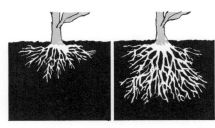

Light watering (left) makes shallow roots. Hot spells may damage plant. Deep watering (right) sends roots down into cool, moist soil.

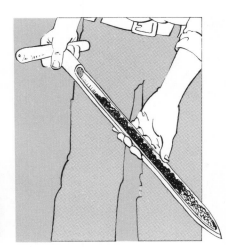

Sample soil core shows top two-thirds of sample is moist, the rest is dry. Longer waterings are needed for deeper soaking. Tube has marked scale.

take a core—it'll reach down to 3 feet. If your soil sample is dry below the first 3 inches, you need to water for longer periods of time. If it's soggy near the top, then hard, then dry, the soil needs to be aerated. If you find a hard layer just below the surface, then your soil should be improved with amendments (see pages 8–10).

Understanding the drip line

Plant roots usually spread as wide as the plant foliage. In taking up water and nutrients, the tips of the root mass play the most active part. The term "drip line" simply means the circle beneath the outer leaves of a plant where most rainwater drips to the ground. The effect is similar to water dripping off an umbrella.

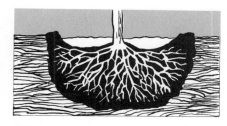

Watering basin *extending outside the drip line directs water to entire root zone of the plant.*

Build a low, circular dike of earth just outside the drip line of a plant and you'll have a watering basin. Fill it with water and let the water penetrate. The roots have time to absorb the water because the branches shade the area, cutting down evaporation. You can use the same watering basin to fertilize the plant.

Wind can steal water

When you turn on a sprinkler on a windy day, much of the water may be carried away before it can penetrate the soil. Some is carried away as windborne particles; some evaporates from the surface before it sinks in. If possible, turn on sprinklers only in still weather. If it's necessary to water on a windy day, use a soaker.

Wind also steals water that the plants draw up and release through

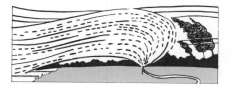

Water *when air is still, not on windy day.*

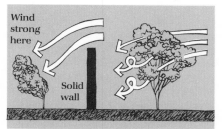

Plant shrubs and trees *as windbreak for your garden. They cut wind speed (solid wall won't), lessening wind's adverse effects.*

their leaves. In still weather, the air around the leaf surface is humid, so the loss of moisture is not as great. Windy weather causes a more rapid water loss from leaves and may dry up plants so much that they burn or die.

If your property sits in the path of a prevailing wind, arrange your garden in such a way that plants will have a windbreak. Trees and tall plants placed on the windy side will help; but solid fences or masonry walls may not. Because wind flows like water, it will come over the top of a solid barrier in a wave, crashing down on the other side. If the windbreak lets some of the wind through, it creates turbulence on the lee side, breaking up the wave into eddies that do less damage.

Roots compete for water

Spade around shrubs growing close to trees and chances are you'll find a network of roots that the tree has

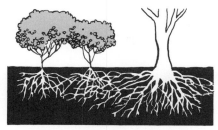

Tree roots *can steal moisture from root systems of nearby plants.*

sent out to tap the moisture supply in frequently watered beds. This is particularly true if the tree is along the street or in some other location that doesn't get regular watering.

Cultivating the soil between the shrubs and the tree two or three times during the season will cut these roots and reduce the competition. Giving the tree its own water rations will help, too.

Weeds also rob soil of its moisture; some do much more so than others. Weeds deplete soil of valuable nutrients as well.

Leaves can tell you when to water

Most leaves show a dullness, a loss of reflective quality, or inward-rolling edges just before they wilt. In many cases when an unwatered shrub or tree drops leaves, that's nature's way of getting the plant through a drought. When water comes to it again, it will grow new leaves.

Shelters for shade plants

Adjusting to the various water needs of plants scattered about the garden is a nuisance. But if you plant all your moisture-loving plants in a bed sheltered from the sun and drying winds, you will save both water and time. Also, in hot dry areas, it's about the only way you can successfully grow such plants as fuchsias, tuberous begonias, and hydrangeas.

Compacted soil causes runoff

Water will run off compacted soil long before the soil is saturated.

If soil in lawn areas is compacted, chances are the root zone is still dry after you water. Best treatment is to aerate the soil: open it up by coring to let in water, air, and fertilizer.

On open beds you can see compacted soil. Spade it up and add a soil amendment (see pages 8–10); spread a 3-inch layer of amendment over the ground and work it into the top 6 to 8 inches of soil.

Mulch saves water & weeding

A mulch is simply a covering for the soil. Gardeners have used almost any material as a mulch, including old newspaper, foot-deep straw, grass clippings, tree leaves, roofing paper, and plastic. These and many other materials will work if they satisfy these two basic conditions: The mulch should help to retain water in the soil on hot days, and it should smother weeds. A third but less important condition is that it looks attractive. Mulch can also insulate plants in cold weather.

If you leave soil uncovered, hot sun and wind will quickly dry it out, forcing you to water more often. The additional water may also produce unwanted weeds. Another disadvantage of bare soil is that the top layer often gets too hot for good root growth. Even if you manage to keep the soil moist, your plants won't grow as well as they should.

Even though sun will heat the surface of a mulch, the soil below is insulated because the mulch holds air. And any moisture in the soil has a hard time evaporating through the differently textured mulch. Mulch prevents sunlight from reaching the soil underneath, so weeds grow with difficulty. Most weeds are smothered, but those that grow are rooted in the loose mulch and come up easily.

You should not let mulches build up against the trunk or stem of a plant (commonly called the "crown") because the trunk may rot if it stays moist too long.

You can use any of the materials mentioned here as mulch, but also check the other materials listed in the soil amendment chart, page 10. (Some of these materials should be used along with a nitrogen fertilizer as indicated in the chart.)

When you choose a mulch, consider the following:

• It should be fairly easy to wet. For example, peat moss dries out quickly, and once dry it won't absorb water easily.

• It should be dense enough not to blow away.

Ground bark is a good choice for a mulch, since it meets all of the above requirements even when finely ground (for certain very windy areas, you may want to use large chips or chunks of fir or other wood).

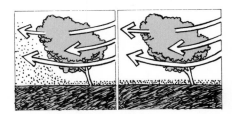

Powdery mulch (left) may blow away in wind; denser mulch stays in place (right).

Most organic mulches should be dug into the soil every year or two and a new layer added. Spade the mulch under as winter begins and replace it just before weed growth starts in spring. Where winters are mild and rainy, you may want to replace the mulch immediately to maintain weed control.

Turn mulch into soil in fall. Add a new layer right away, or wait until spring. Dig no more than 3–4 inches deep inside the drip line.

Black polyethylene plastic is a valuable mulch in the vegetable garden. It tends to absorb extra heat and warm the soil, promoting fast root growth at the beginning of the season and greater crop yields.

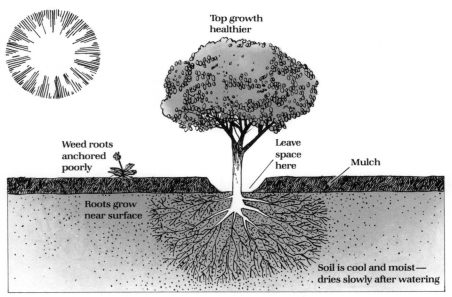

Top growth healthier

Weed roots anchored poorly

Roots grow near surface

Leave space here

Mulch

Soil is cool and moist— dries slowly after watering

Three-inch layer of mulch keeps the root zone of a plant cool and moist even in hot weather. Mulched plants may grow twice as big as those without a mulch, produce better flowers and fruit. Plant roots grow thicker, and water won't evaporate as rapidly. Weeds may grow on mulch surface but are easy to pull out.

Installing a sprinkler system

1) *Dig 8-inch-deep trenches for pipes. String tied to stakes helps digger keep trench line straight.*

2) *Attach control valve with anti-siphon valve to water-source pipe at least 6 inches above ground.*

3) *Assemble pipe, from water source outward, with sprinkler head and riser already fitted. Keep riser upright.*

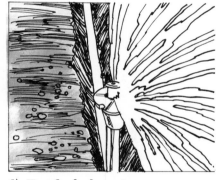

4) *Test for leaks and proper coverage after welds are dry and after first flushing out pipes with sprinkler heads removed.*

5) *Fill in trenches, mounding loose soil above ground level along center of each trench.*

6) *Tamp soil firmly along length of trenches with heavy soil compactor to minimize visible settling.*

It's not difficult to assemble a sprinkler system from solvent-welded PVC (polyvinyl chloride) pipe. You'll need a shovel or spade, pipe wrench, hacksaw, file or sharp knife, pipe-cleaning compound, PVC solvent cement, tape measure, and soil tamper.

The first step is to make a plan; most sprinkler supply companies will help you do this. They'll need some basic information: the area to be watered, the kind of lawn you want, the plantings and buildings next to it, and the location of your water source—a scale map of your garden helps.

They should also know the diameter of the water supply pipe and whether it's galvanized iron or copper, your water pressure (most sprinkler companies will lend or rent you a pressure gauge), and the size of your water meter (look on the meter to see if it's marked or call the water company).

The company that sells you the parts for your sprinkler system will also give you a sheet of assembly instructions. The drawings here give a general idea of what to do.

It's helpful to attach an extra valve first to let you shut off water to the sprinklers while you install them—without turning off the whole water system. (In step 2 you see the extra valve.)

Put the system together one piece at a time. The pipe comes in 10 or 20-foot sections. As you need shorter lengths, measure carefully and cut with a hacksaw, keeping the cut end as square as possible. Remove burrs with a file.

When you're ready to weld parts together, you must work quickly. The plastic solvent adheres quite readily—and once welded, joints cannot be broken apart. (You might want to practice welding a few times.) First apply the cleaning compound, then before it dries daub plastic solvent on both parts. Shove the parts together tightly, and give the parts a half twist to make a good seal.

After installing the control valve on the first section of pipe (see step 2), let the welds dry for 6 hours, then test the pipe for leaks; this section will remain under constant pressure.

Garden hoses, sprinklers, & accessories

Almost everyone needs a hose and attachments for it—nozzles, soakers, sprinklers—even in areas that receive a lot of rain.

Garden hoses come in different sizes. Hose *diameter* is an important consideration. Regardless of what your water pressure happens

What size garden hose?

1/2-inch hose. In 15 seconds, a 50-foot length of 1/2-inch hose filled this 5-gallon jar approximately 1/3 full. If you have big, thirsty trees and shrubs to water, buy a larger size. Advantages of 1/2-inch size are light weight (6 pounds), easy storage. Fine for watering container plants; can be maneuvered by a child.

5/8-inch hose. A 50-foot length of 5/8-inch hose delivered twice the amount of water as the size at left, in same period of time. This size is practical for almost any home garden. Middle-sized 5/8-inch hose weighs only 1 1/2 pounds more than the 1/2-inch hose, sells best in regions with fairly large lots or low water pressure.

3/4-inch hose. Big 3/4-inch hose, 50 feet, filled jar in 15 seconds. With pressure of 50 pounds per square inch, it put an inch of water on 1,500-sq. ft. lawn in 39 minutes. "Big daddy" of garden hoses, 3/4-inch size is heavy (11 pounds) and hard to store. It's long wearing and is a necessity with some kinds of sprinklers.

Hand nozzles

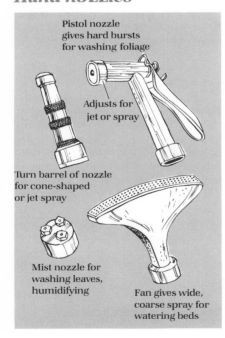

Pistol nozzle gives hard bursts for washing foliage

Adjusts for jet or spray

Turn barrel of nozzle for cone-shaped or jet spray

Mist nozzle for washing leaves, humidifying

Fan gives wide, coarse spray for watering beds

Seven soakers

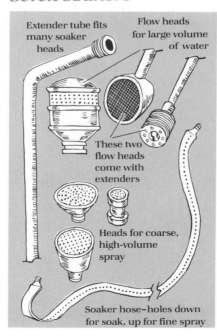

Extender tube fits many soaker heads

Flow heads for large volume of water

These two flow heads come with extenders

Heads for coarse, high-volume spray

Soaker hose—holes down for soak, up for fine spray

Three ways to store hoses

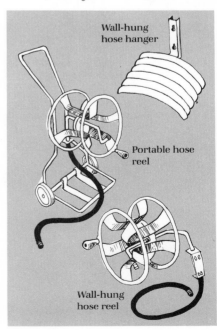

Wall-hung hose hanger

Portable hose reel

Wall-hung hose reel

to be, the output from a hose is in direct ratio to the hose's inside diameter. Standard sizes for general garden use are 1/2, 5/8, and 3/4-inch diameter.

With the hose, you'll need equipment for using, storing, and possibly repairing it. When you buy hose repair parts, be sure you have the right kind. Many can be used on both plastic and rubber hoses, but check the package to make sure. Also, you must buy the right parts for the diameter of hose; check your hose diameter before selecting repair parts.

Subsoil irrigator *puts water right where the roots can use it. It's most useful with deeply rooted trees and shrubs.*

Sprinkler patterns

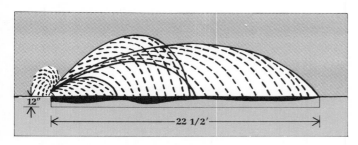

12"

22 1/2'

If you move sprinkler *to obtain overlap, this pattern is effective. Oscillating type makes this pattern, as does the rotating "machine gun" type, which shoots rapid-fire jets.*

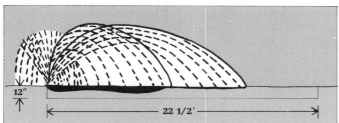

12"

22 1/2'

Most water *drops on inside; you must make successive overlaps. Several sprinklers work this way, including "fixed head" and whirling baffle types.*

12"

22 1/2'

Useful but erratic; *most water falls from 4 to 8 feet out. Some examples: plastic tube soakers; types with revolving arms; those which squirt from holes in sieve pattern.*

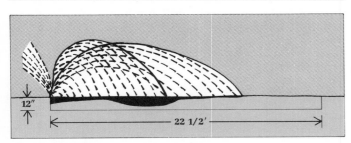

12"

22 1/2'

Cone spray *soaks only a small area; for best results, turn water to half-pressure, move sprinkler often. One cone spray has two big holes like owl's eyes.*

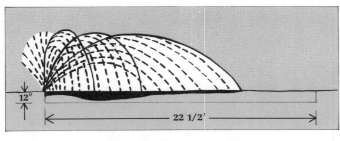

12"

22 1/2'

Fan spray *throws most water 7 to 14 feet from sprinkler head. Example: nailhead spike type, which sprays water through a slit in its head.*

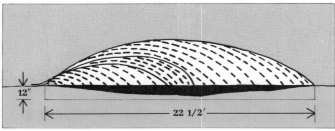

12"

22 1/2'

Drip irrigation

A drip system delivers small amounts of water to individual plants through a network of narrow tubes or porous tubing. The water is delivered slowly, over a long period of time, so that it soaks each plant's root area. You use less water than by sprinkling, but it takes a longer time to apply the needed amount of water to each plant.

In sandy soil, in which there is very limited lateral spread of delivered water, you will have to space the points where water is released closer together than you would for clay soil.

A drip system can be on or below the ground, or underneath mulch. In mild climates you can leave it in place year round. If you'll be recultivating the soil for annuals or vegetables, you may prefer to remove the tubing after each growing season. Where the ground freezes in winter, take up the system in autumn and detach any controls that might hold standing water.

For the best results, put together your own system from the numerous manufactured components—hoses, emitters, pressure reducers, filters. Some components can turn your present garden hoses into drip irrigators. To locate what you need, check under "Sprinklers" or "Irrigation Systems & Equipment" in the Yellow Pages.

Hoses and tubes. Usually black or dark-colored to prevent algae growth, hoses and tubes graduate downward in size to thin "microtubes." Sometimes the main tube is rigid plastic—more of a pipe than a hose—with narrower flexible tubing leading from it.

Arrange the hoses and tubes to extend from your water source to the plants you wish to water (use pins to keep the tubes in place). Tubes can be arranged in many ways.

Porous tubing. Excellent for watering rows of vegetables or flowers, these tubes deliver water along their whole length. They're not soaker hoses—water leaves them more slowly than it does through a standard hose with holes punched along it. They take the place of emitters. You can loop porous tubing around plants, but don't put it right against the trunk or base.

Emitters. These devices are attached to the basic hose and tube system to actually deliver the water. They let the water drip, bubble, or squirt out. Sometimes they pierce a hose; in other systems they're attached to the end of a tube (with very narrow tubing they're not necessary).

By selecting emitters that deliver different quantities of water, you can give more water to a shrub that requires it and less water to the next plant on the drip system.

Pressure regulators. Drip systems slow the flow of water by reducing its pressure. Most do this either by a regulator at the beginning of the system or by pressure-reducing mechanisms in the emitters themselves.

If you attach a drip system to the domestic water supply for an extended period of time, you must install an antisiphon valve where the drip system connects to your outdoor water supply.

Water filters. Most drip systems are equipped with some kind of screen or filter to keep narrow-bore tubes or emitters from clogging with sediment, soil organisms, and mineral deposits.

Filters should be attached to all drip systems; cleaning a filter isn't as difficult as cleaning out clogged emitters. Several times a year—once a month if your water is less than clear—clean the filter and flush the line.

If algae do grow, use diluted swimming pool chlorine or a commercial inhibitor. Diluted mineral acid (like muriatic acid) will clear mineral deposits.

Emitters of several types attach to lengths of tubing, use a built-in pressure-reducer to slow the water flow to a trickle. System can be buried.

Flexible tube system can run unobtrusively along a fence or wall to reach individual plants.

Porous tubing delivers water where roots are concentrated; it's useful along row plantings, can form loops.

Watering plants in containers

Keeping container plants moist is often difficult because there is only a limited amount of soil to hold moisture. Also, water can evaporate through the sides and bottom of many containers. In warm weather, some container plants may need water several times a day.

You should water whenever the top inch or so of soil feels dry. Be sure to water until the water begins to run out of the drainage holes.

The frequent watering that containers require depletes nutrients, so fertilize often.

By checking the soil moisture of your plants every day or so, you'll quickly learn which plants need more water and which ones need less.

Ways to keep containers moist include the following:

• Repot plants regularly. Pot-bound plants have no reserve of moist soil outside the root area.

• Soak the soil. Periodically submerge pots in a tub of water until air bubbles stop rising.

• Use double pots. Put small pots inside larger ones and insulate the space between with gravel or moist peat moss.

• Group container plants close together. Five or six pots placed together help to protect each other from heat.

• Move pots into a little more shade and a lot less wind.

• Spread a mulch over the soil surface.

Repot   Use   Submerge   Set on
          two pots   gravel

Rinsing off foliage isn't a good watering practice. Water soil first, then spray foliage to remove dust, pests.

Don't use a strong jet of water from hose; it may gouge out a hole in the soil. A soaker head, with or without a long handle, is best. Or use a hose with water flow at a trickle.

Special watering situations may require special tools: large hardware stores and nurseries stock watering accessories. An on-off valve may help conserve water, but be sure your hose is solid.

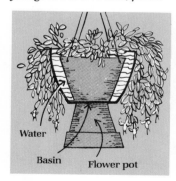

Water

Basin   Flower pot

Soaking a plant with trailing branches can be difficult. Set a basin on overturned pot, put plant container inside, and fill with water.

Dry root ball may shrink away from container sides so water runs around the outside without soaking the soil. If there is space between soil and pot, scrape soil from root ball to fill the gap or add extra soil mix. Water until soil is soaked.

Watering vegetables

Good-tasting vegetables require a steady supply of moisture for uninterrupted growth from seeding to harvest. Too much water will encourage foliage rather than fruit development; too much can also suffocate the roots so they're unable to grow. On the other hand, allowing the roots to dry out will stop growth completely and damage or kill the plant quickly on a hot day. Your watering goal is to keep the moisture level as even as possible, penetrating the soil below root depth and repeating before the soil dries out enough to cause the plants to wilt.

For most gardens, slow soaking of water into the soil is the safest method. It works well for level beds or terraced slopes and in small gardens where you want to avoid sprinkling certain vegetables.

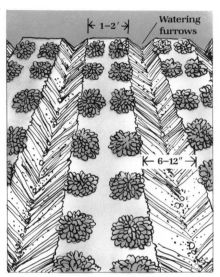

Watering furrows run parallel to long, low mounds of soil. You'll need a soaker for this method to make sure that water flows the length of the furrow.

Watering basins encircle large plants. Linking them together makes watering easy. Mound in center keeps plant above water level.

For vining plants whose fruit lie on the ground (pumpkins and squash, for example), plant seed in a central hollow and train vines to grow outward.

Perforated sprinkler hose makes it easy to water shallow-rooted crops. Turn holes up to sprinkle vegetables, holes down to soak the soil.

Piece of pipe stuck in ground at planting time directs water down to plant's roots where it's needed. Slowly run water through a hose, into pipe.

Controlling Weeds

- How to get rid of weeds: page 60
- Chemical weed killers: page 62
- Crabgrass & other lawn weeds: page 63

How to get rid of weeds

Weeds do well enough on their own; when you help them along with water and fertilizer, they really flourish. If not controlled, they can crowd out annuals and perennials and even small shrubs.

Pulling weeds by hand, using tools, and following weed-controlling gardening practices are all methods of control that are effective if you start early and are persistent. The size of the area involved, the extent of the weed invasion, and the type of planting are the factors that should determine your plan of attack. Occasionally, but not often, you may have to kill weeds by chemical means (see page 62).

Here are some suggestions on weed control and gardening practices that will keep your garden free of weeds.

Hand weeding

It's easy to get rid of shallow-rooted weeds: just pull them up. If you're in the proper frame of mind, you'll derive a certain pleasure out of this. For the deep-rooted kinds, you'll need one of the many convenient weed-digging tools available at garden centers.

Several days before you start weeding, water the area thoroughly so you'll be pulling weeds while the soil is still moist.

Hoeing

Nothing can replace the hoe, the gardener's most useful tool for more than 4,000 years. Using a hoe gives good aeration and water penetration, as well as weed control.

Garden supply stores stock hoes of every size and shape; which is preferable depends on the type and condition of the soil you're working with and the particular job at hand. Narrow and pointed hoes are especially good for weeding around young bedding plants. Scuffle hoes (flat-bladed, disk type, or U-shaped) are easy to use in close quarters or under spreading plants.

Advance toward the unhoed weeds as you go, rather than backing into them and trampling them under foot.

If you keep an eye out for small weeds and destroy them when you first see them, your garden should be neat and you'll never have to struggle with large weeds. So, become acquainted with the wide variety of hoes and cultivators your garden center carries; many of them are fun to use and the end result is a weed-free garden.

For larger areas (orchards, roadsides, vacant lots), rototilling is effective, especially where there are no summer rains to germinate late weed crops. Rotary tillers not only knock down weeds but also incorporate them into the soil, where they decay to form humus.

Using shade

Shade considerably reduces weed seed germination and weed growth. This is a good reason for encouraging shrubs to develop a wide foliage canopy. Gardeners often remove lower branches to make weeding and cultivating easier; but the increased sunlight then encourages weed seed germination and compounds the problem.

Planting ground covers and spacing annuals and vegetables close together are effective in blocking sunlight from weeds, too.

The importance of mulch

After you have cleared weeds from the flower bed or shrub border, apply an organic mulch 2 to 3 inches deep. This cuts off light from

Between paving blocks, use screwdriver or ice pick to pry up stubborn weeds. Notched weeder helps dig out tap-rooted weeds.

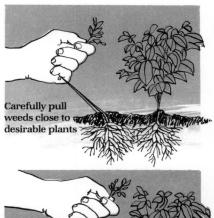

Carefully pull weeds close to desirable plants

Roots may be entwined

Hand-pull weeds that grow close to garden plants. Top sketch shows right method—pull up and away.

the soil surface and makes it impossible for most weed seeds to germinate. Peat moss, well-rotted manure (seed free), leaf mold, composted ground bark, and composted saw-

Hoe weeds away

Six-inch-wide hoe is the most commonly used. Sharp front edge cuts weeds off at ground level.

Scuffle hoe has many variations. This push-pull weeder-cultivator scrapes soil surface to cut weeds.

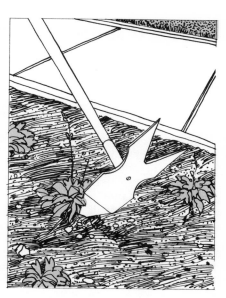

Weeding hoe combines two tools: triangular point on one side works to cut weeds, other side acts as puller.

Three ways to fewer weeds

Spreading shrubs shade the ground, allowing few weeds to prosper in their shadow.

Spaces between young ground cover shrubs invite weeds; no room for weeds to grow after the shrubs have spread.

Use a mulch (see page 52) to cover open ground and prevent weeds from growing back.

dust serve well for this purpose.

Under a mulch, weed seeds that may be present on the soil's surface are completely cut off from sunlight. Most seedlings die before they can reach the surface to get the sunlight they need. The few that fight their way through the mulch are easily controlled by pulling or hoeing. Weed problems are virtually eliminated within a year or two if a uniform mulch is maintained over planting beds.

Mulching to control weeds ultimately saves gardening time.

Chemical weed killers

Chemical weed killers come into our lives mostly as overflow from agriculture and institutional landscape maintenance work. In those endeavors, chemicals are used to reduce time spent hoeing, hand-pulling, or cultivating large fields.

Using chemicals in a home garden risks damaging valuable plants. If you feel you must use chemical weed killers, be very careful with them. Some can be used in established plantings (read product label for cautions) to control specific weeds, while others will destroy all vegetation. Chemicals that are applied to the soil to kill weed seeds before or as they germinate are the pre-emergence controls. Liquids that you spray or sprinkle on the undesired plants are the contact killers. A third category, translocated chemicals, contain an active ingredient that is absorbed by the plant and interferes with its metabolism, causing the plant's death.

Always follow label directions exactly and be careful not to let the chemicals come in contact with anything but the weeds you're trying to kill. Some weed killers are so persistent that traces remain in a sprayer even after rinsing. Don't use that sprayer for other purposes.

Hose-end sprayer is good for large areas. Drift is a problem in spot treating weeds with chemicals.

The chart lists common chemical names, not brand names. Read the label of any weed killer you purchase to check the chemical name, the specific weeds it will control, and the types of plants you can apply it to.

Selecting the right weed killer

Chemical	Effect	Comments
Amino triazole	Kills poison oak and other woody perennials; annuals; quack grass.	Will also kill or damage desirable grasses and ornamentals.
Ammate	Kills annual and woody vegetation (poison oak).	Respraying probably necessary. Clean sprayer thoroughly after use.
Cacodylic acid	Kills all top growth. Best on young weeds.	Won't kill perennial plants.
Casoron	Kills weeds around roses and other selected woody ornamentals.	Work into soil or water in.
Cyanamid	Temporary soil sterilant (used before turf is planted).	After application, wait 24 to 30 days before planting turf.
Dacthal	Kills annual grass, including crabgrass, in established plantings.	Destroys germinating seeds.
Dalapon	Controls grasses, including Bermuda.	Don't irrigate for 24 hours after applying.

Chemical	Effect	Comments
Diphenamid	Controls grasses, some other weeds, in ground covers, dichondra lawns.	Spray on established ground covers. Repeat sprays probably needed.
EPTC	Grass control around shrubs and trees.	Work into soil.
Fortified diesel, stove, or weed oils	Destroys top growth of all the vegetation it contacts.	May smell oily for several days.
Prometon	Kills all top growth, prevents seed germination for a season or more.	Medium-term control of all vegetation. Often mixed with pentachlorophenol.
Simazine	Kills seedlings on germination. Many special uses.	Granules often used for weed control in orchards, vineyards.
Trifluralin	Controls annual weeds in established plantings.	Work into soil or water in.
Vapam	A soil fumigant that kills many seeds before they sprout.	Don't breathe fumes or get the material on your shoes.

Crabgrass & other lawn weeds

Hairy crabgrass looks like its name. Both this and the smooth type are pale green in summer; husky in appearance. They root at lowermost stem joints.

The term "weed" can be applied to any undesirable plant you find growing in your lawn. For example, you may enjoy the early spring appearance of English daisies dotting the grass, while other gardeners might feel it spoils the lawn's otherwise even texture.

Lawn weeds should be removed before they have a chance to spread. Ways to do this include pulling them up by hand or with a tool and using lawn maintenance practices that prevent weeds from prospering. If chemical controls are necessary, refer to the chart on page 62.

Two effective weeding tools are the screwdriver and the long-shanked dandelion weeder pictured on page 60. When your lawn is moist, use these tools to pry out deep-rooted weeds such as dandelions and plantain, or to lift up weed runners like those on bur clover.

Crabgrass. A hot-weather annual, crabgrass sprouts in the spring and spreads vigorously, crowding out other grasses. When cool fall weather arrives, crabgrass turns reddish brown, then dies, leaving its seed in your lawn.

Hand-pulling may be a perfectly good way of removing some weeds, but this isn't true of crabgrass if it's an established growth—hand-pulling actually pulls buried crabgrass seed into sprouting position. You could attempt, though, to pull out a light growth of seedlings.

One effective nonchemical method for controlling crabgrass is to set your lawn mower at a higher setting; taller grass prevents sunlight from reaching the crabgrass seeds. A second way is to avoid wearing lawn grass down to bald spots so crabgrass can get a foothold. A third way is to water the lawn infrequently and deeply—the lawn surface will stay fairly dry, cutting down seed germination.

Bermuda grass. In hot climates, Bermuda grass grows better than cool-season grasses (bluegrass and bent grass). You can encourage its growth by putting your lawn mower at a low setting—a close cropping weakens other grasses and encourages growth of Bermuda.

To *discourage* Bermuda grass, try pulling out isolated sprigs before the grass is deeply rooted.

Quack grass. In cool climates, quack grass spreads by rhizomes (underground stems that root). Quack grass also spreads seed heavily; some of the seeds sprout quickly while others lie dormant for years. In addition, quack grass poisons other grasses. Hand-pulling usually won't get rid of it.

If quack grass gets out of hand in your lawn, you may want to have a professional sterilize the ground with a fumigant or sterilant (ask your nurseryman for the name of a contractor who does this work). You can then plant new grass seed.

Other weed grasses. Many grasses that are too coarse or the wrong color for lawns can be hand-pulled easily. Most of these grasses have dense roots that leave a hole when removed. Dig a little peat moss into the bare patch to bring it up to lawn level, then reseed.

If an unknown lawn weed continues to grow despite your efforts at removal or chemical treatment, pull up a sample of the weed and take it to a nursery worker or county agricultural advisor for identification and advice.

Broad-leafed weeds. These are easily distinguishable for pulling. Some lawn fertilizers contain additives for leafy weed control.

Smooth crabgrass is less common than hairy crabgrass. It has rather narrow leaves and is smaller, smoother than hairy crabgrass.

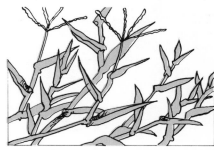

Bermuda grass can be considered a useful lawn grass. But its roots invade shrubbery and flower beds; can become very difficult to eradicate.

Quack grass flourishes in cool climates and almost any soil. Leaves are usually dark green; in dry areas quack grass has a whitish bloom.

Propagating Plants

- Starting seeds in the ground: page 65
- Planting seeds in flats & containers: page 66
- Dividing bulbs: page 67
- Dividing perennials: page 68
- Softwood & semihardwood cuttings: page 70
- Hardwood, root, & leaf cuttings: page 72
- Ground layering & air layering: page 73
- Grafting techniques: page 74
- Grafting techniques—cleft grafting: page 75
- Grafting techniques—bark grafting: page 76
- Budding techniques— T-budding: page 77
- Budding techniques— patch-budding: page 78

Starting seeds in the ground

Generally speaking, you'll have healthier plants and an earlier and longer bloom period if you sow seed directly in the open ground —especially with the faster kinds of summer annuals. The shock of transplanting is entirely eliminated.

In choosing seeds, first check the instructions on the package for correct planting times. Spring is the best time to plant in most regions: wait until frost danger is past and soil has begun to warm up; soil should be just at the crumbly stage and not too wet. In mild-winter areas, you can plant many hardy annuals and perennials in autumn for late winter, early spring bloom.

Before you start preparing the seed bed, turn to the section on soil and soil amendments (pages 6–10). Tender seedlings require perfect conditions to grow quickly and well. Count on a week or two for the seeds to sprout and another period of sparse growth before growth fills in and becomes sturdy.

If you want cut flowers, you may prefer to plant in rows (seed tape is handy for this). Vegetables are often sown in rows too.

Some of the many flowers that do well sown in the open ground are sweet alyssum, aster, coreopsis, gaillardia, marigold, nasturtium, phlox, portulaca, and zinnia.

Seeds in rows

Hoe used with board makes straight furrows; run them north-south so new plants will receive even sunlight.

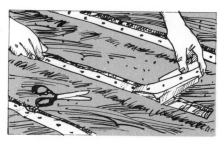

Seed tapes have seeds already spaced—just unroll tape in furrow and cover it with prepared soil. Plants will grow in straight rows.

Sowing a patterned planting

1) Prepare soil, water it, then work out a planting plan. Outline planting areas with gypsum, flour, or stakes and string.

2) Shake fine seed in a can with corn meal or white sand; you can then see where seed falls as you sow it. Or use pelletized seed.

3) Sow seeds evenly, then lightly press seed into soil with back of spade. Cover with a thin layer of sifted compost or peat moss.

4) Use fine spray of water to dampen surface, then keep barely damp until seeds sprout. Avoid puddling of water over newly planted seeds.

5) Transplant or thin out beds when seedlings have two sets of true leaves. Remove weeds, protect seedlings from snails, insects, birds, strong sun.

6) Water older plants with a soaker. Allow top 2 inches of soil to dry out before watering again. Fertilize only when watering.

Planting seeds in flats & containers

1) *Sow seed* in furrows made in prepared soil, cover lightly with more soil. Carefully submerge container in water to seed level, and soak.

2) *Transplant seedlings* when they have two sets of true leaves—lift carefully by a leaf.

3) *In a few weeks* to a month, plants will reach garden-planting size. Until then, keep watering and fertilize weekly.

Indoor planting in flats or other containers is the best method to use for expensive or very fine seed, for seed that takes a long time to germinate and grow (including most perennials), and for some annuals and vegetables that you want to start early when the ground outside is still too cold or wet. You can control the soil mix, you can move the flats or pots around so plants get the right amount of sun or shade, and pest damage is more quickly noticeable and easier to control.

It will take about two months for the seedlings to mature enough so you can set them outside. If you sow them too early, the seedlings will be leggy and rootbound when planting weather arrives.

Almost anything that will hold soil and has provision for water to drain off will do for a seed-starting container. Your choice will depend on what you have available and how many seeds you have to plant. Plastic or wooden nursery flats will accommodate the largest number of seeds; other choices are clay or plastic pots, peat pots, aluminum foil pans (the sort sold for kitchen use), styrofoam or plastic cups, cut-down milk cartons, or shallow wooden boxes that you make yourself. Remember to punch holes for drainage in the bottom of any container that will hold water; if you make your own wooden flats or boxes, leave about a 1/4-inch space for drainage between boards that form the container's bottom.

If you use containers that have held plants before, give them a thorough cleaning to avoid the possibility of infection by damping-off fungi, which destroy seedlings. A vigorous scrubbing followed by a few days of drying in the sun usually will suffice.

Use a commercial potting mix, or combine equal parts of light topsoil, fine ground bark or peat moss, and sand. Sift the soil through a 1/4-inch mesh screen. To kill any weed seeds and fungus in the soil, bake it in a hot oven for an hour before using (smells terrible). You may prefer to start seed in a sterile medium such as vermiculite or in one of the mixes on page 11.

Fill the container 1/2 to 3/4 inch from the top with the soil mix. Firm it with a block of wood or the palm of your hand.

Check the seed packet directions for recommended planting depth. You can cut planting furrows as shown in the drawing at left or scatter the seeds on the surface and sift a layer of soil on top (most fine seeds should not be covered). Then lay a dampened piece of newspaper over the soil, unless seed packet indicates the seeds need light to sprout.

Water carefully. One method is to place the container in a sink or tub, slowly add water to just below the seed level, and allow the soil to soak up the moisture until saturated.

Place the container in a warm spot, but not in direct sun. Keep the soil mix moist but not soaking wet.

After three days, begin checking daily for signs of sprouting. When the first sprouts appear, remove the paper and put the container in more light or filtered sun.

When the seedlings have developed two sets of true leaves, transplant them to 2-inch pots or to another flat where they are spaced 1 1/2 inches apart. Use moist planting mix. To transplant, loosen soil around each seedling, gently grasp one of its leaves, and carefully pull out the plant. Use a pencil to poke a hole in the new planting mix; drop in the seedling, and gently firm the soil around it to previous depth.

Keep the plants in the shade a day or two, then move them into the light again. Water plants occasionally—daily if weather is hot. A light application of liquid fertilizer once a week is a good extra step. Several weeks later, you'll have plants ready to go in the ground (see pages 20–21).

Dividing bulbs

Bulbs, tubers, corms, and rhizomes have the same happy characteristic as perennials: start with a few and in a few years you can have many—if you know how to go about it. Some of the most common techniques are described here.

Daffodils

Daffodils and other narcissus can be left in the ground undisturbed for several years and still bloom freely each season. When flowers begin to get smaller and fewer in number, it's a sure sign that the bulbs are ready to be dug and divided.

Don't dig until the bloom season is well past and foliage has dried and withered. You will find the mother bulb surrounded by several bulblets; separate only those that break away easily. Replant in fall.

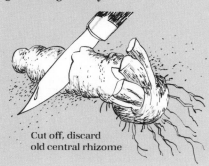

Dahlias

When early winter frosts turn dahlia foliage brown, it's time to dig and store the tubers. Whether you store the clumps for dividing next spring or divide them on the spot, be sure to let them dry out first.

To divide, use a sharp knife and cut the new tubers so each has part of a crown attached to it and at least one dormant eye. Store them in dry sand or peat moss in a dry, cool place.

Each division must have bud here

Gladiolus

Gladiolus corms do best if they're dug up in fall and stored during winter. Do this after bloom season is well past and when leaves have turned a yellowish green.

Sometimes you'll find that two large corms have developed. Break them apart. Or you can increase plants by cutting a large corm into halves or thirds. Also, cormels (see sketch) can be grown to full size in 2 or 3 years.

Cut off foliage 1–2" above new corm

Dust cut edge with sulfur

Pull off old corm and discard

New corms

Cormels Roots

Choose large corms —make clean cuts

Iris

Bearded iris and other plants that grow from rhizomes begin to show signs of being crowded every 3 years or so. Divide them in late summer or early fall. Lift out the root mass with a spading fork, then use a sharp knife to cut off the new rhizomes growing on the outer edge. Discard the rest.

Cut foliage back halfway, then replant. Some should go back into ground right away.

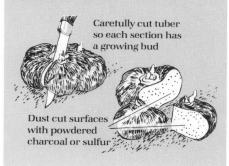

Cut off, discard old central rhizome

Lilies

When lilies become crowded, lift and remove old stems. Separate large bulbs and replant. Also plant smaller offset bulbs or bulblets that form along stems, and any loose bulb scales that fall off. Scales will eventually form new bulbs. Preserve roots, keep barely moist, and replant as soon as possible.

Break off a few outer lily scales—plant bulb and scales

Tuberous begonias

When new shoots first appear on begonia tubers, you can cut them up to increase the number. Take good-size tubers with 3 or more shoots and cut from top to bottom of the tuber between the shoots so each piece has a growing shoot.

Dip cut surfaces in powdered charcoal or sulfur; allow to dry for 3 or 4 days before planting, or store in cool, dry, frost-free location.

Carefully cut tuber so each section has a growing bud

Dust cut surfaces with powdered charcoal or sulfur

Dividing perennials

Each year the typical perennial gains in girth by growing new roots and stems, usually around the outer perimeter of the previous year's growth. Eventually (usually in 2 or 3 years) these clumps get too big for their space. Or perhaps growth has become weakened due to competition and crowding. It's time to divide the plant.

Each root segment or division is actually a plant in itself or is capable of becoming a new plant. Divide an overgrown clump into separate parts and you get that many new plants. It's a fast and inexpensive way of increasing your supply of favorite perennials.

Divide in autumn or early spring, when plants are dormant. Autumn is generally the best time to divide the perennials that bloom in spring or early summer (in cold-winter regions, this may be *early fall*). Late-blooming kinds, such as chrysanthemums, may be divided and transplanted in early winter, if you live in a mild climate; in cold-

If you can't divide and replant the same day, you should 1) cover clumps with wet burlap; 2) tie plastic bag over roots; or 3) put clumps in shallow trenches, cover with damp soil.

How to divide daylilies

1) *To divide* without cutting through many roots, insert two spading forks in center of clump, spread handles. Put separated clumps back in the ground as soon as possible.

2) *Divide smaller daylily clumps* with hand fork, knife, or hatchet. Unlike most evergreens, old leaves of daylilies may be cut back one-half. Don't cut the young center leaves.

3) *To prevent rot* later on— especially in heavy soil—dust roots of each daylily division with sulfur before replanting. Daylilies should be divided every 4 or 5 years.

winter areas, wait until spring to divide them.

After dividing, keep roots moist and plant as soon as possible. If you can't replant the same day, cover the clumps with wet burlap, wrap them in polyethylene, or bury roots in a shallow trench. Keep shaded.

The clumping perennials that you can divide with a spading fork—like the daylily shown at left—include acanthus, agapanthus, and kniphofia (red-hot poker). Plants with dense roots that need cutting apart—like the columbine —are asparagus fern, iberis, Shasta daisy, and yarrow. With coral bells, chrysanthemum, and primrose, pull off the rooted outside pieces for replanting and discard the woody center.

For more information about perennials, see pages 41–43. The drawings on those pages show some of the most commonly planted kinds.

Some perennials are difficult to divide

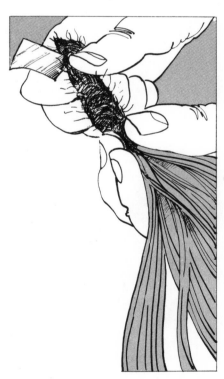

Plants with tap roots, such as this perennial alyssum, cannot be divided. Try propagating such plants from seed or cuttings.

Because of sparse roots and matted top growth, dividing arabis is difficult. Instead, take cuttings (see pages 70–73). Aubrieta is increased same way.

Dividing columbine

Divide every year or two by pulling apart carefully with hands or by cutting through clump with sharp knife. Cut back old stems. Columbine also grows readily from seed.

Making coral bell divisions

1) *Pull off* separate divisions by hand. Discard old woody pieces; keep only the young vigorous sections. Divide clumps when they are about 3 to 5 years old, in fall or in spring (colder areas).

2) *Make clean cut* across the bottom of each rooted division of coral bells. If mealybug is a problem in your region, dip the roots in a malathion solution before planting.

Softwood & semihardwood cuttings

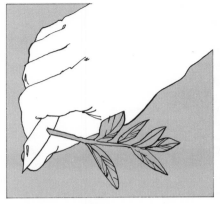

1) *Make clean cut just below a leaf or leaf node. Four to 5-inch-long cutting should be from new growth that is firm. Remove any flower buds.*

A common gardening dilemma: Your neighbor has geraniums that are just the right color for your patio, but you've never seen anything like them at the nursery. Or you visit a friend who has splendid azaleas, but she can't remember what variety they are. What can you do?

The answer is simple: just ask your friend if you can take cuttings from these plants and start your own. All you need are a few branch tips. Wrap them in moist paper, then hurry home and set them in a special potting mix (see description following).

Cuttings will produce plants exactly like those you took them from, whereas seeds may produce plants that are unlike their parents, and take longer to grow.

Softwood cuttings, which can be taken from spring until late summer during the active growing season, are the easiest and quickest rooting of stem cuttings. You can take them from soft, succulent new growth that has some flexibility but does break when bent sharply. You take semihardwood cuttings from the same plants, later in the season.

Semihardwood cuttings are taken after the active growing season or after a growth flush, usually in summer or early autumn, when growth is firm enough to snap when the twig is bent sharply (if it just bends, the stem is too mature for satisfactory rooting).

In choosing cuttings, look for normal, healthy growth; avoid fat or spindly branches. Softwood cuttings root best if you can snap them off cleanly from the parent plant. If they crush or bend, the wood is too old. Generally you should cut just below a leaf bud (node), but some plants can be cut between nodes. Keep all cuttings cool and moist (not wet) until you can plant them.

Rooting the cuttings

For both types of cutting, the procedures are the same. You'll have a better percentage of successful rootings if you start cuttings in a container of some sort—pot, can, flat or box, or cup. Be sure the container will drain water; if it has no drainage holes, poke or punch holes in its bottom so excess water will be able to drain out.

Fill the container with a blend of half sand and half premoistened peat moss, firming it down slightly so that the surface is a half inch below the top of the flat. Open a container of rooting hormone powder and place it beside the flat. One by one, remove the cuttings from their moist wrapping and make a clean, slanting cut with a razor blade or sharp knife just below a leaf or bud.

If the leaves are very large, snip off about half of each leaf with scissors. Strip off any lower leaves so only the stem will be buried in the planting mix. Dip the stem in the hormone powder and tap it gently to remove any excess. Use a pencil to poke a hole in the sand and peat moss mixture and set in the cutting, firming the soil around the stem.

When you've finished planting the cuttings, cover them with transparent kitchen wrap, a plastic bag, or a jar. Remove this cover once a day for a few minutes to allow air to circulate, then cover again.

If you can keep the temperature of the soil mix at 75° to 80° F/ 24° to 27°C (see discussion following), the cuttings will root more quickly. When new growth appears, the cutting has rooted. Gently lift one out, carefully removing some of the soil until you see roots. Then transplant the cutting to a slightly larger container to give the roots more growing room. Never move

any plant from a tiny pot to a very large one. Use a size that allows for an inch or two of new soil around the root ball.

When the new growth is full and sturdy, you can set the plants in the garden. Plants that cannot be set out when they're ready—because of very hot or very cold weather—may have to be transplanted to still another larger container to keep them from becoming rootbound.

Bottom heat speeds root growth

Softwood and semihardwood cuttings root more quickly if soil temperature remains constant at 75° to 80°F/24° to 27°C. If your house has radiant heating in the floors and you have only a few cuttings, you can just put them in an out-of-the-way corner and let the house heat do the job.

For a larger number of seedlings or cuttings you can use the age-old practice of laying a bed of fresh manure several inches thick in a coldframe (see page 87) and setting the flats or pots on top. As the manure rots, it produces heat.

A third way to keep soil temperature constant is to use an electric coil heater. Most nurseries carry two different types. The best known is simply a long flexible coil that you

2) Insert cutting *in hole made with pencil after dipping stem in hormone powder. Remove any leaves that would be buried in the soil.*

3) Cover cutting *with jar or plastic bag to create humidity. Lift once a day for air circulation and to prevent mold from growing.*

4) Check root growth *when new leaves form. Azaleas may need 3 months to root. Transplant to slightly larger pot with acid soil mix.*

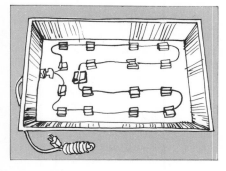

Electric heating cable is held in place with clips attached to plastic flat; soil goes on top, stays warm.

wind around under your planting flats. Different lengths of coil, or differences in materials, determine the price. The other type of heating unit consists of a flat with the coil built in. These flats are about the size of an ordinary flat and cost about the same as the more expensive coils.

Some plants to try

The following list is by no means complete, but cuttings from these plants will root fairly easily.

Softwood cuttings: Perennial alyssum, arabis, aubrieta, begonia, candytuft, chrysanthemum, dahlia, dianthus (carnations, pinks), fuchsia, geranium (includes ivy gerani-um, pelargonium), penstemon, sedum, thyme.

Semihardwood cuttings: Azalea, bougainvillea, ceanothus, daphne, gardenia, heather, hibiscus, honeysuckle, hydrangea, ivy, lavender, oleander, plumbago, pyracantha, star jasmine, thuja, willow, wisteria.

A miniature greenhouse

If you fail to root softwood cuttings using the usual methods, try planting them in a plastic bag filled with perlite. You can use this miniature "greenhouse" for rooting house plants, perennials, shrubs, or trees.

Put two handfuls of perlite (see page 6) into a medium-size plastic bag and wet it thoroughly. Then turn the bag upside down, keeping the neck loosely closed while you squeeze out the water. The perlite should be damp but not wet.

Prepare the cuttings as described on the opposite page and put the bare stem into the perlite. Then close the bag (to root succulents, leave it open) and put it in a spot that has good light but no direct sun. For air circulation, open the bag briefly each day but don't lift or disturb the cutting.

It may take from a week to a month for the cutting to root. To test its progress, gently pull up on the

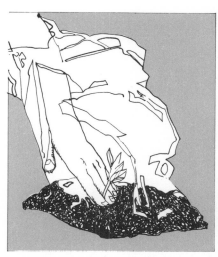

Plastic bag with moist perlite is good container for rooting softwood cuttings. The plastic holds in humidity.

cutting. If the perlite moves, there are roots running through it. Lift out the cutting and transplant it into a small pot or directly into the garden if weather permits.

A second rooting method utilizing a plastic bag is suitable for quick-rooting plants. Fill the bag with a moist mixture of half sand, half peat moss. Tie it closed and hang it in a well-lighted, wind-free place. Punch rows of holes in the bag, about 1 1/2 inches apart, and poke stems of cuttings into the holes.

Hardwood, root, & leaf cuttings

additional soil, and water thoroughly.

Hardwood cuttings are a way of increasing your supply of certain deciduous shrubs and trees; root cuttings may be taken from the roots of any plant that produces sprouts from the roots; and leaf cuttings are possible with fleshy-leafed plants.

Hardwood cuttings

Take these cuttings in autumn when plants are dormant, after leaves have fallen but before winter freezes come. Most hardwood cuttings are slow in getting established—sometimes as long as a year.

Hardwood cuttings can be made of deutzia, forsythia, figs, grapes, kolkwitzia, philadelphus, and weigela, to name just a few examples.

Take the cutting by severing the top of a branch at the point where wood is about the size of a lead pencil; each cutting should be 6 to 9 inches long and include at least two leaf nodes. Make the bottom cut a slanting one just below a node or leaf joint. Leave the tip intact or, with longer cuttings, make the top cut square across and just above a node.

Store the cuttings in a shallow trench in well-drained soil or in a pot or box of soil. With trenches, cover cuttings with about 2 inches of soil. Where the ground freezes, add enough mulch to keep cuttings protected from frosts. In boxes, cover cuttings with damp peat moss or soil; keep moist through the winter.

By the time weather warms up in spring, the cuttings will have formed calluses and roots and can be set in an open cutting bed.

Root cuttings

Plants that can be propagated from root cuttings include Japanese anemone, Oriental poppy, trumpet creeper, plumbago, blackberry, and raspberry.

Take root cuttings in early spring or in late summer at the end of the plant's growth period. Select roots 1/8 to 1/4 inch in diameter from vigorous plants.

Cut roots into pieces 1 to 3 inches long. Fill a box or flat to within about 1 inch of the top with light garden soil; place cuttings 2 inches apart, horizontally, on top of the soil. Cover with about 1/2 inch

Cover with glass or newspaper and place in the shade. Check every week for moisture and for sprouts and remove the covering when growth shows.

If you have just a few cuttings to root, place them upright in a pot of the rooting medium. The thickest end of the root cuttings should be upright, the tops of the cuttings just at soil level. Water the cuttings and place the pot in the shade, covered if you wish by glass or a sheet of cardboard.

Leaf cuttings

You can take leaf cuttings to propagate African violets, gloxinias, Rex begonias, and many succulents.

Sometimes the entire leaf is used to start a new plant, in which case the leaf stalk is inserted in sand. In other cases the leaf is shortened or cut into triangular sections. There should be a section of leaf vein in each portion. Plant these pieces 1/2 inch deep in moist sand. Bottom heat helps to speed rooting.

Rex begonia or African violet leaves will root if they are placed flat on top of moist sand and held down with toothpicks. Keep these moist, shaded, and at constant temperature.

Making a leaf cutting

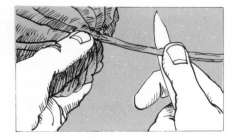

1) *Trim leaf stem* to 1 or 2 inches (don't crush the stem).

2) *Place stem* in moist potting mix. Keep shaded, at constant temperature.

3) *Check for new growth* by carefully lifting up the leaf.

Ground layering & air layering

The two layering methods—ground layering and air layering—tend to be slow to produce results, but with some hard-to-root plants you are more sure of success with layering than with cuttings. The reason that layering is more successful is that you don't remove the branch from the plant until it has formed roots.

Try your hand at ground layering

By using this technique, it's possible to propagate plants that are not easily rooted from cuttings, such as magnolias, pieris, and rhododendrons. You can increase your stock of vines, shrubs, perennials, and even some small trees this way. Azalea, rhododendron, daphne, forsythia, tree peony, cotoneaster, rosemary, dianthus, sarcococca, juniper, and penstemon layer quite easily.

Early spring is the preferred time for layering woody plants, although layers made in autumn or winter are usually successful. Ivy, star jasmine, ceanothus, junipers, and several other ground covers will spread much faster if you make several layers along each branch without separating it from the parent plant.

New plants you get from layering should be transplanted in late autumn if your climate is mild; if your winters are cold, wait until spring. Keep slow-rooting shrubs, like rhododendrons, in place for another full year to permit the development of a sturdy root system. You can leave perennials in place and transplant in fall.

Air layering: for house plants, too

The principle here is the same as for ground layering; the difference is that air layering applies to branches higher on the plant, which are covered with sphagnum moss and plastic instead of buried in the ground.

This is an excellent method for increasing your supply of choice shrubs and trees, as it often works on plants that are difficult or impossible to root by other means. It's especially useful with some of the large house plants.

If the rooting is successful, you'll see roots appearing in the sphagnum moss in several months. Then you can sever the newly rooted stem from the mother plant and pot it or plant it out on its own. At that time it usually is wise to reduce the number of leaves by half.

The three steps in ground layering

 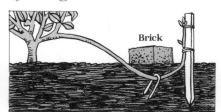 

1) *Insert a pebble* into notch cut halfway through a low, flexible, pencil-size branch. Notch should be just below a leaf joint about 8 to 12 inches from branch tip. Dust cut with powdered rooting hormone.

2) *Dig wide hole* about 4 inches deep. Anchor notched part of branch with wire loop or rock; bend end of branch up and out. Fill hole, firm soil, and water. Stake end of branch. Put weight on soil surface.

3) *New growth* indicates success. When you're sure new roots have formed, cut new plant from the parent plant, dig it up, and move it to new location. Some plants may take 2 or more years to form roots.

Here's how to air layer

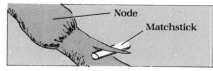  

1) *Below leaf node* on a branch from pencil size to 1 inch in diameter, make a slanting cut one-third through. Insert matchstick.

2) *Or, remove a ring* of bark about 3/4 inch wide, scraping it down to hard core of wood. Dust lightly with rooting hormone powder.

3) *Wrap the cut* with a generous handful of damp sphagnum moss. Tie a piece of polyethylene securely around the moss.

Grafting techniques

Whip grafting

Whip grafting is most suitable for grafting small scions on small-diameter stock. Try it on small ornamental plants or fruit trees, such as apricot and plum.

The knives you use should be high-quality steel, kept very sharp, to ensure cleanest cuts.

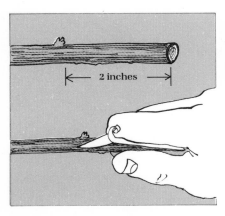

1) *Cut a branch* of stock plant about 2 inches beyond a bud. Beginning right next to the bud, use a razor-sharp knife to make thumb-length diagonal slice. Surface of cut must be absolutely flat; use a very sharp knife.

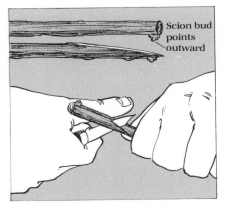

Scion bud points outward

2) *Select a scion* that's same diameter as stock. Scion bud should point outward. Measuring against cut on stock, nick the scion at beginning and end of cut; slice scion diagonally to fit stock.

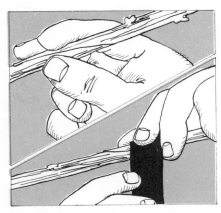

3) *Place cut surface* of scion against slice made on stock to check fit. Working from middle to end, wrap 6-inch length of plastic electrical tape around joint, overlapping 1/2 inch. Then wrap to other end.

4) *Add three or four more layers* of tape, winding tightly. New shoots show that graft is successful. Fruit trees will grow vigorously. Tape can stay in place permanently or be removed in the third year.

Grafting can make one fruit tree bear several varieties with different ripening times—perhaps once each month. If a fruit tree (such as a cherry) needs a pollinator, you can graft a branch of the pollinating variety onto it instead of planting a second tree. You can even graft several different kinds of fruit onto the same tree (apricots and plums, for example).

An ancient horticultural art, grafting is the operation of inserting a short piece of stem, the *scion* (SIGH-un), bearing one or more buds into another plant (*stock* or *understock*) to form a union that grows together. For the graft to take, the thin *cambium* layer (between the bark and wood) of both scion and stock must be perfectly aligned.

When you fit the cut surface of the scion against the stock, be sure bark edges meet all around.

If the graft succeeds, a branch grows from it and carries the flowers and fruits of the plant from which the piece of stem was taken; the rest of the plant will continue to show its own growth pattern and other characteristics.

The stock plant can be a pencil-slim seedling to be grafted near ground level—or an old fruit tree to be grafted at the top of its trunk or on its major limbs.

Theoretically, for a graft to take, the scion and stock plants must be close botanical relatives. However, that rule has its exceptions. Your safest first try at grafting probably would be to graft one variety of fruit (such as apple or peach) onto another variety of the same kind, or one variety of camellia onto another variety of camellia, wisteria onto wisteria, and so forth, until you become skilled. Then, try grafting from one plant onto another that you believe to be closely related.

Grafting of deciduous trees and shrubs should be done before growth buds swell in the spring. You can graft evergreens just before the surge of spring growth.

With bark and cleft grafting, shown on the next two pages, you would trim off all but one strong graft after the scions begin growing. The whip graft method, left, does not require this trimming.

Grafting techniques —cleft grafting

The cleft method, useful for grafting fruit trees, can be performed during the dormant season on most plants. You use small scions and a thick branch or trunk of the stock plant.

Cleft grafting is a popular method, but it's not ideal: it allows only two to four scions; the cleft split can go awry; rot can enter; the cleft heals slowly; and the union can be weak.

1) Prepare stock by smoothly sawing off a straight-grained branch or trunk. Position a cleaver, heavy knife, or grafting tool; split evenly 6 inches deep. New branches grow from here.

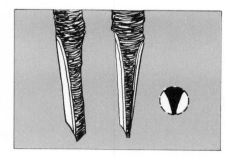

2) Prepare the scion by shaping one end into a long, gradually tapering wedge. The outside edge of the wedge should be slightly thicker than the inside edge.

3) Use a splitting wedge (or hook end of grafting tool) to hold cleft open. Here, two scions are inserted into a stock, one at each end of cleft (insert bigger scion first).

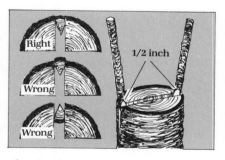

4) Check position of scions to be sure cambium layers are in contact. Be sure to leave 1/2 inch of cut surface of scions exposed above surface of the stock, for stronger union.

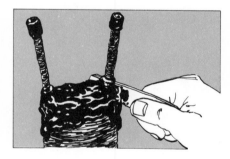

5) Cover entire union and all cut surfaces with grafting wax. If it rains within 24 hours, you may need to apply more. And until growth begins, rewax any splits in grafting wax.

6) If the weather is very cold or dry before grafts are well started, cover with paper bags punctured for air. Be sure to remove bags if the temperature goes above 85°F/29.4°C.

7) After new growth has begun, tie or tack 1 by 2-inch strips of lath to the trunk as support for the grafts. This is an extra precaution to prevent movement if grafts aren't well anchored.

8) By selective pruning, prevent growth of a weak section of tree that could be subject to splitting. At the end of the first year, cut back unwanted branches.

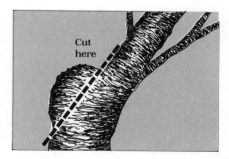

9) If only one scion grows, slice off the dead shoulder on opposite side of stock. Make a straight, smooth cut following growth angle of new branch. Apply pruning compound.

Grafting techniques —bark grafting

Often used as a substitute for cleft grafting on fruit trees, bark grafting is the best method to use on older trees. It's also the most successful for novices. In bark grafting, stock is much thicker than the three or four scions.

You do bark grafting in the early spring, when bark pulls away from wood easily. This means taking scions in winter (during dormancy) and storing them in plastic bags in the refrigerator.

1) *Smoothly saw off* a branch or trunk from stock. Cut a slit for each scion, slicing through bark and cambium layer of stock into the wood. Space slits evenly.

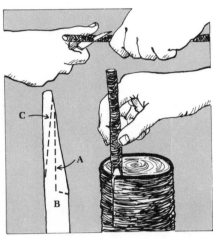

2) *Trim scions* to fit, leaving three or four buds on each one. Make a slanting slice (A) on inner side. Optional ledge at top of inner slice (B) will fit over stock. Taper outer side (C).

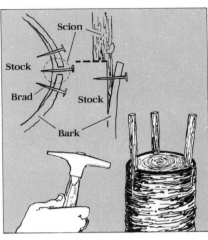

3) *Lift bark* on stock and insert scion under one flap or down middle— whichever makes the snugger fit. Drive a wire brad through bark and scion into stock. Extra brads go through flaps.

4) *Immediately after placing* and nailing scions, cover all cut surfaces with grafting wax or asphalt emulsion grafting compound. Until new growth begins, rewax any splits in grafting wax.

5) *When new growth begins,* tie or tack 1 by 2-inch strips of lath to the stock as support for grafts. Prune back unwanted branches at end of first year; leaving a selected branch alone.

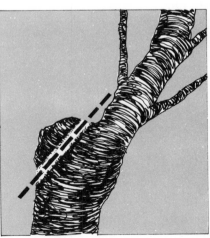

6) *If only one* of the scions grows, slice off the dead shoulder on opposite side of stock. Take off all dead wood, cutting smoothly at an angle that follows branch.

Budding techniques —T-budding

You have nothing to lose in experimenting with budding: if the bud fails, the tree or shrub isn't harmed. (A graft that doesn't take, on the other hand, disfigures the plant.) With budding, you can convert a plant to a better variety or add another variety to an existing plant —even furnish a pollinating variety within a fruit tree's structure.

The technique is to insert a bud from one plant under the bark of a related variety. If the two varieties are compatible and if you are skillful (or lucky), the bud and the plant will unite and grow well.

Plan to do budding in summer and early autumn. Through the rest of the year, the live, plump bud remains dormant. In spring, when the surge of growth comes to all the buds on the plant, the implanted bud also starts to grow and you cut the branch back to just above the bud.

All the growth from the implanted bud—flowers, fruit, and leaves—will have the characteristics of the plant from which you took the bud.

The plant and the section of branch into which you place the bud is called the *stock* or *understock*. The buds come from the base of leaf stalks on the *budstick*, which should be about the same diameter as the stock.

The T-bud technique is used with plants (roses, for example) that have thin bark. It's very important that the bark pull away easily; this partly depends on the time of year.

1) *Make vertical cut* 1 inch long in branch of 1/4 to 1/2-inch diameter. Slice down into wood; remove any foliage in the way of potential scion growth.

2) *Make horizontal cut* through bark and into wood, across top of vertical cut. Circle about one-third the distance around branch.

3) *Pry up corners* gently. If bark won't budge or chips away, it's either too early or too late in the season. If too early, try again in week or two.

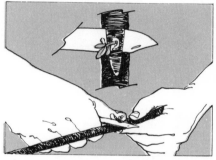

4) *Slice under a strong bud* on budstick, starting 1/2 inch below bud, finishing 1 inch above. Cut down into the wood.

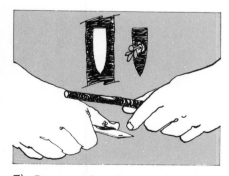

5) *Crosscut* down into wood, 3/4 inch above bud. Push shield-shaped piece out sideways. Leave a layer of wood attached to back.

6) *Push bud shield* downward under loosened bark flaps, being careful not to damage bud. Align top of shield with horizontal cut.

7) *Bind* with plastic electrical tape, leaving bud exposed, or use budding tape. Remove tape when bud shows new growth.

Budding techniques —patch-budding

Use patch-budding instead of T-budding (page 77) with shrubs and trees that have thick bark, such as walnuts, pecans, and avocados.

Double-bladed tools for patch budding are manufactured but aren't widely sold. You can make one with two knife blades mounted on a block about 1 1/4 inches apart. Knives for any kind of budding should be kept very sharp.

In cutting the budstick, also keep the leaf and its stalk that grow next to the bud. Use the leaf stalk as a handle and also as an indicator: the leaf stalk will wither a week or two after budding, but if the bud remains plump and green, then the procedure is a success. But if the entire bud shield or patch (bark, bud, and leaf stalk) withers or turns dark, the operation has failed.

In late winter, cut off the stock branch just above the new bud. The bud will sprout into a flourishing new branch in the spring.

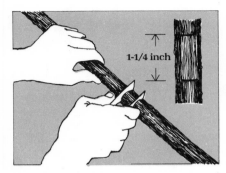

1) Make parallel cuts one-third the distance around stock. Join two of the ends with one cut, forming a square C shape with the cuts.

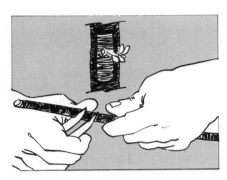

2) On budstick, make parallel cuts above and below the bud. Make vertical connecting cuts on each side of the bud. Don't cut too close to bud.

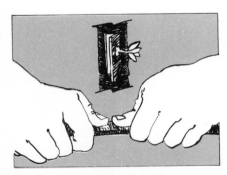

3) Press the bud patch out from budstick with sideways pressure. Leave a core of wood attached behind the bud, well under the layer of bark.

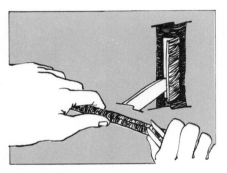

4) On the stock, lift the vertical edge of the square C made in step 1. Bud patch will slide underneath this flap. Lift flap very gently.

5) Slide the bud patch underneath the lifted flap until patch sits flat on bare wood. Trim overhang on flap and on bud patch.

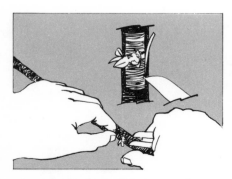

6) If the bud patch is thinner than bark on the stock, pare bark on stock so that tying will hold patch tightly. Surfaces should be as flush as possible.

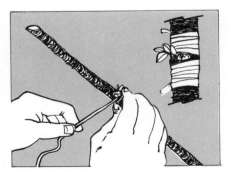

7) Tie as for T-bud (see step 7, page 77). Or, you can secure bud patch with gummed paper or polyethylene tape. Don't use fabric tape.

8) When the bud begins to swell and grow, remove tape. Prune stock branch above bud, making a slanting, clean cut. Remove any foliage that's in the way.

Summer Heat & Winter Cold

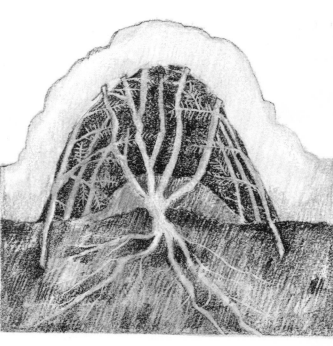

- Shade devices: page 80
- Protecting plants from occasional frosts: page 82
- All-winter protection: page 84
- Hot-weather planting: page 85
- Coldframes & hotbeds: page 86
- Planting in autumn: page 88

Shade devices

Reasons for needing shade are many. Seedlings and young transplants—even those of sun-loving plants—get a much better start if some temporary shade is provided. This is particularly true in hot-summer climates, but in almost any region a sudden and unexpected surge of hot weather can damage young plants.

Other plants are by their nature shade-loving, for example tuberous begonias, cinerarias, cyclamen, and fuchsias.

Look for ready-made material when building sunshades. The lath-and-wire fencing and bamboo blinds shown on the opposite page are examples. You can also buy inexpensive reed fencing or screening, or plastic blinds.

Versions of the shadecloth used by professionals, usually black or green and made out of polypropylene or saran, are widely available. This shade cloth casts a soft, even light and spans big areas with just a perimeter support structure.

An easy-to-make plant screen

1) Lay out framework by placing lengthwise pieces 6 inches in from ends of crosswise pieces. Nail together. Lay diagonal brace under crosspieces; nail it.

2) Lay laths so they fit snugly together; starting at one end of frame and working toward the other. Post along the left side is to help you align the laths.

3) Nail down alternate lath strips, keeping the aligning post in place. To build a 6-foot shade frame you'll need about 22 nailed strips.

4) Remove loose strips, then nail each lath to diagonal crossbar. Attach to legs or prop against fence. See example in drawing below.

Portable shade

A portable shade device such as any of those shown here can be pressed

Sunshades give temporary

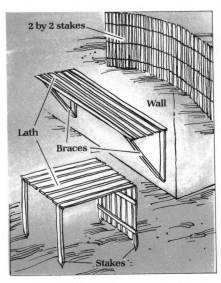

Simple shades of lath, bean poles, or lath-and-wire fencing give plants temporary protection from hot sun. Attach to wall or tack to stakes.

5) Lath screen on a frame can be placed over beds of new seedlings as shown here, or you can prop it up on south side of a planting bed.

into service at a moment's notice. It will protect foliage, keep roots cool, and conserve moisture. Even a few days of such protection can save you the frustration of watching young transplants wither and die. When weather returns to normal and plants have become established, the shade device can be stored in the garage or some other out-of-the-way place.

A lath sunscreen should always be placed so the laths run north and south. (As the sun moves across the sky, strips of sun and shade move across the plants.) Also, since the sun is always a little to the south, let the south edge of the sunscreen extend beyond the plants to keep them all under shade.

Permanent shade

For a permanent planting of shade-loving plants, you might consider building a roof over a patio or along a fence or wall, using either lath or some of the plastic or metal panels available. You may even want to build a completely enclosed lath shelter.

If the shelter you choose is just a roof, try to face it to the east or north and cut off all light from the south and west. The sketch at right shows the reason. Early-morning sun will shine into the shelter while the air is still cool, stimulating bloom and good leaf color. Then as the sun climbs higher and air temperatures rise, the roof will protect the plants.

Where you have no choice and must face the covering to the south, the overhang will have to be deeper to provide shade in late summer and early fall when the sun is low in the sky.

Before building, check on the width of roof you'll need by standing an 8-foot pole vertically at the spot where you want the overhang to end. Do it in late September, when the sun has dropped lower in the sky but the air is still warm, and note where the pole's shadow stops. Sun will penetrate that far into your shelter at that time of year. By December it will penetrate still farther, but the air will be colder.

Another approach to providing shade is to plant deciduous trees or vines. These will leaf out in the summer, when you need the most shade, yet will allow sun to shine through during the winter. Some

Overhang casts shade on plants from mid-morning on, but admits early morning light. East-facing wall needs a fairly deep overhang to be effective.

vines are illustrated on page 48.

Remember that shade plants usually need high humidity as well as protection from direct sunlight. During part of the year fog cover and natural humidity may be enough, but in many areas you should consider adding protection from drying winds: fences, louvers, or windbreak plantings. Wind protection helps keep humidity high by reducing air motion.

protection from intense sun

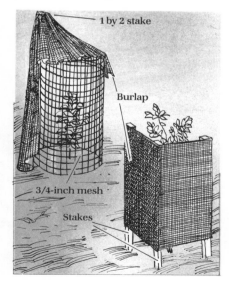

Wire cylinder draped with burlap acts as shade, windbreak. For tall-trunked plant, use burlap nailed to stakes set firmly in the ground.

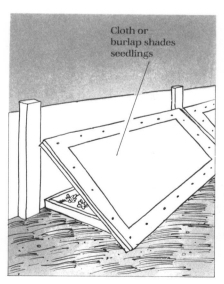

Burlap tacked onto lath or stake frame shades flats of seedlings or new transplants in ground, is easy to prop against wall or sturdy fence.

Roll shades of plastic or bamboo come in many widths and lengths. Use various kinds of pole frames to support the shades.

Protecting plants from occasional frosts

The surroundings make a difference

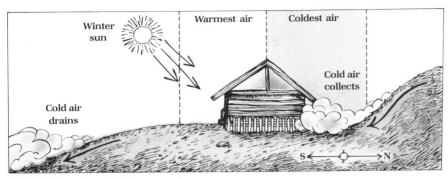

Take advantage of garden microclimates to grow plants that require varying conditions. Hills and hollows, points of the compass, and structures influence microclimates. Cold air "drains" on slope, collects in low, enclosed places.

Arrows represent heat loss. Plants exposed to open, cloudless sky—especially the north sky—are more subject to frost damage than ones grown under trees or overhangs.

Open-ended frame can be covered with heavy plastic or burlap to make a temporary winter greenhouse.

Protecting plants from cold weather is second nature to gardeners in regions where winter means snow and zero-degree weather (see page 84).

In mild-winter regions, though, where frosts and occasional hard freezes do occur, gardeners are not as likely to be winter-conscious. They may grow many half-hardy and tender plants that thrive in their climate, and quite frequently several winters will pass with no damage whatsoever. Then along comes a winter with temperatures dipping to just a few degrees lower; this is when unprotected plants can be killed.

There are landscaping and plant care practices that will pre-

Here are ways to save

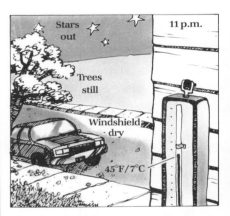

Check at bedtime for signs that hard frost is on the way; cover any tender plants until temperatures rise.

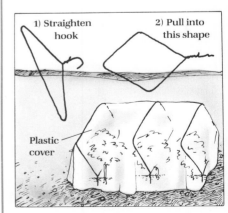

Wire coat hangers make frame for plastic film tent. If wind is a problem, anchor with rocks.

vent frost damage. First, build your basic landscaping—shade trees, screening and foundation plantings, hedges—with thoroughly hardy plants. Use more tender plants as fillers, as summertime display plants, in borders, or in areas of secondary interest; plant them in sheltered sites (entryways, courtyards); or grow them in containers and move them to sheltered sites when the weather turns cold.

Fertilize and water while plants are growing fastest in late spring and early summer. Taper off use of nitrogen fertilizer in late summer to discourage production of new growth that would not have time to mature before cold weather hits.

Actively growing plants are more susceptible to cold than dormant or semidormant plants. Reducing water will help harden growth, but soil around plants should still be moist at the onset of the frost season; moist soil holds and releases more heat than dry soil.

A hard, ruinous frost seldom strikes completely unexpectedly. There are almost always several nights of light frost—the kind that nips but doesn't kill—before you get a frost that really means business. You can trace the pattern of danger by watching for any areas where plant foliage has been nipped or for frosted stretches of lawn or bare earth, and know pretty well where frost will occur later on in the season.

The most likely spots to be hit by frost are stretches of open ground exposed to the sky on all sides, particularly to the north sky. Plants in hollows or in enclosed areas where cold air is held motionless are also in danger of being damaged by frost.

If plants have been damaged by frost, don't hurry to prune them. Premature trimming may stimulate new, tender growth that will be hurt by frosts. And you may cut out more than necessary, mistaking still-alive growth for dead. Wait until new growth begins in spring, then remove only wood that's clearly dead.

plants from frost

All-winter frost protector might as well look nice. This one has Japanese design. Cover with cloth on cold nights.

Cardboard box, upside-down. Cut bottom on three sides to make lid. Open during day, close at night to retain heat.

Bamboo or other flexible stakes make frame for small "tent" of polyethylene. Anchor plastic with rocks.

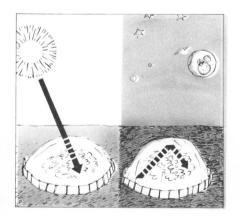

Hotcap's paraffin-treated cover allows some sun to penetrate soil in daytime. Trapped heat protects plant at night.

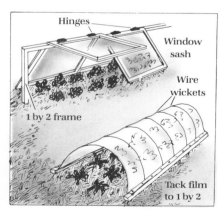

Two variations of cloche: a tent of sash, a portable tunnel. Plastic film makes a good glass substitute.

Evergreen branches break under snow loads. To prevent this, brush off or shake branches to remove snow.

All-winter protection

Preparing roses for snow & frost

Mound of soil

Conifer boughs, straw

Protect roses where ground freezes by mounding soil over trunk or covering entire plant with boughs or straw.

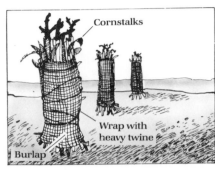

Cornstalks

Wrap with heavy twine

Burlap

Insulate taller roses against hard freezes by wrapping them with cornstalks; secure with tied burlap.

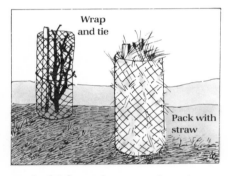

Wrap and tie

Pack with straw

Tack chicken wire to a stake, using wire as tall as your plant and long enough to form cylinder around plant. Put stake into ground next to plant, circle plant with wire, and secure the ends. Pack cylinder with straw.

Styrofoam rose cones require canes be tied together; cut down to fit cones. Mound soil over bud union and place cone over bush; put brick on top of cone and place soil over flared base to hold cone in place.

"Minnesota tip," time-consuming but successful, involves digging up roots on one side of plant, bending bush over into trench, covering all with soil. Set plant upright again in the spring.

Where soil freezes hard and temperatures drop below zero, gardeners do not grow tender plants outside. But many do grow roses, and a few attempt broad-leafed evergreens—boxwood, euonymus, holly, pieris, and rhododendrons. All of these plants need help to get through such winters alive.

Roses and other plants that can't take the cold are bundled up or buried under piles of leaves or straw. Container plants are moved to sheltered locations. Outside pipes are drained and water is turned off.

With roses, which are basically deciduous, your aim is to keep roots and bud union (at the very least) alive, and to preserve as many live canes as possible. In regions that regularly get down to 15°F/ −9°C or lower, wait until a couple of hard freezes have hit, then tie rose canes together and mound soil to 12 inches high over bud union and base of canes.

After soil mounds freeze, cover mounds with straw or secure cut evergreen boughs so that they cover mounds and canes; you want to keep mounds and canes consistently cold, rather than leaving them exposed to repeated freezing and thawing (and the drying effect of winter winds). Early spring weather often brings warm days alternating with freezing ones, so remove protection cautiously and gradually as garden soil thaws.

Some broad-leafed evergreens will survive fairly low temperatures but succumb to windburn and sunburn when low temperatures, strong sun, and cold, drying winds combine forces. Protect these plants with shelters of burlap, lath, sheets of plywood placed on the windward side of the plant, or evergreen boughs stuck in the ground around the plant like shocks of corn. The best garden location for these plants is a spot where winter's bright sun will not strike frozen plants.

Above all, keep soil moist and keep moisture available by means of a thick mulch that will prevent soil in the root area from freezing. Greatest damage comes to these plants when they transpire water and can't replace moisture.

Hot-weather planting

In most regions, the best times to plant are spring and autumn. But gardeners who move to a brand-new house may want to plant right away, even if it's mid-summer; and in desert and southern regions the weather may almost always be warm.

When you set out plants in summer heat, you'll not only observe the usual planting practices —you must also take extra steps to protect against high temperatures, low humidity, and drying winds.

Here we show the steps for planting a shrub in hot weather. The same principles apply regardless of what you are planting.

Plant late in day. Be sure your new plants don't suffer while they are awaiting planting; keep the roots and foliage moist and in the shade. Plant in the late afternoon or evening, or wait until an overcast day; this will give plants at least 15 hours or so to adjust to their new location before the heat comes on strong once again.

Use lots of water. Notice the lavish use of water in nearly every step. You must water the planting hole and the ground around it, the soil mix used for backfill (don't make it soggy), the root ball of the plant while it's still in the container, and the soil mix as it goes into the hole. Finally you water the plant after it is settled and a watering basin is formed. (*Caution:* You will be working with soaked soil and wet backfill. Be especially careful not to pack it as you dig and refill.)

Supply shade. All plants set out in warm weather should be protected from wind and sun with a temporary shade of lath or burlap. Be especially careful to cover the exposures to the south and west. If you use burlap, moisten it when the wind blows to make a type of air conditioner. More ways to provide shade are shown on pages 80–81.

1) *Dig planting hole* and fill with water. Let water drain thoroughly before you plant. Also moisten the soil you removed and let it dry a bit as the hole drains. Be careful not to compact any of the soil as you are working.

2) *Moisten soil amendment* (a quantity that would fill half the planting hole). Peat moss must be kneaded with water, then squeezed dry. Toss amendment with equal volume of moist soil to mix without compacting.

3) *Water plant thoroughly,* then let it drain. While you're waiting, place a layer of amended backfill in the hole and mix in a tablespoonful of superphosphate to insure proper root growth. Level the backfill.

4) *Place plant* in hole so top of container soil is level with the ground. With water running slowly into the hole, spade backfill evenly around plant. Don't let water run in so fast that it can't drain away quickly.

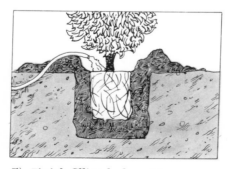

5) *Finish filling hole* and form watering basin by mounding soil around the plant. Fill the basin with water several times and let it drain. Water will keep plant moist until the roots have a chance to take hold.

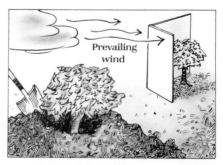

6) *Conserve moisture* by shielding plant from sun and drying wind for several days and by piling mulch, 3 inches thick, in, over, and around watering basin. In a week to 10 days, remove mulch from trunk of plant so trunk won't rot.

Coldframes & hotbeds

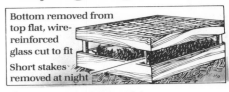

Bottom removed from
top flat, wire-
reinforced
glass cut to fit

Short stakes
removed at night

Flat uses second flat with bottom
removed, fitted with wire-reinforced
glass, as top. Short stakes prop open.

Experienced gardeners consider a coldframe an indispensable tool to successful year-round gardening. In fact to many, a well-built, well-tended coldframe is nearly as useful as a small greenhouse. And it takes up far less space and can cost almost nothing if you build it with scrap lumber.

A useful coldframe can be anything from a simple frame with a cover of plastic sheeting to a more elaborate structure with its own heat source. You may want to start with something fairly simple until you see just how much you'll use it.

For cold weather

In milder climates, coldframes protect plants against frost and help to keep temperatures warm enough for plant maintenance through the winter and to keep off excessive rain. In cold-winter regions, an unheated frame helps plants survive by preventing rapid fluctuation in temperature.

If the unit has an auxiliary heating system, the structure is commonly known as a "hotbed." The text on these two pages uses the term coldframe exclusively; however, if you live in a cold climate, the term also means "hotbed."

Whatever the climate, a coldframe is especially useful for early planting of summer annuals and seeds, protecting tender plants in winter, helping cuttings to root faster, starting perennials from seed in summer, and growing many kinds of plants you wouldn't otherwise attempt to grow.

What happens inside

A coldframe is a passive solar energy collector and reservoir. During the day, the sun's radiation comes in through the transparent lid or roof, warming the air and soil inside the frame. At night, heat stored in the soil radiates out and keeps your plants warm. Night temperatures inside a coldframe can be 10° to 20° higher than the air outside.

Also, the nearly airtight structure minimizes loss of moisture through evaporation—and cuts down on your watering chores for the plants inside.

The simplest piece of garden equipment that uses this principle of a heat, moisture, and light trap is the "hotcap," a dome of heavy waxed paper used to protect tomatoes, melons, and other young plants from late spring frosts (see page 83).

Planning your coldframe

To gain maximum solar heat, orient your coldframe to face south or southwest. Building its lid with a 6-inch back-to-front slope will trap the most heat inside and will let rainwater run off.

When planning its location, consider the microclimates in your garden. A stand of trees will deflect wind and keep the coldframe warmer inside. The wall of a nearby building will reflect additional heat that the coldframe can absorb. Sink it 8 to 10 inches into the ground, and you'll increase heat retention even more.

Whatever location you choose for your coldframe, make sure it's in a part of the garden that has good drainage, since you don't want water to collect around or in the frame after every rain.

Building hints

In planning a coldframe, start with dimensions of the cover. If you are not restricted to a size, choose dimensions that will fit some multiple of a standard planting flat. Flats come in several sizes, but two

A closer look at a coldframe

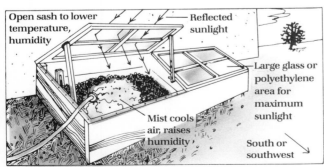

Open sash to lower
temperature,
humidity

Reflected
sunlight

Large glass or
polyethylene
area for
maximum
sunlight

Mist cools
air; raises
humidity

South or
southwest

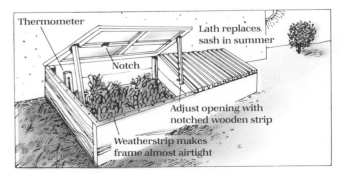

Thermometer

Lath replaces
sash in summer

Notch

Adjust opening with
notched wooden strip

Weatherstrip makes
frame almost airtight

Coldframe cover acts as a heat trap; wall behind reflects sunlight, shields frame from winter winds. Thermometer hung at rear should stay near 85°F/30°C. Notch any transverse mullions to facilitate water runoff.

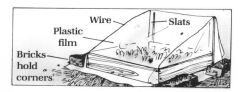

Over a bed with just a few seedlings, drape plastic over wires strung from slats. Bricks hold corners.

Plywood boards at each end of planting bed seal plastic hung over wire hoops. Boards weight edges.

Raised bed is half full of soil. Sash leans against the wall; sides are closed with plastic.

commonly used types measure 14 1/2 by 23 1/2 inches and 18 1/2 by 18 1/2 inches. Make your frame with enough leeway so you can lift flats in and out without pinching your fingers.

If you want to use scrap pieces of lumber and glass you have on hand, then the size of your cold-frame will be dictated by the dimensions of these pieces.

For the cover panel, glass, acrylic plastic, fiberglass, and polyethylene sheeting are readily available materials. (You can also buy ready-made sash, usually 3 by 6 feet, or snap-together aluminum sash in which you install polyethylene film.)

Glass is most expensive and, barring breakage, most durable. Check house-wrecking companies, glass companies, and salvage yards for old windows before you buy new glass.

Clear acrylic plastic is usually sold in precut sheets. It resists decomposition by sunlight, but it scratches easily.

Fiberglass comes flat or corrugated in 2, 4, and 6-foot-wide sheets. Flat fiberglass is slightly more ex-pensive, and it's harder to find. Sunlight does deteriorate fiberglass slowly; expect it to last 5 to 10 years.

Clear polyethylene film is the least expensive—but least durable—lid material. You'll probably have to replace it every year. It's cheapest to buy in large rolls—6, 8, 10, or 12 feet wide. Store unused polyethylene away from sunlight.

For the frame itself, the material that's easiest to work with, most commonly available, and least expensive is wood. Rot-resistant construction heart redwood and select tight-knot cedar are ideal. But plywood or scrap lumber will do, and they're both far less expensive. You could also use poured concrete, concrete blocks, or metal.

Other equipment you'll need

A good thermometer is essential if you want your coldframe to work. Most plants that will grow well outdoors in North America will continue growing at temperatures from about 40° to 100°F/4° to 38°C, and do best at about 85°F/30°C.

When your thermometer reaches 85°F/30°C, you can prop open the top of the frame to let out some heat. Then in late afternoon, when the outside temperature starts to fall, shut the top to trap the heat radiated by the soil. You'll probably need to open your coldframe on all but the coldest, cloudiest days.

You could also use a heat motor, a device that automatically opens the top when the interior gets too warm.

In really hot weather you'll have to whitewash the glass, or make a second cover of lath to cut down on the light.

To help your coldframe absorb heat most efficiently, paint the sides black, inside and out. Introducing a thermal mass (something that holds heat well), such as glass or plastic gallon jugs filled with water, keeps night temperatures higher. If the jugs are painted black, the water inside them can reach 135°F/57°C, heating very effectively.

On very cold nights, cover the coldframe with carpet, straw, or sheets of styrene foam to prevent trapped heat from radiating back into the atmosphere.

Sunken coldframe

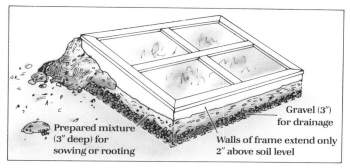

Partially buried coldframe far surpasses on-the-ground model in heat retention.

Hotbed protects from severe cold

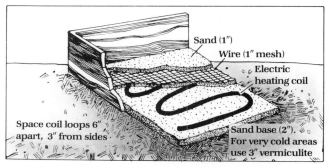

*A **hotbed*** is a coldframe with an electric heating cable added—here, buried under sand and wire.

Planting in autumn

Wherever winters are fairly mild, shrubs, trees, ground covers, and even some herbaceous plants will get a head start if you plant in autumn. But if you're likely to have cold periods or even just a hard frost or two, be sure the plants you've chosen are kinds that withstand cold.

For best results, set out plants early enough to begin to grow while soil is still warm. Late September or early October is about the right time. Try any of the plants listed.

Annuals and vegetables. Calendula, Iceland poppy, nemesia, pansy and viola, primrose, snapdragon, stock, pea family, cabbage family, other early bloomers.

Perennials. Any that flower in spring or early summer.

Shrubs. Azalea, camellia, ceanothus, conifers, daphne, privet, rhododendron, roses, lilac, native shrubs.

Trees. Use any that are not tender.

Ground covers. Chamomile, mondo grass, rosemary, strawberry, star jasmine, ice plant.

1) *Warm soil* forces root growth, but mild autumn air temperatures won't wilt or burn the plant's foliage.

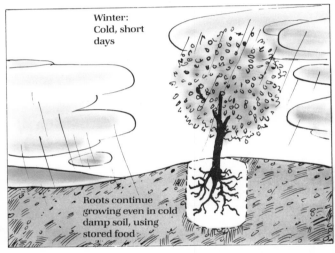

2) *Rain* waters the plant, and root growth continues into cold weather, even after the soil has cooled.

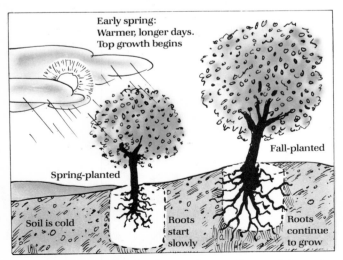

3) *Autumn-planted shrub* on right. is well rooted; its spring-planted neighbor gets slow start in cold soil.

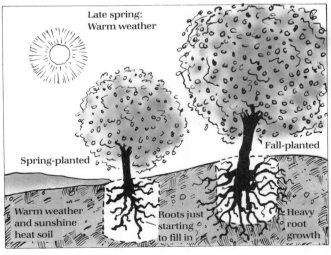

4) *Warm weather* brings top growth on rooted plant, but spring-planted one has too few roots for big spurt.

Garden Specialties

- Vegetables fresh from the garden: page 90

- Fruits & berries... decorative edibles: page 96

- Herbs for flavor & fragrance: page 98

- Roses, the all-time favorites: page 100

- Succulents & cacti... undemanding, sometimes spectacular: page 102

- House plants take the garden indoors: page 104

Vegetables fresh from the garden

It's surprising how many vegetables you can grow in a small garden plot. You can even interplant vegetables with flowers and small shrubs in your garden: many vegetables are highly decorative plants. And some are suitable for planting in containers—to take advantage of that sunny spot on your patio or deck.

To grow their very best, vegetables need all the sunlight you can give them and just the right amounts of water and nutrients. Before you buy any sets or seeds, choose a planting site that gets full sun for most or all of the day. Then rough out a plan on paper to show where each crop will go. Prepare the soil as described on pages 6–10, adding necessary amendments and a complete fertilizer or well-rotted manure and bone meal or super-phosphate.

Plant seeds according to package directions, or set out young plants from the nursery. When the plants are a couple of inches tall, mulch them (see page 52) to conserve moisture and stop weed growth. See page 58 for advice on watering. Fertilize vegetables once or twice as they grow.

If pests become a problem, see pages 120–130 for control methods. Never use an insecticide on vegetables that you plan to harvest within a week or so; read product labels carefully for instructions on how long to wait between spraying and harvesting.

Warm-season vegetables. The summer crops need soil warmth to germinate and long days and high temperatures (or short days and early heat)—without significant cooling at night—to form and ripen fruit. Most warm-season vegetables are grown for their fruit rather than their leaves, roots, or stems.

Cool-season vegetables. Most cool-season vegetables are leaf and root crops. A few are grown for other reasons: peas and broad beans for edible seeds; artichokes, broccoli, and cauliflower for edible flowers.

Cool-season vegetables grow steadily at average temperatures 10 to 15 degrees below those needed by warm-season crops. Many will endure some frost. Success with cool-season crops depends on bringing plants to maturity in the kind of weather that favors vegetative growth rather than flowering.

In general, you plant in very early spring so the crop will mature before summer heat settles in, or in late summer so the crop matures during autumn or even winter.

Vegetables for many salads grow here in a 7-foot circle surrounded by lawn. Young and mature plants are chard, parsley, chives, celery, and several kinds of lettuce.

A cornucopia of summer squash includes seven different colors, sizes, shapes: golden zucchini, straightneck, crookneck, green zucchini, scallopini, round zucchini, and scallop (patty pan).

Artichokes

Highly decorative, massive perennial that can spread to 8 feet wide. Needs long, mild winters and cool summers. Plant root divisions in early spring (available from nurseries and by mail order, or divide a mother plant in autumn after foliage has died back). Harvest period is late winter through midsummer, earlier where winters are warm. If not harvested, buds open to spectacular purple, thistlelike flowers.

Asparagus

A hardy perennial that needs a winter dormancy period. Spears push up from root masses from early spring until warm weather. Feathery plumes on mature plants manufacture food reserves and should be left on until they have begun to dry in late autumn. Plants are long-lived but take several years to come into full production. Start from roots, available in late winter at nurseries or by mail order.

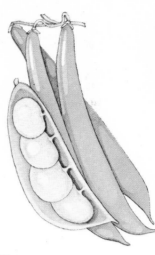

Beans

Two types most frequently grown by the home gardener are snap beans and lima beans. Each is available in low-growing (bush) types and tall-growing (pole) types. Beans require warm soil (65°F/18°C) to sprout reliably. Snap beans in bush form require 6 to 7 weeks to mature in warm weather; pole beans take 10 days to 2 weeks longer. Lima beans require warmer soil to sprout reliably, and they mature 3 to 5 weeks later than snap beans.

Beets

Biennial planted as annual. To have beets throughout summer, plant seeds at monthly intervals, starting as soon as soil can be worked in spring. Mulch lightly, keep moist. Thin plants to about 2 inches apart while they are small. Tops and roots of pulled plants can be cooked and eaten; choice leaves can be harvested while roots are still in ground. Grown as cool-season crop in the west. Harvest when 1 to 3 inches in diameter.

Broccoli

Hardy cabbage relative. Easy to grow; bears over long period. Plant to mature in cool weather: in mild climates, plant in late summer, autumn, or winter for winter or early spring crop; in cold-winter areas, set out young plants in late winter or early spring, about 2 weeks before last frost. Cut heads before clustered buds begin to open. After central head is removed, side shoots will produce additional heads.

Brussels sprouts

Require long growing period of cool weather. Where summers are short but cool, buy young plants early and transplant to garden as soon as soil can be worked in spring; plants will bear in autumn. In mild climates, plant in autumn or winter for winter and spring harvest. Sprouts grow along tall stem; snap or trim off when they are still firm and green (begin at bottom of stem, leaving sprouts on upper stem to mature).

Cabbage

Early varieties mature in 7 to 8 weeks; late varieties in 3 to 4 months. Plant to mature during cool weather. You can grow spring and autumn crops where the cool but frost-free growing season is 5 months or longer. Plant early varieties in spring, late varieties in midsummer for autumn harvest. Harvest and store before heavy freezes.

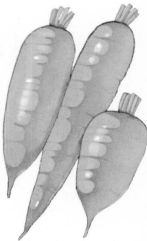

Carrots

Because they germinate unevenly, sow carrot seeds rather thickly (20 to 30 seeds per foot), in rows at least 12 inches apart. Keep soil moist and free from a crust on top. When seedlings are 2 inches high, thin them to leave 1 1/2 inches between each one; apply a thin band of commercial fertilizer 2 inches from row. Sow seeds at any time of year, but avoid hot summer months and winter months with freezing temperatures.

(Continued on next page)

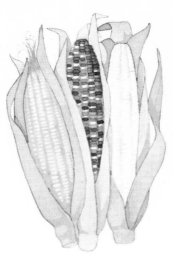

Cauliflower

Of all the cole crops, cauliflower is the most difficult to grow successfully. It grows best in a cool, moist climate. Daily sprinkling is helpful, especially if a dry, hot spell comes along. Set out plants in late summer for autumn harvest (winter harvests are possible in mild western or Gulf Coast climates). Plant in early spring in east and cold-winter west.

Celery

Plant celery only if you're looking for a challenge. It doesn't tolerate very high or low temperatures, is a heavy user of water and nutrients, and needs sandy or silty soil. Can be planted in early spring in most regions. Seeds are slow to germinate, so it's best to start them indoors 2 months ahead of planting time.

Corn

Plant corn after the soil has warmed and frosts are past. It must be planted in a series of parallel rows so that wind can distribute the pollen effectively. Corn needs lots of water after growth starts, especially at tasseling and after silking stages. It thrives on heat. If kernels spurt milky juice when punctured with your thumbnail, corn is ready to be picked. If juice is watery, corn is immature; if doughy, corn is overripe.

Cucumbers

Owners of small gardens often have difficulty finding room for any of the vine crops because they need at least a 5 by 5-foot ground area. Because of their light weight, cucumbers adapt well to being trained up trellises, thereby saving space. Plant them 18 inches apart, train the center stem vertically up the trellis to the top, then pinch the top off and train the lateral branches sideways. Otherwise, grow like squash, melons.

Tubbed cherry tomatoes enjoy reflected heat from paved surface of patio. Half-barrel allows room for roots.

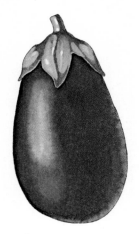

Eggplant

Heat-loving, frost-tender summer vegetable, best grown from nursery plants because it sprouts and grows so slowly from seed. Space plants 3 feet apart in rows 3 to 4 feet apart. Pick fruits when glossy, dark purple, and about 6 inches long. An attractive container plant; choose a tub or box with a capacity of at least 2 cubic feet.

Garlic

Seed stores and some mail-order seed houses sell "mother" bulbs for planting. They look like garlic bulbs from the grocery but are firmer. Break bulbs apart into cloves, and plant cloves with bases downward, 1 to 2 inches deep and 2 to 3 inches apart in rows 12 inches apart. One or two dozen cloves will be plenty for an average crop. Culture is the same as for onions.

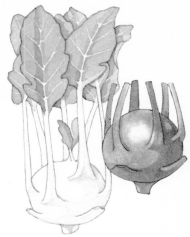

Kale

Curly kale makes a decorative garden or container plant and supplies edible leaves. Cooked like spinach or shredded in salads, kale is delicious but strong in taste. Nurseries seldom sell started plants, so you'll most likely have to buy seed and sow it. Plants are easy to transplant. Kale can be grown into summer more easily than other cole crops; it doesn't head and isn't as inclined to go to seed in hot weather.

Kohlrabi

Like kale, kohlrabi must be grown from seed. Sow seeds about 2 weeks after average date of last frost; follow with successive plantings about 2 weeks apart. The edible part is the swollen stem section above ground; it's especially good sliced like a cucumber, or cooked like a turnip.

Leeks

A relative of the onion, a leek doesn't form a bulb. Sow seeds in early spring (in cold-winter areas, sow seeds indoors and set out plants in June or July). As the plants grow, mound the soil around the fat, round stems to make the bottoms white and mild-tasting. Begin to harvest in late autumn.

Lettuce

Basic types are crisphead, butterhead, loose-leaf, and romaine. Crisphead is most difficult for home gardener to grow as it requires a constant temperature of 55 to 60°F/13 to 16°C. Butterhead varieties are loosely folded with smooth yellow center leaves. Loose-leaf lettuces are best for growing in hot climates. Romaine stands heat moderately well. Stagger lettuce planting for continuous supply.

Melons

To ripen to full sweetness, melons need from 2 1/2 to 4 months of heat. They will not tolerate foggy or cool summer days. You grow melons in the same way as squash and pumpkin. Watermelons need more heat than other melons and more space than other vine crops (8 by 8 feet). Of all melons, cantaloupes are easiest to grow because they ripen the fastest.

Onions

All onions (including green onions and shallots) are especially easy to grow as long as they have a fairly rich soil and regular watering. You can plant onion sets (tiny onions from seed stores) all winter in mild climates; in harsh-winter climates, plant them in early spring. Seeds need about 5 months to mature; sets need 3 to 4 months. Green onions can be picked in about 3 weeks.

(Continued on next page)

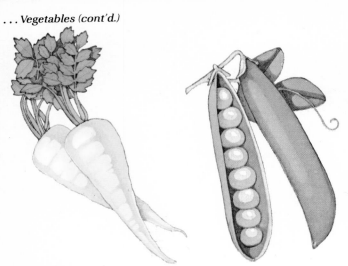
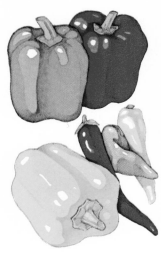

Parsnips

Parsnips are related to the carrot, but growth is much slower—4 months from seed to harvest. In cold-winter areas, sow seeds in late spring, let plants grow through summer, harvest in autumn, and leave excess in the ground to be dug up during winter. In milder climates, parsnips will rot if left in the ground; sow seeds in autumn for spring harvest. Parsnips need deep, loose soil; in heavy soil, sow in holes or trenches filled with sand or 3/4 sand and 1/4 soil.

Peas

Peas are a cool-weather crop; plant them in autumn, winter, or early spring. An easy crop to grow when conditions are right. Peas require water-retentive but fast-draining soil. Bush types need no support. If you have the space, you can grow tall (vining) peas on trellises, strings, or screen; they reach 6 feet or more and bear heavily. Edible-pod or snow peas are available in both vine and bush types; pick pods when they are 2 to 3 inches long and while seeds are still undeveloped.

Peppers

The two basic kinds of peppers are sweet and hot. Sweet peppers grow on stiff, rather compact, large-leafed bushes about 16 inches high. Hot pepper plants are taller, more spreading, and have small, narrower leaves. Sweet peppers mature in 65 to 80 days and can be grown anywhere in the country except in high elevations or extreme northern areas. Hot peppers ripen later, are better suited to areas with long, warm seasons, but are grown in northern states. Set-out plants are fastest.

Potatoes

White potatoes are commonly grown in average-size gardens, but sweet potatoes take up too much space for most home gardens (vines will spread to 6 feet or more across). Plant white potatoes early in spring or in midwinter in sandy, well-drained soil. Buy certified seed potatoes at a seed store. Cut into chunky pieces (1 1/2 inches square); place chunks, eye facing up, 4 inches deep and 18 inches apart. Dig new potatoes when tops begin to flower, mature ones after tops die back.

Pumpkins

Pumpkin varieties range from tiny jack-o-lanterns to giants weighing more than 100 pounds. They need lots of space; even the bush types spread over 20 square feet in rich soil. Start pumpkins in early summer from seeds sown in circles of three on mounds raised slightly for drainage and warmth. Space groups of vining varieties 10 feet apart, bush varieties 4 to 5 feet.

Radishes

You can harvest some kinds of radishes 3 weeks after you sow the seed. Speedy growth and relatively easy culture make this vegetable popular. Sow seeds as soon as soil can be worked in the spring and at 2-week intervals thereafter except in hottest time of the summer. Work in a light application of balanced fertilizer, plant seeds 1/2 inch deep and 1 inch apart, and water often. Space rows about 12 inches apart.

Rhubarb

Rhubarb is a perennial that dies back or goes dormant each autumn and shoots up new leaves in spring. The plant needs a dormant period and doesn't do well where winters are warm. Sow seeds or set out plants or roots in late spring. Water slowly and deeply. Let plants grow through two seasons before harvesting. Never eat the leaves—they're poisonous.

Spinach

You can sow seeds from July to September so plants will grow to maturity in autumn, winter, or spring (depending on your climate). The long daylight hours of late spring and heat of summer make it go to seed too fast. Spinach requires a rich soil that drains well. When seedlings get a good start, thin plants so the remaining ones are 6 inches apart. In summer, you can grow a similarly flavored plant called New Zealand spinach.

Squash

There are two basic types of squash. Summer squash (such as zucchini or scallop) takes only about 2 months to grow. Winter squash takes 3 or 4 months. (Spaghetti squash looks like any other winter squash, but the flesh is made up of long spaghetti-like strands.) Plant squash seeds in spring. Harvest summer squash when small and tender. Leave late squash on vines until thoroughly hardened; harvest with an inch of stem and store in a cool place.

Swiss chard

Ideal for any vegetable garden, chard is easy to grow and yields continually through a whole summer without going to seed. Grow it in any sunny spot— even among flowers. Rhubarb chard has red stems, reddish-green leaves, and is attractive in flower arrangements. When cooked, it is sweeter and stronger-flavored than green chard. Plant chard seed outdoors as soon as the soil can be worked in spring. Harvest outer leaves as needed.

Tomatoes

Tomatoes outrank all other vegetables in popularity with home gardeners. Varieties differ in size of plant; size, shape, color, and taste of fruit; and in climate adaptability. Nurseries sell the best varieties for the local climate. Plant seedlings at least 3 feet apart. Set plants in deeply; you can bury as much as 1/2 or 3/4 of the leafless part of the stem. Stake plants or support them on wire cylinders (see page 109). Water often, especially early in season.

Turnips and rutabagas

These cool-season, frost-hardy vegetables produce huge crops of edible roots and greens. Both spring and autumn crops of turnips are possible, but rutabagas are almost always planted in midsummer for autumn harvest. Turnips can be globe shaped or flattened globe. Colors are white, white topped with purple, or creamy yellow. Plants can reach 18 inches in height and spread. Rutabagas are larger, with large yellowish roots. Space plants to allow full root growth.

Vegetables thrive in series of raised beds. Portable greenhouse-type lid at left gives plants an early start and protects them from late frosts.

Fruits & berries ...decorative edibles

Fruit trees, grapevines, and berry plants can be among the most rewarding additions to a home garden, giving you years of satisfaction from the eye appeal of colorful blossoms and fruits and pride in harvesting delectable crops. It's important to find out which varieties are best suited to your climate and soil.

Fruit trees

Apple

Apples are among the most cold-tolerant of fruit trees, but climate adaptability varies according to variety. Mature trees may reach 20 feet tall with a 40-foot spread. Many varieties available on dwarfing or semi-dwarfing rootstocks that will grow to 8–15 feet.

Apricot

Apricots flower very early in spring, so fruit production is chancy in regions subject to late frosts that follow warmer weather. In such regions, plant trees in northern exposure so they will warm up slowly (but don't plant in shade). In mild-winter areas, choose varieties with low chilling requirement.

Cherry

All cherries—sweet and sour—have a high chilling requirement (need many winter hours below 45°F/7°C) and therefore are not adapted to mild-winter areas. Plant sweet cherries about 30 feet apart, sour cherries as close as 20 feet. Two trees are needed to produce fruit on sweet cherries; ask at your local nursery for advice about the best combination of trees to produce fruit.

Citrus

Check for varieties best suited to your climate. Ripening time will vary according to variety. If your area is likely to have late frosts, cover plants with paper or burlap or keep under protective overhang. Dwarf varieties make good container plants, which can be moved to a sheltered place when necessary.

Fig

Varieties differ in climate adaptability, some thriving under cool coastal conditions, others needing prolonged high temperatures to bear good fruit. Figs for the home garden do not need pollenizing. Most varieties produce two crops the first in June or July, the second in August or September.

Peach & nectarine

Peaches and nectarines differ by variety in their tolerance to cold or mild winters. Generally, they are a risk where winter temperatures drop below −15°F/ −26°C. In warm-winter regions, select from varieties that need less than the usual chilling requirement. Plant in autumn wherever possible, no less than 20 feet apart; in cold-winter areas, plant in early spring.

Pear

Pears will accept poor drainage and neglect better than other fruit trees. Plant about 20 feet apart. Prune only to shape, as heavy pruning may stimulate vigorous growth that's especially susceptible to fireblight.

Plum & prune

Most varieties are derived from either European or Japanese species. Both grow 15–20 feet high and about as wide. European varieties bloom late and are better adapted to areas with late frosts or cool, rainy spring weather than are the early-blooming Japanese kinds. Many varieties need another variety growing nearby as pollenizer.

If you plant berries, give them ample growing room—many can run rampant in your garden, so keep under control through pruning and sucker removal. Support tall-growing kinds by a trellis or other training device. Strawberries are easily grown plants that thrive in strawberry barrels and specially designed strawberry pots as well as in the open ground.

Fruit trees are popular subjects for espaliering, and for good reason. Espaliering exposes a maximum of branch surface to the sun, stimulating heavier flower and fruit production. Apples and pears top the list of favorites to espalier.

For techniques of pruning fruit trees, see page 117; for training vines, see pages 114–115. For the espalier method, see page 118.

Grapes

Grapevines are favorites for growing on a trellis or an arbor, or along a wall or fence. (If you train them on a wall, make sure they get afternoon sun.) Grapes take 3 years to grow to maturity. If planted and pruned properly, watered regularly, and fertilized each year, even a single vine will be one of your garden's outstanding features.

She's sampling *juicy grapes from vine trained along arbor.*

Berries

Blackberries

(This group includes boysenberries, loganberries, youngberries, and nectar berries.) Deep-rooted plants; won't stand shallow, poorly drained soil. Grow them as bushes or train them tall, in a supporting framework.

Blueberries

Need cool, moist, acid soil that drains well. Keep well watered. Prune to prevent overbearing. Most varieties are upright to 6 feet or more; a few are rather sprawling and under 5 feet. Plant two different varieties to assure pollination. Highly ornamental, with attractive small flowers, fruit, and good fall color.

Raspberries

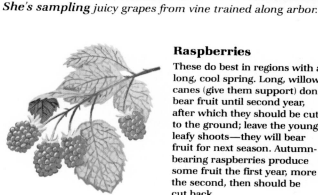

These do best in regions with a long, cool spring. Long, willowy canes (give them support) don't bear fruit until second year, after which they should be cut to the ground; leave the young, leafy shoots—they will bear fruit for next season. Autumn-bearing raspberries produce some fruit the first year, more the second, then should be cut back.

Strawberries

Easily grown plants that require no special training. They can be grown in any fertile, well-drained soil. Plant in spring or, if you live in a mild climate, in autumn (you'll get berries the first spring).

Herbs for flavor & fragrance

The fragrance, flavor, and healing qualities of herbs are woven into the rich tapestry of Biblical stories, ancient classics, quaint herbals, and scientific works. Yet with all this background in antiquity, herbs are remarkably up-to-date, free-wheeling plants. Today few people have space or need for a formal herb garden, but there's always demand for an attractive and serviceable ground cover, edging, shrub, or container plant. Herbs fill all these needs.

A raised bed near the kitchen door, a planter box near the barbecue, or a corner of the vegetable garden make ideal locations for the herbs you use for cooking and garnishing. In winter, herbs grown in containers can be moved to an out-of-the-way place during dormancy. Some drought-resistant herbs make good soil binders on slopes. And many shrubby herbs combine well with other plants in perennial or shrub borders.

Herbs as a group are vigorous, undemanding plants that require only average soil and moisture. Most are sun lovers, but some will take part shade.

Many herbs can be grown inside the house.

Sunny marigolds spark planting of culinary herbs: marjoram, Italian parsley, and lavender-flowered lemon thyme.

Anise
Pimpinella anisum

Likes light, fertile, well-drained soil. Annual; start seeds as soon as ground warms up in spring. Use leaves in salads, seeds for flavoring cookies, pastries, confections.

Basil
Ocimum basilicum

Annual. Grows readily from seed sown in spring. Plant in full sun or part shade. Leaves have a spicy, clovelike flavor; especially good in tomato dishes.

Borage
Borago officinalis

Likes sun or filtered shade, slightly poor soil, moderate amounts of water. Annual; grows readily from seed sown in spring. Use leaves in salads or pickling, or cook as greens.

Burnet
Poterium sanguisorba

Small burnet or salad burnet is a perennial. The leaves have a pleasant, cucumberlike flavor; use them in salads, iced drinks, vinegar, butters. Thimble-sized, rose-colored flowers.

Caraway
Carum carvi

Seeds develop in second year, then plant dies. Harvest in midsummer when seeds are ripe but before they drop. Use to flavor pickles, cabbage, Brussels sprouts, cookies, bread.

Catnip
Nepeta cataria

Likes light, rich soil, sun or part shade, moderate moisture. Perennial; sow seeds in spring or late autumn. Protect seedlings from cats. Use leaves for tea. Plants are 2–3 feet tall.

Chamomile
Chamaemelum nobile

Roman or English chamomile is the one most often used in herb gardens. Good ground cover around garden paths. Sow seeds in early spring or late autumn. Brew tea from blossoms.

Chervil
Anthriscus cerefolium

Sow seeds in slightly moist garden soil in part shade. Annual; reseeds readily. Similar to parsley but with slightly aniselike flavor. Use with other herbs to enhance, or add to salads.

Chives
Allium schoenoprasum

Usually bought as small plants but can be grown from seed. Plants can be divided. Use chopped chives in salads, cheese and egg dishes, gravies, and soups.

Coriander
Coriandrum sativum

Sold in markets as Chinese parsley or cilantro. Use seeds in potpourris and to flavor beans, stews, sausage, pastries; leaves to flavor fowl, meats, spicy sauces.

Dill
Anethum graveolens

Annual. Plant in full sun in well-drained, good garden soil. Use leaves fresh or dried, or ripened seeds, in fish, chicken, lamb dishes, stews, sauces, salad dressings, bread.

Fennel
Foeniculum vulgare

Propagate by seeds sown in spring; likes full sun and light, well-drained garden soil. Leaves and seeds have pleasant anise flavor. Good seasoning for fish, cheeses, vegetables.

Lemon balm
Melissa officinalis

Lemon-scented and flavored perennial. Slow to germinate; sow seeds in fall for spring plants, or propagate from plant divisions or cuttings. Use fresh or dried leaves for tea and in potpourris.

Marjoram
Origanum majorana

Sow seeds early in spring or propagate from cuttings or divisions. Can be grown indoors in sunny window. Use fresh or dried leaves to flavor meats, salads, vinegars, and casseroles.

Mint
Mentha

Perennial. Most varieties grow almost anywhere and spread rapidly by underground stems and runners. Best contained in pots or boxes. Use as garnish, add to lamb, jelly, fruit cocktails.

Oregano
Origanum vulgare

A good container plant, but replace about every 3 years. Grow new plants from seeds or divisions. Annual in cold climates. Use leaves in same foods as marjoram or thyme.

Parsley
Petroselinum crispum

Biennial, treated as annual. Grow from nursery plants or sow seeds in spring. Soak seeds in warm water for 24 hours before planting. Part shade or sun; water regularly. Use as garnish.

Rosemary
Rosmarinus officinalis

Will tolerate poor soil if it's well drained; likes hot sun. Perennial shrub in mild climates. Good in containers or indoors. Use leaves fresh or dried with chicken, stews, vegetables.

Sage
Salvia officinalis

Likes poor but well-drained soil, full sun; fairly drought resistant. Annual in cold climates; grow from seed or cuttings. Use fresh or dried leaves with lamb, stuffings, sausage.

Savory
Satureja

Start summer savory (annual) from seed, winter savory (perennial) from cuttings or divisions. Use leaves fresh or dried with meats, fish, eggs, beans, and in soups, vinegars.

Sweet bay
Laurus nobilis

An evergreen shrub or tree. In hot-summer regions, grow in filtered sun or afternoon shade; in cold areas, bring indoors in winter. Use leaves fresh or dried in stews, spaghetti, meat loaf.

Sweet woodruff
Galium odoratum

Attractive, low-growing perennial; spreads rapidly as ground cover in shade. Start from plants or increase by root divisions in autumn and spring. Use flowers for May wine or tea.

Tarragon
Artemisia dracunculus

Rather prostrate, woody perennial. Does not produce seeds; grow from cuttings or divisions. Use leaves fresh or dried in salads, egg dishes, cheese, vinegars, and with fish.

Thyme
Thymus

Many species and varieties. Perennial; start from seeds or cuttings. Use leaves fresh or dried in vegetable juices, stuffings, soups, and with fish, poultry, meats, vegetables.

Roses, the all-time favorites

The rose is one of the most popular of all flowers—and for good reason. The matchless beauty of the blooms is in itself enough to qualify this ancient shrub for top ranking. Add to the lovely flowers their fragrance, unending variety of forms, long bloom season, and wide adaptability.

When you start a rose garden, buy good plants. Be sure those you select have three to five thick, healthy canes and roots that are not dried out. If you order plants by mail, buy them only from a reputable nursery company.

For advice on how to plant a rose bush, see page 17. For tips about pruning, see page 116.

There are many kinds of roses, encompassing literally thousands of varieties. The types described here are those most popular in today's gardens. We've also suggested a few varieties as a good starting point for beginning rose gardeners. Remember, though, that many magnificent varieties are introduced each year, and some will replace the current favorites.

Combination planting of roses includes two climbers, 'Handel' and 'America'. In the foregound is a floribunda, 'Cathedral'.

Hybrid tea

These are the aristocrats of the rose world. Flowers are beautifully formed and generally large, and buds are long and graceful. Examples: 'Peace', 'Miss All-American Beauty', 'Mr. Lincoln', 'Perfume Delight', 'Double Delight', 'King's Ransom', 'Paradise', 'Pascali'.

Floribunda

Smaller-flowered and generally lower-growing than hybrid teas, this class is famed for its masses of bloom borne almost continuously from spring to autumn. Examples: 'Redgold', 'Sarabande', 'Angel Face'. Polyantha types: 'Margo Koster', 'The Fairy'.

Grandiflora

Descended from crosses between floribundas and hybrid teas, this class combines many good features of both. Plants are vigorous and usually tall growing. Examples: 'Queen Elizabeth', 'Granada'.

Climber

Many of the best varieties are mutations of hybrid teas, floribundas, and grandifloras. Examples: 'Golden Showers', 'Climbing Mrs. Sam McGredy', 'Handel', 'Climbing Cecile Brunner'.

Massed petunias in pink and white complement blossoms on a pair of tree (standard) roses.

They're really just this size. Miniature roses like 'Judy Fischer' are dainty, scaled-down replicas of floribundas or hybrid teas.

Tree rose

Many hybrid teas, floribundas, and grandifloras are budded on tall-caned understocks and sold as standards 24 to 40 inches tall. They are excellent for lining walkways or adding a tall accent wherever needed.

Shrub type

Noted for their landscape value as individual plants more than beauty of individual blooms, some species roses and their hybrids make excellent "living fences." Examples: 'Belinda', 'Blanc Double de Coubert', 'Harison's Yellow'.

Old rose

It's getting harder to find the fragrant, enchanting favorites of yesteryear, but some are still obtainable by mail order. Examples: 'Reine Victoria', 'Souvenir de la Malmaison', 'Tuscany'.

Miniature

These tiny specimens are excellent for rock gardens and container planting. Buds the size of popcorn kernels open into blooms often less than an inch in diameter. Examples: 'Starina', 'Popcorn', 'Judy Fischer'.

Succulents & cacti...undemanding, sometimes spectacular

Succulents are one of the most fascinating groups of plants in the entire plant world. Cacti, euphorbias, crassulas, and agaves are all succulents, but each appears distinctively different.

All cacti are succulents, but all spiny succulent plants are *not* cacti. If the plant has spines or sharply pointed hairs arranged in clusters separated by areas of spineless skin, the plant most likely is a cactus.

Succulents are found in every part of the world where plants have difficulty in getting and keeping water—particularly in desert and high mountain regions.

To duplicate the conditions of their natural habitat as closely as possible, plant succulents where they get ample sunlight (though they will tolerate some shade). Water very sparingly the year around, letting soil dry out between waterings. Overwatering can cause succulents to rot.

A few hardy types, such as sempervivum and sedum, can survive cold winters, but most succulents are killed by freezing temperatures. In cold climates, grow them in pots or other containers, and move them to a well-lighted indoor location for winter. If you live in a region where winters are mild, you can grow them either in containers or in permanent outdoor locations protected from frosts.

Welcoming trio of containers holding kalanchoe, echeveria, dudleya, and sedum brighten entry with its dark blue door.

Aeonium

Rosette-forming plants, growing in a clustering base in bushier species or atop sturdy stems in others. Brightly colored flowers in yellow, white, or pink.

Crassula

Most crassulas thrive in containers and can remain in same pot for years. White, pink, yellow, green, or red flowers in late summer, fall through spring.

Gymnocalycium

Small cactus, often grown as house plant. Long-lasting flowers in red, pink, white, or sometimes yellow. Easy to grow. Dislikes scorching sun.

Opuntia

Three distinct groups: prickly pears with flat-jointed pads, one growing out of another; tall cylindrical-jointed chollas; dwarf species with globular or cylindrical stems. Vivid blooms.

Agave

Known for its toughness and tolerance to adverse conditions. Popular in desert landscapes, especially where bold forms are needed.

Aloe

Ranges from dwarf sizes to tree types. Clumps of fleshy, pointed leaves, often green or gray-green with contrasting bands or streaks. Orange, red, or yellow flowers in clusters.

Cereus

Easy to grow, strong, vigorous plant. Wide variety of sizes, forms. Some form candelabra-shaped crown; others branch at base. Nocturnal white flowers. May grow to tree-size cactus in ground; often miniature in pots.

Cotyledon

Prized for bold form and interesting leaves. Grows 1 1/2 to 3 feet tall. Orange flowers in spring, summer. Do not water from above.

Echeveria

Handsome, fleshy-leafed rosettes. Much hybridizing has produced many echeverias that are highly prized for their shape, color, leaf texture. Commonly called hen and chicks.

Echinocactus

Many kinds of large, cylindrical cactus with prominent ribs and stout thorns. Among the easiest cacti to grow. Varied in shape and size.

Echinopsis

Small cylindrical or globular cactus usually grown in pots. Flowers to 8 inches long in white, yellow, pink or red.

Euphorbia

Strong, boldly shaped. Each species is unique. Excellent indoors, serving same function as sculpture. Striking in form, attractive in texture and color, slow-growing.

Haworthia

One of best choices for potted indoor plant because of compact size (to 1 foot tall), tolerance for shade, fascinating leaf formations.

Kalanchoe

Kalanchoes are tropical natives, preferring a moist environment with little threat of frost. Good indoors or outdoors; attractive potted plants.

Lemaireocereus

Tall, columnar plant that branches into many ribbed stems. Commonly called organ-pipe cactus. Requires sunny location and minimum winter temperatures above 35°F/2°C.

Lithops

Many species. One of the most unusual plant groups, commonly called "pebble plants" or "living rocks" (they look like rocks and pebbles). Best grown indoors.

Sedum

Small succulents, usually under 8 inches high. Unusual coloring, fast growing. Excellent potted plants. Hardier species make colorful ground covers or rock garden plants.

Sempervivum

Popularly called houseleeks. Small, rosette-forming plants, some less than 1/2 inch wide. Popular rock garden plant.

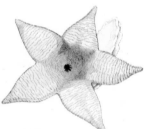

Stapelia

Succulent resembling cactus; clumps of 4-sided succulent stems. Large 5-pointed flowers in summer. Good desert succulent, tolerating extreme heat. Best in pots.

Yucca

A desert tree or shrub. Does best in full sun. Most take considerable drought when established but many will accept garden watering. Creamy white bell-shaped flowers in spring.

House plants take the garden indoors

African violet
Fuzzy, heart-shaped leaves
grow in rosettes. Varieties of
Saintpaulia ionantha have plain
or scalloped, green or variegated
leaves; purple, violet, pink,
white, or variegated flowers.
Likes bright light, high humidity.

House plants have come a long way
since the days when wealthy Victo-
rians grew ferns in their conser-
vatories and only those who could
afford it had potted palms gracing
their houses. In today's homes,
house plants of all sizes, shapes,
and varieties are displayed wherever there's space.

If you've never grown house
plants, or if you've tried with little
success to keep them healthy and
attractive, it's important to know
that finding a good location for your
house plant is crucial.

Almost all plants, for instance,
dislike dry heat. And though a few
plants will survive in a dark hall—
both Howea palms and aspidistra
have been known to do so—most
plants will die without adequate
light. Indirect or north light is best
for most indoor plants. Never set
any plant in an uncurtained south
or west window: hot sun coming
through these exposures can
quickly bake or burn tender plants.

Every so often, you might want
to group your indoor plants under
special fluorescent tubes that can
stimulate plants to bloom, if used
12 to 14 hours per day.

How much water do indoor
plants require? You'll find through
experience that each plant has its
individual watering needs. A good
way to check is simply to feel the
soil every few days—when the top
inch or so feels dry, it's time to add
water. Keep in mind that a soggy
plant will die sooner than a dry one.

Fertilize your house plants
regularly with one of the numerous
products available, including tab-
lets, liquids, powders, and capsules. Most of these fertilizers are to
be dissolved and diluted in water
for application. Some types are
scratched into the soil surface; tab-
lets and slow-release capsules are
placed on top of or in the soil.

Boston fern
Nephrolepis exaltata 'Bostoniensis' has graceful, drooping,
sword-shaped fronds. Easily
grown. Likes bright light, cool
house temperatures, some
humidity, regular fertilizing,
good drainage. Keep moist.

Dieffenbachia
Striking dark green to yellow-
green leaves with white or
cream variegations. Callalike
flowers form on mature plants.
Likes north light; turn occasionally. Water only when surface of
soil seems dry.

Indoor plant collection hangs from
12-foot-long ceiling track. Included
here are Boston fern, ivy geranium,
wandering Jew, spider plant, bridal veil,
creeping Charlie, and split-leaf
philodendron.

Asparagus fern

Not a true fern but has same feathery qualities, and arching or drooping stems. Myers asparagus is a fast grower. Likes good light, ample water, frequent misting. Leaves will turn yellow in inadequate light.

Aspidistra

Sturdy, long-lived foliage plant. Tough, glossy, dark green leaves. Prefers high humidity, cool temperatures, regular watering. Light can range from dark shade to filtered sun. Responds to fertilizing in spring, summer.

Begonia

Extensive group of plants, most of which make good house plants. Generally prefer filtered light, regular fertilizing, rich potting mix that is slightly acid. Keep moist with perfect drainage.

Bird's nest fern

Showy, apple-green, undivided fronds with black ribs unfurl from heart of *Asplenium nidus*. Fronds dislike being touched. Avoid water accumulation in center of plant; it may cause crown rot.

Coleus

Brilliantly colored, velvety leaves, often ruffled or scalloped, in many shades. Needs good light, warm temperatures, regular fertilizing, ample water, standard potting mix. Pinch stems repeatedly.

Columnea

Trailing stems; good in hanging baskets. Paired, shiny leaves. Brilliantly colored, tubular flowers to 3" long, in red, orange, yellow, or combinations. Likes average temperatures, high humidity, good light.

Creeping Charlie

Plectranthus is one of several trailing plants known as creeping Charlie. Good plant for hanging baskets. Likes light shade or bright light. Water thoroughly, don't water again until surface is dry. Also called Swedish ivy.

Croton

Tropical plant (*Codiaeum variegatum*) grown for colorful leaves that may be green, yellow, red, purple, bronze, pink, or combination. Likes bright light, warm temperatures, high humidity, ample water.

Dracaena

Bladelike foliage, green or variegated. Can become tall. Likes bright light, high humidity, regular fertilizing and watering, but will tolerate low light, low humidity, infrequent watering. Effective planted three to a pot.

Ficus benjamina

Drooping branches, delicate appearance. New growth pale green, older leaves dark green. Likes bright light, standard potting mix, regular fertilizing. Let soil dry between waterings. Very popular indoor tree.

Fiddleleaf fig

Large, dark green, glossy, fiddle-shaped leaves to 15" long, 10" wide. Tolerates low light. To increase branching, pinch back *Ficus lyrata* when young. Keep leaves clean. Can grow to tree size inside house.

Grape ivy

Cissus rhombifolia has dark green leaves divided into diamond-shaped leaflets 1–4" long with sharp-tooth edges. Easy to grow. Tolerates low light. Not fussy about soil, water, or temperature.

(Continued on next page)

Howea palm

Slow growing. Feathery leaves, clean green trunk ringed with leaf scars. Likes warm temperatures, standard potting mix, ample moisture. Tolerates low light, some watering neglect.

Peperomia

Plants have a variety of interesting foliage. Tiny flowers in dense, small, slender spikes. Likes filtered light, standard potting mix with good drainage, high humidity, not too much water. Protect from direct sun.

Philodendron

Treelike types grow 6–8' high with sturdy, self-supporting trunks. Vining types need support. Self-heading types form short, broad plants. All types like good light, some humidity, ample water.

Piggy-back plant

Tolmiea menziesii has heart-shaped, apple-green leaves with delicate fuzz and toothed edges. New plantlets grow on top of older leaves. Likes filtered light, cool temperatures, ample water. Tolerates wet soil.

Pothos

Epipremnum aureum has variegated, heart-shaped leaves. Attractive trailing plant for pots, window boxes, large terrariums. Likes good light, regular watering, fertilizer, but tolerates some neglect.

Prayer plant

Maranta leuconeura has large green leaves with paired brown spots along midrib. At night, leaves fold together, resembling praying hands. Likes filtered light, high humidity, regular fertilizing, lots of water.

Schefflera

Fast-growing, tropical-looking plant with long-stalked leaves divided into leaflets with spread like fingers of hand. Prefers rich soil, occasional fertilizing, bright light. Let dry between waterings. Wash leaves, mist.

Spathiphyllum

Dark green, large, oval leaves narrowing to a point. White callalike flowers. Likes bright light but tolerates less; high humidity, frequent watering, regular fertilizing, fibrous potting mix.

Spider plant

Chlorophytum comosum forms clumps of green or variegated, grasslike leaves. Miniature duplicates of mother plant, complete with root, form at end of stems and can be potted individually. Good in hanging baskets.

Split-leaf philodendron

Large vining plant (*Monstera deliciosa*). Needs good support to climb. Leathery, dark green leaves, deeply cut; small leaves that do not split indicate poor light, low humidity; leaves on youngest plants uncut.

Threadleaf false aralia

Dizygotheca elegantissima has lacy, evergreen leaves, dark green and glossy above, reddish brown beneath. Likes bright light, good drainage, high humidity. Waterlogged or dry soil will cause leaf drop.

Wandering Jew

Tradescantia, one of several "wandering Jews," is a fast-growing, trailing plant. Needs frequent pinching to control size, keep compact. Likes normal watering, and light ranging from sun to shade.

Pruning, Pinching & Tying

- Staking and tying: page 108
- Pruning—to preserve beauty & health: page 110
- Pruning—good technique & the right tools: page 112
- Small steps in directing growth: page 113
- Training vines: page 114
- Pruning roses: page 116
- How to prune fruit trees: page 117
- Espaliering: page 118

Staking & tying

Nothing is sadder than to see a beautiful young tree or a flowering plant beaten down by a sudden storm or collapsed under its own weight. You can avoid this disappointment if you follow proper staking procedures.

Some plants, particularly taller ones, obviously need staking if they are to stand up against the elements. Others, while they may not

The method depends on the plant

Delphinium *stake must be long enough to support flower. Use ties that won't cut into the stalks or stems.*

Dahlia *stake is placed 2 inches away from tuber (left) at planting time; as plant grows (right), tie stem at intervals.*

Gladiolus *at left grew crooked before it was staked. At right, the stake was put in next to bulb at planting time.*

Sprawling plants, *whether grown singly or in rows, can be supported with stakes and wire or twine.*

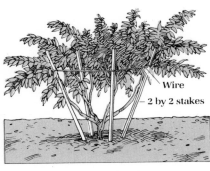

Multiple-trunked shrubs *or small trees can be supported and trained on a frame of wood stakes and wire.*

Single weak-stemmed plant *owes support to figure-eight tie. Loop string around plant, cross over; tie firmly.*

Clump of plants *needs just one stake. Place strong stake in center of informal group, tie plants to it individually.*

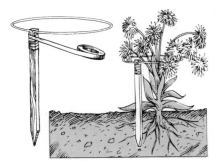

Heavy flowers *lean against coat hanger bent to form a circle, then taped to the top of a stake.*

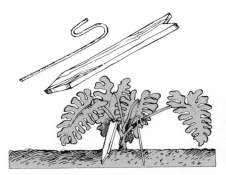

Low-growing plants *are propped up by notched plant labels or bent wire. Props can be moved as the plants grow.*

absolutely require staking, will only perform their best when given proper support.

Always stake a plant securely and in as natural a position as possible; try to keep the stake and tie as unobtrusive as you can. Never make the tie too tight.

Adapt the staking technique to the plant's growth habit and the way it is used. For example, plants such as dahlias, tall delphiniums, lilies, and top-size gladiolus and tuberous begonias are usually staked individually. Multiple staking, on the other hand, is the most efficient method for plants in rows, as in a cut flower garden; it also works well in group plantings.

Stake early to prevent damage to roots, to keep the plant straight, and to allow growth to adapt to and cover the stake and tie material.

Green-painted bamboo and wood stakes are regular items at most garden centers. Also available are green plastic stakes and metal ones. You'll find that ties hold more securely on rough wood than on smooth surfaces.

Anchoring trees

To protect young trees against winter storms, use three guy wires attached to a rubber or plastic-covered tree tie. Anchor the wires to 2 by 4-inch stakes driven 2 feet into the ground. Set stakes, making sure the pull of the tree is against the 4-inch side. Use turnbuckles on the wires to keep them taut.

Ground cover "hairpins"

Many ground covers will sprawl and spread out with no special training. Others, such as star jasmine, will hug the ground better if you pin branches to the ground with 6-inch staples, starting when plants are young.

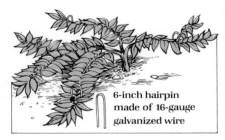

6-inch hairpin made of 16-gauge galvanized wire

Train ground covers with wires.

Precautions for staked trees

Watch staked trees carefully. The ties become tighter on growing trunks, and if they're too tight they'll constrict the flow of nutrients and weaken the trees. Ties can also rub and cut into tender bark.

Tie loops around trunk between stakes.

Loosen or remove tight ties or replace them with ties that are larger, more elastic, or padded. Where a tree has been cut or worn by a tie, clean the wound and paint it with pruning compound.

Stakes that no longer provide support for the now-stronger tree may be slowing down its growth. Remove the stakes if you don't expect strong winds and if the tree doesn't fall over with removal. This will allow the tree to develop its own strength independently.

A selection of plant ties

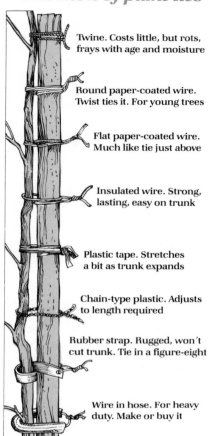

Twine. Costs little, but rots, frays with age and moisture

Round paper-coated wire. Twist ties it. For young trees

Flat paper-coated wire. Much like tie just above

Insulated wire. Strong, lasting, easy on trunk

Plastic tape. Stretches a bit as trunk expands

Chain-type plastic. Adjusts to length required

Rubber strap. Rugged, won't cut trunk. Tie in a figure-eight

Wire in hose. For heavy duty. Make or buy it

Plant ties ranging from twine to hose and wire are sold at nurseries. Use the top six ties for small plants.

Training tomatoes in a wire cylinder

Tomato vines, by nature, ramble over the ground. If the fruit is not to rot and be eaten by insects, it must be kept off the ground. This wire mesh cylinder, placed over the tomato plant while it's young, not only keeps the fruit healthy and easy to pick, but also allows you to cultivate around the plant easily. With it you can grow tomatoes in narrow beds; and once filled with tomatoes, it is decorative enough for borders with flowering annuals. Use concrete reinforcing wire for the cylinder; it is rigid enough to be self-supporting. If you use wire with 6-inch mesh, you'll find that the tomatoes are easy to pick and the vines easy to train. You can paint the cylinder to prevent rust and add to its attractiveness. Make a watering basin about 2 feet wide around each plant.

Some tomato varieties, the *determinate* types, are bushier than most tomato vines and not as suitable for staking or trellising.

Pruning—to preserve beauty & health

Some plants require considerable pruning; others may need little or none. You should prune to maintain plant health by cutting out dead, diseased, or injured wood; to control growth when an unshapely shrub or tree might result; to restrain plant size; and to increase the quality and yield of flowers or fruit.

When should you prune?

Some kind of pruning is necessary for many plants just before or at the beginning of the growing season. Major pruning on deciduous plants like fruit trees and roses is usually done in late winter when branches are bare. But you can also clean up, pinch back, or shear many plants in summer and autumn—in fact, you may have to if you want to keep a plant a certain size or shape.

Shrubs and trees that produce flowers can be pruned after the flowers fade and just as new leaf growth is beginning. Since the plant is in an active growth stage, the cuts you've made will heal quickly.

If you grow a plant specifically for cut flowers, cut off every bloom with a view to shaping the plant; cut above a bud facing the direction you want growth to take.

Importance of terminal buds

Terminal buds are the growing buds on the ends of all branches and branchlets.

During the season of active growth, these tip buds draw plant energy to themselves and grow, adding length to the stems. But if any growing terminal bud is cut or nipped off, growth ceases at that part of the plant and the growth energy that would have gone to the terminal bud goes instead to lateral (side) buds you can see easily and to less-apparent dormant (latent) buds along the branch.

Removing (pinching off) the terminal bud doesn't change the direction of plant growth—it just increases the number of stems and buds. To change the direction of a

branch, you must find a fat bud growing in the direction you want the branch to grow. You then snip off the whole branch just above the bud. That bud will take over.

For the same reason, you never cut off just the tip of a branch that's vigorously growing faster than the rest of the plant (this will only give you several vigorous branches). Instead, you cut off the branch at the base, or at least to a bud located well below the rest of the foliage.

Where to make cuts

Whenever you approach a plant that you are going to prune for any reason—to take its flowers, to improve its shape, to make it bushier, or to make it more open—remember this: *never make a cut at an arbitrary point along a branch.* Instead, cut just above a bud or a good branch, or make the cut flush with the trunk or base, trying to make the wound fairly small so bark will cover it quickly.

If you leave a stub, no nourishment will pass through the tissue below the cut. The stub above the bud or main branch will wither and die, offering a breeding ground for disease organisms that can damage the whole branch.

If you have a choice of which bud or branch to cut back to, choose the one that points in the direction you'd like new growth to take. And if you have no preference

Buds direct growth

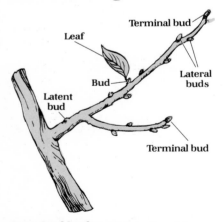

Terminal buds lead growth out in new direction. Removing them causes lateral buds and latent buds to grow. A leaf often shows bud location.

Removing the terminal shoot or bud (pinching) activates the buds below into strong growth. Plant will become bushy at that point.

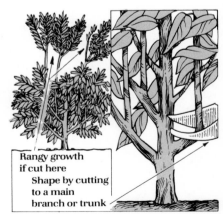

Twiggy growth may happen if you trim off just the ends of vigorously growing branches. Instead, cut off runaway branches at base.

Here's where to make your cuts

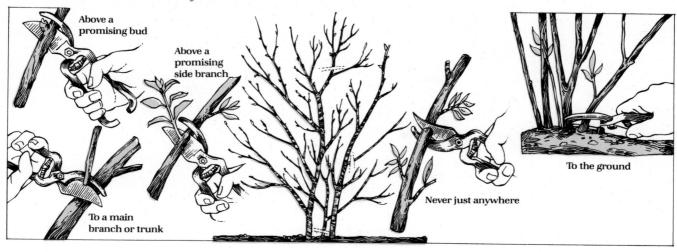

Above a promising bud

Above a promising side branch

To a main branch or trunk

Never just anywhere

To the ground

for the branch's direction, remember that generally it's better for the plant if the new branch can grow toward an open space rather than toward another branch. Crossing branches are troublesome: they rub against each other and they spoil a plant's looks.

The only situation where pruning to a growing point does not apply is in shearing. In this case you are cutting such small, twiggy growth that the dead stubs are of no consequence. For example, you shear hedges and the spent flowers on some annuals and perennials (see page 113).

How a plant wants to grow

A veteran gardener looks at a plant and considers how it grows before assisting its growth by pruning. Cuts should enhance the plant's natural shape and assist its growth.

You can train a tree or a shrub to grow almost any way you want if you watch how it grows naturally and learn (by trial and error if necessary) how it responds when you've pruned a terminal bud, part of a branch, or a whole branch.

For example, privet will often sprout lush growth if you cut it back to bare twigs. But you'll find that pruning some shrubs and trees will produce little new growth. A good example of this is the camellia—pinch it back by cutting off the terminal bud and you may get only one replacement branch. To produce several branches, you must cut back to the point where last year's growth stopped and this year's began (look for a difference in bark color).

In contrast, perennials such as marguerites may not survive the kind of extreme cutting some trees and shrubs thrive on.

Special pruning situations

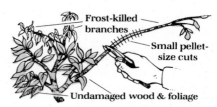

Frost-killed branches

Small pellet-size cuts

Undamaged wood & foliage

Frost-killed branches *should be cut back when frost danger is past and new growth is just beginning. Make small pellet-size cuts up to green wood.*

Wrong

Right

Shear hedges *so that sides slope in somewhat at top. If hedge flares out at top, lower leaves and branches won't get enough light.*

Cut here

or here to force lower buds

Not here. No dormant buds to force

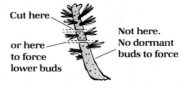

Conifers *normally don't require pruning. But if a conifer must be pruned, cut selectively back to another branch or bud on the whorl-branching types; generally, you can shear random-branching plants.*

Prune to enhance shape

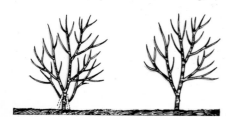

Thinning*—removing entire stems, limbs, or branches—opens up and simplifies the plant structure.*

Heading back*— cutting off lengths of stem—reduces size of plant, yet encourages fullness.*

Pruning—good technique & the right tools

Most gardeners depend on four basic tools for pruning: a pair of shears, a set of long-handled loppers, a pair of hedge shears, and a pruning saw, perhaps with an extender. Many other tools are available for more specialized pruning jobs.

When making any pruning cut, avoid leaving a stub. Also avoid undercutting the bud or branch. The best cuts place the lowest part of the cut directly opposite and slightly above the upper side of the bud or branch to which you are cutting back.

Keep a can of tree-sealing compound on hand to seal any big cuts you make—it helps keep out any disease organisms.

Shears. Of the various cutting tools, you'll probably most often use a sturdy pair of pruning shears that fits your hand. They're light enough to carry with you whenever you go into the garden. You might also want to get the little specialty shears meant specifically for cutting flowers, but these are too small to serve as your only pruning tool.

Hook-and-blade   Anvil

When your shears begin to crush or tear the plant tissue, it's time to have them sharpened. Ragged edges on a pruning cut heal more slowly than clean cuts. Use shears that are strong enough for the job. If you can't get them to cut easily through a branch, the shears are too small, too dull, or both. Switch to a pair of loppers or use a pruning saw instead.

With hook-and-blade pruning shears, remember to place the blade, not the hook, on the side toward the plant. If the hook is on the side toward the plant, you will leave a small stub.

Loppers. Long-handled loppers reach up higher and further into dense foliage than hand shears. And they will cut through thicker branches. When using them, follow the same principle as with hook-and-blade shears: put the blade, not the hook, on the side toward the plant.

Hedge shears. These won't cut through thick stems or branches; use them for shaping or shearing hedges, shrubs, some perennials, ground covers, and faded flower heads.

Pruning saws. You'll find these invaluable when you need to cut limbs that are too thick for shears or loppers or when a plant's growth won't allow your hand and the shears to get into position to make a good cut.

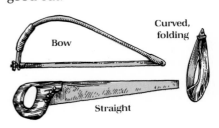
Bow   Curved, folding   Straight

Large limbs are heavy; if you cut down through one with a single cut, it's likely to split or tear before the cut is finished (possibly splitting further back than you intended). See drawing at left above.

The right way to cut

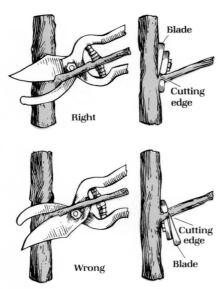
Blade / Cutting edge / Right
Cutting edge / Blade / Wrong

Hold pruning shears with the blade closest to growth that will remain; stub results when you reverse the shear position.

Second cut / First cut / Bisect

Cut heavy limbs in three stages. The first cut is under branch; make a second cut to remove the limb, outward from first cut. Final cut should bisect the lower angle that branch forms with the tree trunk.

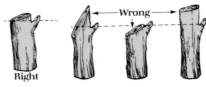
Wrong / Right

Correct pruning cut (left) has lowest point even with the top of growth bud and slants upward at a 45° angle. Be sure tools are sharp.

Small steps in directing growth

Any of the cultural practices shown on this page can be done in minutes—seconds, perhaps—while you stroll through your garden.

Though these grooming techniques aren't absolutely essential to the health of the plant (with the exception of sucker removal), many plants will look their best with a "pinch here" or a "cutback there."

Pinching

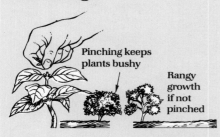

Removing the tender growth tip of a branch with your thumb and finger forces development of the side shoots—keeps plants bushy, well branched. So to achieve a bushy plant with many branches, pinch off the terminal bud or shoot of every branch before plant becomes rangy.

To encourage a taller-stemmed plant or one with a trunk and branches at the top, pinch off growth tips of the side branches. Let main stem grow to height you want, then pinch.

Disbudding

Some plants—for instance, certain varieties of camellias and roses—produce more buds than they can mature properly. For this reason, many gardeners (especially those who enter flowers in shows) remove some of the buds so that the plant's energy can be concentrated in the remaining ones to make them grow better.

Of course, some varieties are famed for their multiplicity of smaller or medium-size flowers; if this is the case, there is no point in disbudding.

Cutting back

Some established perennials (at least a year old) won't be top performers next year unless you cut them back in summer, right after they bloom. But be careful not to cut them back too far—one-third to one-half is sufficient.

Use hedge shears to trim soft-stemmed ground covers such as arabis.

Thinning fruit

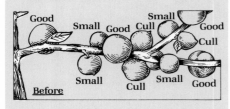

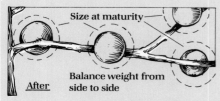

During the weeks when heavy crops are beginning to develop on fruit trees, you should thin them. The remaining fruit will then have space to mature fully. For example, leave 4 inches between peaches (shown here) or nectarines, 6 to 8 inches between apples.

Removing suckers

A sucker is a shoot that grows from a root, from an underground portion of a stem, or from an understock below a bud or graft.

Wherever it sprouts, a sucker can slow plant growth by diverting nutrients for its own growth. If not removed, it can even kill the upper, more desirable part of the plant. To keep a plant free of suckers, rub off the tender buds as soon as they appear; pull off suckers flush with root, stem, or understock. Just cutting them off will permit new suckers to grow.

Removing flowers

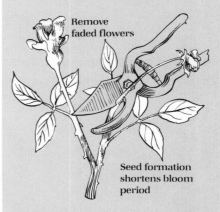

Many plants will bloom longer if you remove flowers as they fade instead of letting them remain on the plant and go to seed. Remove the spent flower and its stem down to the first leaves. This flower removal can help to shape the plant if you trim to well-placed buds.

Training vines

In landscaping, vines are often the best choice in places where no other plant has room to grow. A long, blank, sun-baked wall with a walk beside it can be softened by covering it with a vine. And a vine growing on a fence gives some of the effect of a hedge but requires less space and maintenance.

Several of the most popular vines are shown in the drawings on page 48. The charts on pages 137-

Vines climb in different ways

Twining stems *spiral around a support. Examples are morning glory and Hall's Japanese honeysuckle.*

Tendrils *wrap around support and around other stems. Passion vine and sweet pea grow this way.*

Disc-shaped suckers *attach themselves to surface. Examples are Virginia creeper and Boston ivy.*

Ways to train vines

On a fence, *train vines by attaching ends to wood strips or securing them with wire; make whatever pattern you like.*

Vine-draped dowel *hung from eaves helps to soften the roofline.*

Lattice screens, *or wood and wire frames, keep vines growing where you want them for privacy, windbreaks.*

Hinged trellis *of vines can be pulled back for painting wall. Hooks hold it.*

152 identify vines to grow for specific purposes, such as fragrance or fast growth.

Most vines come equipped with "built-in" devices that make climbing easy—twining stems, or tendrils or rootlets along the stems. Others have no way of holding on and merely ramble aimlessly unless you train and tie them. But this does not necessarily mean that they are harder to manage.

The tie you use depends on the vine and the kind of structure that's supporting it. Various kinds of ties are illustrated on page 109.

For a lightweight vine, use soft twine, raffia, wide rubber bands, or plastic or reinforced paper ties. The ties can serve as an adjunct to the vine's own holding mechanism; by the time the ties weather and finally give way, the twining stems or tendrils will already be holding the vine in place against its support.

For heavy-stemmed vines, particularly those that have no device for holding on, use heavier, longer-lasting materials: pliable insulated wire, heavy rubber tree ties, sections of clothesline (woven cotton or plastic-covered), or strips of canvas. Your hardware store is full of heavy-duty possibilities (see below).

Check ties from time to time; add new ones as needed.

Rootlets *along stems fasten to wall. Plants that grow this way include several kinds of ivy.*

Tying *to a support holds up vines with no other means of attachment: jasmine, climbing rose.*

Hardware that's useful for supporting vines

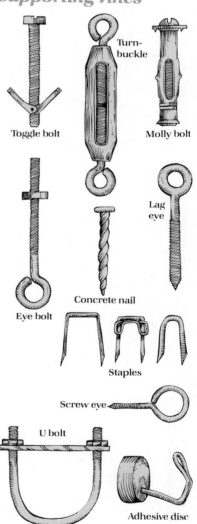

Turn-buckle

Toggle bolt

Molly bolt

Lag eye

Concrete nail

Eye bolt

Staples

Screw eye

U bolt

Adhesive disc

Special hardware *solves most of the problems involved in attaching both vines and trellises to wood, masonry, and plaster walls. Drill holes in masonry with a star or carbide tip drill.*

Vines in containers

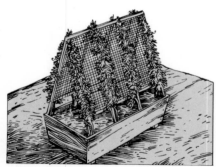

Trellised *container-grown vines give a quick, pleasing effect.*

For a vertical focal point, *choose fast-growing vines.*

Following the path *laid by rows of string or wire, vines can flourish.*

A wire frame *shapes a tree pattern; ivy is particularly well-suited.*

Pruning roses

Though there are different schools of thought on rose pruning, here is one bit of advice to remember: in addition to the major once-a-year pruning, prune a little all year long, cutting off spent flowers and trimming back branches that cross and tangle. Light-to-moderate pruning will produce the best possible roses.

How to prune hybrid teas, grandifloras & floribundas

Cuts to bud union should be flush. A stub could die back into the union, becoming entryway for disease. Paint with pruning compound.

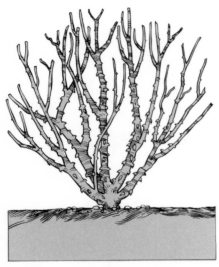

1) Ready for pruning, dormant bush is leafless or nearly so. Time the pruning of most rose bushes from January (mildest climates) to March or April (30 days before last expected killing frost in coldest areas). Swelling, growing buds are easy to see.

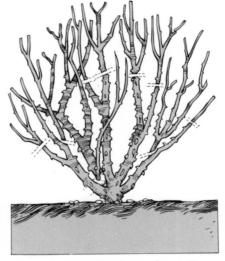

2) Remove all dead wood and all weak, twiggy branches. Cut old canes that produced no strong growth, branches that cross through bush's center, and weak stems. Shorten the remaining branches (see next two steps for directions).

Pruning a climbing hybrid tea

During annual pruning, remove only the old and obviously unproductive wood. Then cut the laterals that bore flowers last year back to two or three latent buds.

Pruning a tree rose

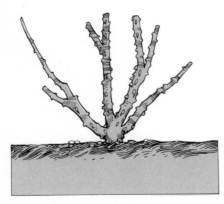

3) In mild climates, healthy growth should not be reduced by more than one-third. This is moderate-to-light pruning. To develop large shrubs, cut only growth that's pencil-thick or less. Try to remove older growth.

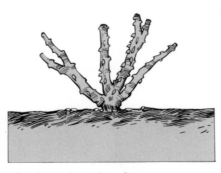

4) Where freezing damages rose bushes, remove all dead and injured wood. This may leave shrub only half to a third the size it was in fall. Use protective coverings, mulches in winter (see page 84 for examples).

Accent is on symmetry when pruning tree (standard) roses. Remove stems extending beyond generally dome-shaped outline. Keep the top open.

How to prune fruit trees

The business of making a fruit tree grow to your eye's satisfaction, while still getting a good crop of fruit, is mostly a matter of knowing how the tree grows by itself, then pruning every year (when the tree is bare) to direct this natural growth as well as you can.

You can afford to be bold when you go about the job. A few wrong cuts can't kill a tree. The tree's growth in spring and summer will hide or correct most of the mistakes. It is usually better to prune and take the risk of making a few mistakes than not to prune at all.

The aim of all fruit tree pruning is to make or keep good tree structure and to force more growth into fewer buds, making bigger fruit.

Apple, pear, cherry

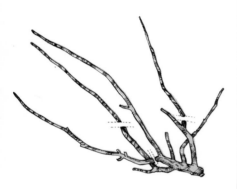

Young, growing tree *is being pruned to increase branch length and remove competing or potentially weak branches. Fruit comes on little spurs that grow very slowly.*

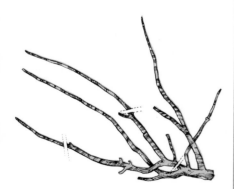

Mature tree's pruning *maintains size by removing last season's growth, stimulating replacement wood. No main branch is left dominant. Remove any damaged branches and twigs.*

Peach, nectarine

Young tree's branches *are shortened to remove two-thirds of last year's growth while directing new growth into selected branches. These trees grow very vigorously.*

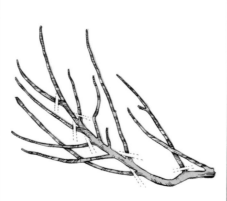

On mature tree, *remove two out of three side branches formed during the last year. These thinning-out cuts don't increase branch length; they leave enough wood for flowers and fruit.*

Apricot, plum

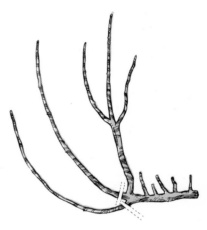

Horizontal branch. *Remove lower branches, especially on apricot. Fruit forms partly on spurs (short, stubby branches growing off main branch), partly on last year's shoots.*

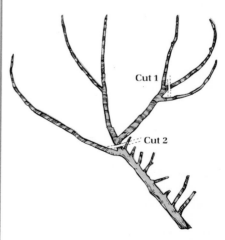

Vertical branch. *Typically, the best cut removes branches, directing growth outward and making tree more spreading (Cut 1). Or subdue one branch (as shown in Cut 2).*

Espaliering

Espaliering—the training of a plant into a definite pattern—is an exacting but rewarding art. You can espalier many kinds of plants simply by varying the technique.

The drawings below show how to espalier a fruit tree. Fruit trees are most often the subject for espaliering, and for good reason: espaliering exposes a maximum of branch surface to the sun and, therefore, stimulates heavier flower and fruit production. Apples, pears, apricots, cherries, and plums are all favorite espalier subjects. Dwarf forms of all five are available, and are a good choice for smaller gardens.

If you live in a cool climate, choose a planting site against a south wall or fence to gain the most from the sun's heat. In hot-summer regions, give plants an eastern exposure so reflected heat won't burn the fruit.

Supports must be sturdy because branches are heavy when loaded with fruit. Use posts of galvanized pipe or wood (4 by 4-inch), with 14-gauge galvanized wire stretched tightly on turnbuckles. Leave 4 to 12 inches between the trellis and wall for free air circulation and for working room.

Train the first pair of cordons (horizontal branches) along the wire about 14 inches above the ground. Space other branches about a foot higher than the horizontal branches just below.

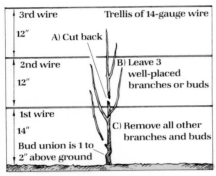

1) Planting time. *Newly planted tree rests against wire support.*

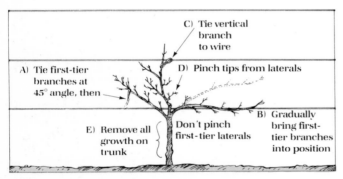

2) First growing season. *Gradually train first tier of branches to horizontal position and tie the growing vertical to the next wire. Choose two young branches for next tier and pinch tips of any others.*

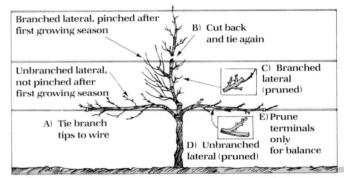

3) First dormant season. *Cut back vertical below the second wire when tree loses leaves. Leave two branches for second tier and cut back any others to stubs with two or three spurs. Stubs will eventually produce fruit along trunk.*

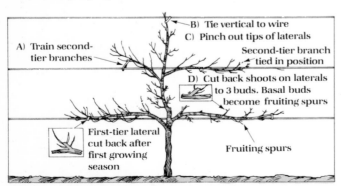

4) Second growing season. *Train second-tier branches as you did first tier during first growing season. Fruiting spurs will form at base of all laterals below second tier; will produce fruit in a year.*

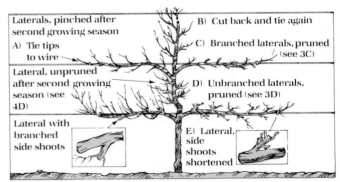

5) Second dormant season. *Cut back vertical branch below third wire. Prune second-tier laterals as you did first tier during first dormant season. Continue training in succeeding years, keeping tree to the shape you want.*

Pests & Diseases

- Effective pest control—
  the basics: page 120
- The insect-size pests:
  page 122
- Using pest controls: page 124
- Plant diseases: page 126
- Rodents, birds & deer:
  page 128
- Pest-controlling
  plants & animals: page 130

Effective pest control— the basics

To keep your garden healthy, keep it clean. Rake up debris often. Wash off foliage regularly, using a hose nozzle to direct the spray of water. Dig mulches into the ground each year, replacing with a fresh layer.

Remove pests *routinely. Check underneath leaves—they hide there. Or leave a board out overnight and they'll hide under it; squash or discard in a bag.*

Soap spray *is the answer to aphid problems if a water jet spray doesn't wash them off. Mix 3 tablespoons soap with a gallon of water. Spray plant, wait, rinse.*

Pests are primarily a problem when one crop is planted over a large area. A pest that attacks only wheat or peaches would find a paradise in a field of wheat or a grove of peaches. Massive destruction by insects is far less likely in a garden with a wide variety of plants.

The loss of a few leaves or flowers does little real harm to a plant. Many lovely and productive gardens contain plants with chewed leaves and less than perfect flowers, but these imperfections are easily overlooked if the garden is healthy in all other respects.

Preventive garden maintenance

You can keep your garden relatively healthy without using chemical sprays by taking these two preliminary measures: keep the soil in good shape by adding soil amendments and nutrients (see pages 6–10) and remove any plant that is badly damaged by pests or that is wilted or moldy. If you want to replace a damaged plant with a similar kind, ask at your local nursery about resistant varieties.

Once you have established a healthy garden, keep it clean. Rake up any debris such as fallen leaves and fruit. (Either compost, see pages 12–13, or discard this debris; be careful, though, not to compost diseased plant parts.)

Dig mulches into the ground each year, and replace them with fresh layers. Wash off foliage regularly, directing spray upward, to keep it free of dust and pests. Remove any spent flowers and foliage.

Spread sticky adhesive *around trunk to frustrate crawling insects.*

Many creatures are helpful

Most creatures you find in your garden are neutral in terms of the well-being of your favorite plants. In fact, many of them affect your garden beneficially: they keep the destructive (and consequently well known) creatures in check.

When you're in doubt about an unfamiliar bug, look at the drawings on pages 122–123 and 130. If the bug isn't illustrated, and if it's not obviously damaging your plants, you can assume that it's a relatively safe inhabitant of your garden.

Using a water jet

Select a hose nozzle that adjusts for different sprays or a pistol type that delivers sudden, sharp blasts of water. Then look for your prey.

Aphids are usually green or dark-colored and collect mainly on young growth and buds. Where they are very dense, put your hand behind the bud or branch to support it against the force of the water as you hose them off the plant; a little rubbing with your fingers will also help. Once on the ground, aphids rarely return to the plants.

Spittle bugs generally appear in spring and hide in little blobs of the foam they create. A direct hit from the water jet will knock them to the ground where they quickly die.

Mites are tiny red bugs that resemble spiders and live in a type of web under leaves. If the underside of the leaf looks dusty or webbed, the mites may already be there. They love dust but hate dampness. Turn your hose nozzle up and spray upward from the base of the plant to clean the underside of the foliage.

If birch trees or other plants feel sticky, aphids are probably at work dripping honeydew. Wash the plant off thoroughly or a nasty black fungus will grow on it.

Picking off plant eaters

Whenever you're out in the garden, be sure to look for pests under a few leaves of each plant. If you squash or rub them off as soon as you notice them, you may not need a pesticide later on. And since many pests are seasonal, they may disappear by themselves if you can keep them under control for the time being.

If a hard squirt of water from a hose won't wash away a few aphids, rub them off by hand. You can squash caterpillars and beetles or you can put them in a bag and burn or discard it. To catch slugs and snails, place a few boards here and there, then turn them over in the morning and remove the pests.

Hunting is especially good at night with a flashlight.

Protection without poison

If you can't control garden pests by washing or rubbing them off, squashing them, or letting their natural enemies do the job, don't give up hope. There are alternatives that are deadly to pests yet harmless to other life.

For sedentary bugs like aphids, make a strong solution of soap or detergent and water using 3 tablespoons of soap flakes in a gallon of tepid water. Using a tank sprayer, cover the infested plant with suds, wait a few hours, and then wash the plant off with plain water. Mineral oil sprays—sold in nurseries—do a similar job.

If plant seedlings are being chewed, try putting a jar or can over each one at sundown and removing them in the morning. Push the jar into the soil a bit to prevent nocturnal chewers from getting under the rim. Don't forget to remove the covers in the morning or your seedlings will cook in the trapped heat under the cover.

Fruit trees are sometimes attacked by such climbing insects as ants and earwigs. Most nurseries carry a sticky adhesive material that you paint around the base of the tree trunk. The pests will stick to the painted area on their way up the tree. You'll need to apply a new layer of material every few weeks because it gradually loses its stickiness as it collects dust or chaff. Check by touching it with your fingers periodically.

Still another way to deal with pests is to place a few twists of newspaper or short lengths of old garden hose in the garden in the evening; these traps will collect those countless earwigs who like to push into tiny spaces.

Because slugs and snails like dampness and protection from sun, a shingle or board placed in the garden will attract them. You then have the option of squashing them or putting them into a bag, adding salt, and discarding. Whichever method you choose, be sure to look out for their eggs, which look like small clusters of pearls.

Certain underground pests such as cutworms and grubs may suddenly appear when you work the soil, but it's easy to chop them up. Spadework, too, is sometimes an effective way to control ants. If you see an anthill, use a spade to turn over the soil, hoping that one spadeful will kill the queen. Without her, the workers will die out.

To control flies, you can use the swatter—still a popular and effective tool. Sticky paper is another well-known method; it does a good job in sheds, lathhouses, and other out-of-the-way corners. The paper comes in a roll inside a cardboard cylinder. Unroll it and pin it in a dark corner near the ceiling. Flies are attracted by its odor.

Spray if you must

Poisonous sprays are a touchy subject with some people because of the reports in books and newspapers about ecological damage and human illness that seem to be traceable to insecticide. But most garden centers carry a number of spray materials that kill insects and disease organisms yet remain harmless to most other creatures.

Some of these products contain sulfur or copper. Others, such as pyrethrum or rotenone, are made from the leaves and roots of certain plants. Limit your use of any of these sprays to afflicted plants only. The small, portable, pressurized tank sprayer is the easiest to use. It holds just enough mixture for small jobs, so you're never tempted to spray other plants with leftover spray.

For more information on pest controls, refer to the chart on page 125.

The insect-size pests

A look at the more common garden pests, illustrated here, will help you recognize them at first glance when you encounter them in the garden. Compare these drawings with the pictures on page 130 of some of the birds and small animals that can *help* you control the population of more destructive garden creatures.

Many pests feed at night. The best way to be on guard against them is to recognize the type of damage they do.

If you see signs of plant damage, you can wait until dark and then go out with a flashlight to search for the marauders. You may see armies of earwigs, slugs, or cutworms that you can immediately pick off or eradicate with a chemical spray (see pages 120–121 for the basics of control; specific chemical and nonchemical controls are explained on pages 124–125).

Two "pests"—beetles and earwigs—can actually keep other pests under control, although they do damage plants themselves. Other marginally destructive, or less common, pests are ants, borers, diabrotica, lawn moths, leafhoppers, and soil mealybugs.

Ants
Some kinds protect aphids, mealybugs, scale; feed on honeydew excreted. Nests may injure plant roots. Some damage plants; others invade houses.

Codling moths
The cause of wormy apples and pears. Larvae enter fruit as it starts to form. Spray after most petals fall; spray twice more at two-week intervals.

Pests are shown larger than life size.

Grubs
Root-feeding beetle larvae that live just beneath soil surface. In lawns they feed on grass roots, whereas lawn-infesting cutworms feed on blades.

Houseflies
These don't damage plants. Good sanitation where garbage and garden wastes are stored, in dog runs, and in stables keeps them under control.

Lawn moths
Larvae, called sod web-worms, live near soil surface, eat grass blades at base. Adults—tan, inch-long moths—hover over lawns at dusk in summer.

Leafhoppers
Small, fast-moving green or brownish insects. Feed on underside of leaf, causing white stippling on upper side. Some kinds spread virus diseases.

Scale
Small insects that attach themselves to stems and leaves; generally covered with protective shell, form colonies. Some secrete honeydew, attract ants.

Slugs, snails
Among commonest, most destructive garden pests. Feed at night and on cool, overcast days, hide on warm, sunny days; leave a trail of silvery slime.

Soil mealybugs
Attach themselves to and feed on roots. Injury to roots interferes with water uptake; causes plants to wilt and die. Controls are not too effective.

Spittle bugs
You can't see the bug because it's surrounded by protective froth. Feeds on stems, frequently on strawberries. Common, not-too-serious pest in spring.

Aphids

Tiny green, black, yellow, or pink insects; sometimes winged. Live and feed in colonies; stunt plant growth. Some excrete honeydew; spread diseases.

Beetles

Many kinds and sizes; chew on leaves, bark. Hand-pick large, slow-moving ones. Kill grubs (larvae) in the soil if you turn them up while cultivating.

Borers

Many kinds; larvae (caterpillars or grubs) bore into stems and trunks. Paint adhesive on base of peach trees for peach borer.

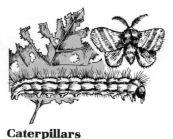

Caterpillars

Larvae of moths and butterflies; some smooth, others hairy; great variation in size and general appearance. Also see codling moths, borers. Most chew leaves.

Cutworms

Hairless moth caterpillars; common leaf-eating pests. Often cut off seedlings at ground level. Some feed at night, hide in soil during the day.

Diabrotica

Also known as cucumber beetle; some closely related kinds are striped. Feed on many different vegetables and flowering plants. Larvae feed on roots.

Earwigs

Night-feeding insects. Feed on other insects as well as flowers and leaves. Leave rolled-up newspapers out overnight, remove in the morning.

Grasshoppers

Late-summer pests with ravenous appetites. Most prevalent in warm winter, hot summer areas. Lay eggs in soil, hatch following spring.

Leaf miners

Insects lay eggs on leaf surfaces. Tiny larvae enter leaves; feeding results in unsightly serpentine effect. Spray to kill adults before they lay eggs.

Mealybugs

Small, white, nearly immobile insects that form colonies at stem joints or toward bases of leaves (usually the undersides). House plants often attacked.

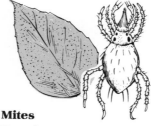

Mites

One of worst summer pests. Finely stippled leaves with silvery webs on underside; you need a hand lens to see mites. One type is the red spider mite.

Oak moths

Larvae eat leaves of western native oaks, particularly in coastal California. Two broods each year—spring and summer. Larvae can strip tree's leaves.

Thrips

Tiny, fast-moving insects that damage plant tissue by rasping surface cells. Feed inside flower buds, so flowers seldom open. Also feed on foliage, new shoots.

Weevils

Many kinds including strawberry root weevil; most are quite small. Adults feed on leaves and fruit at night, hide by day. Grubs feed on roots.

Whiteflies

Very small, common pests. Scalelike nymphs (young) attach to (and feed on) underside of leaves. Pure white adults flutter about erratically.

Wireworms

Waxy, yellow, inch-long worms (grubs) cut roots and bore into bulbs, large roots, and stems, leaving irregular, deep pits. Also attack germinating seed.

Using pest controls

An introduction to effective pest control is on pages 120–121. The pests themselves are shown on pages 122–123; and some of their natural predators and parasites are described on page 130.

The chart on the opposite page suggests ways to control common garden pests. You'll find the nontoxic controls listed on the left side of the dark line and the chemical controls listed on the right. Some of these chemicals are used as active ingredients in other chemical mixtures. These mixtures are scientifically tested for the compatibility of each ingredient—you should never try to mix different ingredients on your own.

Chemical controls should be handled and stored carefully. Before using one, read the instructions on the label. If you're spraying vegetables, the instructions will suggest how long to wait before harvest (guard against cutting these time periods short).

When you're finished spraying, thoroughly wash your equipment, your hands and other exposed skin, and any clothing that came into direct contact with the spray. Then, for the safety of children and animals, store the chemical under lock and key. Make sure that any measuring spoons you use to measure quantity are stored the same way so they will not be used accidentally in the household.

To avoid mixing too much spray, use a 1-quart, graduated measuring cup rather than a 1-gallon measure so that you can easily calculate the amount you need. Remember that three teaspoons equal one tablespoon.

Tank sprayers are easier to handle (and less wasteful) than the extremely fast hose-end sprayers. If you intend to use any chemical that kills vegetation, such as weed oil, use a separate sprayer for it.

When you have finished spraying, be sure to wash and rinse sprayers and sprayer parts. Before you spray another time, rinse and wipe off all parts. A bit of chaff, a speck of dirt, or a little dried-up spray material can block tiny holes.

Following are suggestions for using some of the controls listed in the chart headings.

Bacillus thuringiensis. This nonchemical control contains bacteria that destroy the digestive processes of caterpillars; it is harmless otherwise. Caterpillars stop eating but remain on the plant, moving slowly until they starve. Sold as Thuricide, Dipel, and Biotrol.

Contact poisons. Pyrethrum, ryania, and nicotine sulfate are all contact poisons—they must come into direct contact with the insect to kill it. These poisons are made from plant parts: pyrethrum comes from a kind of chrysanthemum, and the nicotine in nicotine sulfate comes from tobacco.

Dusting sulfur and lime sulfur. Before using these controls, carefully read the instructions on the label to make sure you are using them in the right season.

Metaldehyde. This chemical is a relative of wood alcohol (methanol). Slugs and snails love it for some reason, even though it's fatal. It comes in liquid or bait form; the bait consists of meal or pellets. Be careful with metaldehyde mixed with bran; it's highly poisonous to birds and pets. Put the bait in a little dish under a garden shed or put it in a paper plate under a porch or deck. Snails or slugs often die on the spot; wash the dish or discard the plate.

Poisonous sprays. When you need a poisonous spray, use it carefully and make it count. Spray only those plants that are suffering from insect damage. First rinse the plants off with water. Then spray the leaves, starting at the bottom of the plant and working upward. Finish by spraying the upper surfaces of the leaves.

Poisonous dusts. Several insecticides are manufactured as powders so finely ground that they are dust. You either use the container the product comes in or put it into a special applicator. If you apply it in early morning when the air is still, the dust makes a large cloud of particles which slowly settle as a thin, even coating. Dusting is convenient: no mixing, fast application, and easy clean-up.

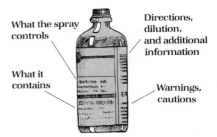

Information on labels is for your protection and knowledge; always heed precautions.

Formula for dormant spray varies according to season; follow label instructions.

Some chemicals kill mainly on contact. Be sure that you cover the entire plant with the substance.

Pests	Adhesive barriers	Bacillus thuringiensis	Hand methods	Dusting sulfur	Oil spray	Soap solution	Water jet	Diazinon	Dursban	Malathion	Metaldehyde	Methoxychlor	Nicotine sulfate	Pyrethrins	Ryania	Systemics
Burrowers																
Borers	×		×													
Codling moths		×						×				×			×	
Corn earworms		×	×		×			×								×
Leaf miners			×							×						
Leaf chewers																
Beetles	×		×						×					×	×	
Caterpillars	×	×	×					×		×				×		×
Diabrotica			×							×		×			×	
Earwigs			×													
Grasshoppers			×					×	×	×						
Japanese beetle			×												×	
Leaf rollers			×							×						
Oak moths		×														×
Snails & slugs			×								×					
Weevils			×					×								×
Nuisance insects																
Ants	×		×							×						
Houseflies & mosquitoes			×							×				×		
Soil pests																
Cutworms			×					×								×
Grubs & wireworms			×													
Lawn moths		×	×					×						×		
Sucking insects																
Aphids					×		×	×		×			×	×		×
Leafhoppers													×	×	×	
Mealybugs					×								×			×
Mites				×			×								×	×
Scale					×		×	×		×						×
Spittlebugs							×						×			
Thrips										×						×
Whiteflies						×		×		×		×	×			×

Plant diseases

Signs of mildew on leaves are white powdery or mealy growth and distortion.

Plants, like all living things, are subject to certain diseases: fungal, bacterial, and viral infections. The surest way to minimize disease is to use *preventive* control measures, such as the following:

1) **Keep your garden** free of weeds, fallen fruit, and dead flowers.

2) **Control** the insect population using the methods described on pages 120–125 and 130.

3) **Replace** plants that show signs of disease year after year. Buy disease-resistant varieties.

4) **Rotate** your annuals from year to year; some disease organisms affecting certain plants can remain in the soil and ruin them again.

5) **Water** plants deeply and infrequently (except plants in containers; see page 57), adding nutrients as they are required.

6) **Give your plants** the proper growing conditions. Don't put sun lovers in shaded areas, and don't crowd mildew-susceptible plants together—it cuts down on air circulation.

7) **Remove** annuals and vegetables after their normal growing season. Old and weak plants are especially prone to disease.

8) **Burn or discard** any diseased plants; don't put them in a compost pile.

Some of the most common diseases are listed here, along with recommended controls. The chart specifies which chemical to use for certain diseases, if spraying becomes necessary.

Anthracnose. Large, brown, irregular blotches on older leaves, twig dieback, and canker on small branches. *Solution:* Cut away infected twigs and branches; spray.

Chemical controls for leaf and stem diseases

All of the chemicals listed in the chart should be available, individually or in mixtures, in small packages at your nursery or garden center. Always follow label directions for mixing and applying the chemicals. Also, use a product only on the plants mentioned on the label.

Common or coined name of active ingredient and formulation Disease	Acti-dione (Cycloheximide) wettable powder	Benomyl wettable powder	Bordeaux* water suspension of copper and lime	Captan dust or wettable powder	Ferbam dust or wettable powder	Fixed copper dust or liquid	Folpet (Phaltan) dust or wettable powder	Lime sulfur liquid	Karathane dust, liquid, or wettable powder	Streptomycin wettable powder	Sulfur dust or wettable powder	Thiram dust or wettable powder	Zineb (Dithane Z-78) dust or wettable powder
Anthracnose		×	×		×	×	×	×				×	×
Damping off				×						×		×	×
Fireblight			×			×							
Leaf spot		×	×	×		×	×	×			×	×	×
Peach leaf curl			×					×					×
Powdery mildew	×	×						×	×	×		×	
Rust								×					×
Scab			×	×	×	×	×	×			×		
Shot hole		×	×	×	×	×		×					×

*Best results only when you mix fresh ingredients immediately before use and agitate the mixture continually while spraying.

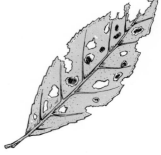

Peach leaf curl distorts the leaves, can weaken the tree. Also infects nectarines, almonds.

Rust symptoms—orange spots in clusters—appear on bottom side of a leaf (right).

Scab disfigures fruit, causes leaf drop in affected plants, spots on leaves and stems.

Attack of shot hole fungus has left its very distinctive marks on this infected leaf.

Black spot. Black spots appear on leaves. *Solution:* Spray with fungicide; discard chronically infected plants. Clean up fallen leaves.

Camellia petal blight. Camellia flowers turn brown. *Solution:* Pick off infected flowers and keep area around plant very clean.

Cherry "dead bud." Disfigures both fruiting and flowering trees. Both flower and leaf buds die. *Solution:* Spray once in October and again as soon as possible after January. Use copper hydroxide at 6 pounds per 100 gallons of water, with highly refined petroleum oil. Bordeaux mixture is also effective if mixed just before use and agitated while spraying.

Damping off. Newly sprouted seedlings develop a stem rot near the soil surface and fall over (or the seeds never sprout). *Solution:* Use sterile planting soil; drench affected plants with fungicide.

Dutch elm disease. After disease is spread by elm bark beetle, foliage wilts, leaves turn yellow and fall off, and eventually the tree dies. *Solution:* Call your county agricultural agent for advice on the best control.

Fireblight. Flowering shoots of pear, apple, crabapple, pyracantha, cotoneaster, quince, hawthorn, or toyon suddenly wilt and look as though scorched by fire. Dark sunken cankers form in bark of lower limbs. *Solution:* Prune out and destroy diseased twigs and branches. Sterilize pruning tools

and cut surface with disinfectant such as rubbing alcohol. Spray at 4 or 5-day intervals through the blossoming period. Where disease is persistent, grow nonsusceptible plants.

Leaf spot, leaf blight. Red, brown, or yellow spots on leaves and stems. *Solution:* Thorough garden cleanup.

Peach leaf curl. Leaves on peach trees become misshapen and curled, eventually falling off. This interrupts the flower/fruit cycle. *Solution:* Spray peach trees with lime sulfur or fixed copper sprays in winter during a period of dry weather and before leaf buds swell.

Powdery mildew. A bluish-white dust that appears on leaves and flower buds. *Solution:* Spray with fungicide; discard chronically infected plants.

Pseudomonas. Causes dieback of smaller twigs in plums, prunes, cherries, apricots, peaches, pears, and other fruit trees. *Solution:* For the home gardener, control isn't practical. Subsequent new growth will hide dead twigs.

Rust. Blisters form on leaves and scatter reddish or yellow spores. *Solution:* Spray with fungicide; discard chronically infected plants.

Scab. Red, brown, or yellow spots on leaves and stems. *Solution:* Use dormant spray of lime sulfur just before flower buds open. Spray with wettable sulfur when blos-

soms show pink and again when three-fourths of blossom petals have fallen.

Shot hole. Red, brown, or yellow spots on leaves and stems drop out, leaving a "shot hole" appearance. *Solution:* Thorough garden cleanup; spray with fungicide.

Texas root rot. Sudden wilting of the leaves signals that at least 50 percent of the root system has been damaged. *Solution:* Add sulfur and organic amendments that decompose rapidly, such as manure and sawdust. Prune to remove half the foliage of affected plants.

Verticillium wilt. This disease lives in the soil and frequently attacks tomatoes. *Solution:* Plant wilt-resistant varieties.

Virus diseases. A number of virus diseases (mosaic, yellows, and others) are apt to strike almost any kind of plant. *Solution:* Pull and destroy any plant that has died for mysterious reasons. Keep aphids, leafhoppers, and other sucking insects under control, as they are known to be virus spreaders.

Also, humans do a fair job of spreading these diseases by propagating infected plants from cuttings, by budding or grafting, by pruning or pinching diseased plants, and by smoking or handling tobacco around plants.

Much research is being done to determine the causes and control of virus diseases, but to date there is little that the home gardener can do to save afflicted plants.

Rodents, birds & deer

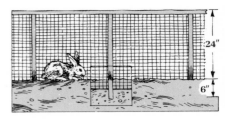

Rabbits are diggers. Bury a piece of wire fence to keep them out of your garden. This may work with gophers.

A number of animals and birds can cause damage to your garden. But you'll probably prefer to discourage rather than destroy birds, deer, and rabbits. They're fun to watch, even while they're munching on your ripe tomatoes or newly transplanted petunias.

Rabbits

Because they're especially fond of tender greens, rabbits can be a terrible nuisance in the vegetable garden. A few cottontails can nearly clear a vegetable patch in a very short time.

The best solution is to build a 2-foot-high fence of fine chicken wire (mesh no larger than 1 1/2 inches) extending 6 inches more underground. Rabbits may ultimately burrow beneath the underground extension, but if you check periodically you usually can discover their holes before they succeed in tunneling completely under the fence.

To protect trees from rabbits' gnawing, encircle each trunk with a wire mesh cylinder 2 feet high; bury the cylinder base 2 to 3 inches in the soil and stake it.

Commercial rabbit repellents are available. They must be reapplied as plants grow, and are not for use on vegetables and other food crops.

Gophers & ground squirrels

Burrowing rodents such as the pocket gopher, the gopher, and the ground squirrel can cause enormous damage in a garden. A gopher will nibble at plant roots, eat plant tops, munch on fruits such as pumpkins and melons, and pile up mounds of loose earth that may partially bury plants he doesn't eat.

The gopher operates from an elaborate system of tunnels usually 6 to 18 inches below the surface. First sign of his presence is often a mound of fresh, finely pulverized soil in lawn or flower bed.

To catch a gopher, poke around until you locate a main tunnel, then excavate to it and place traps. Cover the opening.

Another way to keep a gopher and other tunneling rodents away is to put lighted road flares, gopher bombs, or chemicals (sold at nurseries) down the hole; some gardeners have even tried automobile exhaust. If the problem is serious, ask for help from a professional exterminator.

Some gardeners prefer to protect their plants with underground barriers. These can be as simple as lining each planting hole with chicken wire, or as complex as digging up an entire planting area and lining the bottom and sides of the cavity with wire.

Mice & voles

These tiny animals may or may not be a nuisance in your garden. The population of voles (small, mouselike rodents) sometimes increases greatly, seemingly overnight. If your garden is in the way, it may be damaged. Though voles and field mice live in abandoned gopher and mole burrows, they feed mainly on above-ground portions of plants.

Roaming cats can solve the problem if they like to hunt, or you can use mouse traps, rat traps, and box traps. Try baiting traps with walnut meats.

Another method is to use poisoned grain in containers punctured with small openings that only a mouse or vole can enter. But sometimes rodents build up a resistance to poison, so mice may turn up again.

Moles

Mostly eating insects, moles dig tunnels as they hunt for underground grubs and worms. As they push along, plant roots may be cut or damaged; whole plants may even be pushed out of the ground. Signs of moles are ridges of raised and cracked soil and little conical mounds of soil.

If you see a mole hill, push the soil down firmly to collapse the tunnel and prevent plant roots from drying out. You can try using mole traps or bait, but since the animals use most runs only once, catching them is very difficult.

Squirrels

These rodents can strip nut trees bare overnight. They will also dig in flowerpots. If you're losing just a few nuts and if you can keep your flowerpots quite close to your house, you may be able to ignore the problem.

But if the damage becomes too great (stripped bark, young tree growth destroyed), you'll probably want to send the squirrels packing. Call your county agricultural office for information on any local program for squirrel control.

Birds

Most birds are wonderful entertainers with their songs and antics, and many eat harmful insects—but

Two ways to get rid of rodents

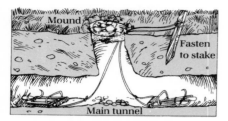

To set Macabee gopher traps, dig through mound to main tunnel; set traps and insert, business end first. String and wire ties, fastened to stake, prevent loss of traps, make them easy to retrieve.

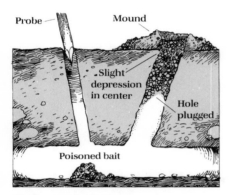

Probe method, for inserting poison bait in tunnel. This is a gopher tunnel; same probing system works for moles and pocket gophers.

Protecting plants from birds

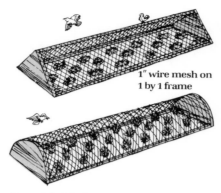

Portable bird protector made of scrap lumber, chicken wire, or cheesecloth.

Enclose fruit trees with broad-mesh netting (3/4 inch) two or three weeks before fruit ripens.

Fences discourage deer

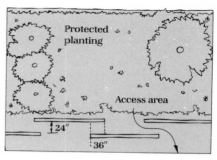

Six-foot-high baffles in staggered rows provide a maze that deer seem to avoid.

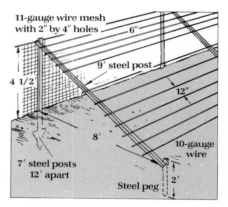

Low fence can be deer-proofed by building an outrigger that extends 8 feet out from the existing fence, as shown.

---

at certain times, certain birds can be nuisances in your garden. They'll eat newly planted seeds, tender seedlings, transplants, fruits, nuts, and berries.

To protect seeds and seedlings from being eaten, spread chicken wire or cheesecloth covers over the beds until the plants are full and sturdy. Check for any openings that might let a bird get through.

To protect small fruit trees, throw a net over the whole tree. Either buy one ready-made or make your own of nylon netting. You can buy nylon or plastic netting in rolls from 4 1/2 to 13 feet wide and up to 200 feet long.

Broad-mesh netting (3/4 inch) is the most popular for trees, since it lets air, water, and sunlight in easily. Enclose fruit trees with nets two

or three weeks before fruit ripens. Tie nets off where the lowest branches leave the trunk. Remove nets at harvest time.

Fine-mesh screen and nylon netting are the most popular for covering rows of sprouting seedlings and maturing vegetables—birds can't get their beaks through them. Tent the material over the rows with stakes and string for support.

Another method—less effective than using netting—is to hang reflectors, noisemakers, or other fluttering objects from the tree's branches. Whatever protective measure you choose, keep in mind that birds are, on the whole, of great value in your garden: many species are omnivorous and help to control damaging insects.

Deer

Though they're nice to watch, deer can ruin the looks of a garden.

Here are some ideas for keeping deer away from your plants: put chicken wire cages around young plants; build fences 6 to 8 feet high; use electric fences; add a horizontal outrigger extension to an existing fence; scatter blood meal fertilizer on the ground or hang it up in small bags; spray strategic spots frequently with commercial repellent; toss moth balls around the garden; leave rags soaked in creosote in various spots; allow a deer-chasing dog to roam at night; use scarecrows or noisemakers.

If none of these measures works, you can always resort to planting only those plants that deer seem to dislike.

Pest-controlling plants & animals

Some plants, insects, and small animals will actually discourage or kill damaging garden pests. You can't always count on this kind of help, but you can learn which plants repel pests and which insects and animals you should protect and encourage to stay.

If you have a problem with nematodes (those destructive relatives of the ordinary earthworm), try interplanting marigolds with other flowers or vegetables. Nematodes apparently find marigolds distasteful.

Some people think that another plant, *Euphorbia lathyrus*, has similar effects on the pocket gopher; the rodent dislikes its bitter and poisonous roots.

Shoofly plant, *Nicandra physalodes*, is an annual that may repel whiteflies.

Among the helpful insects, the most commonly found are lacewings and lacewing larvae, mantids (the big praying mantis is the best known), ladybugs, stink beetles, and earwigs. You might also want to introduce a tiny and helpful wasp called *Trichogramma* to your garden. You just buy the eggs of this wasp and of other insects (order from biological garden supply outlets) and place them in the garden; they hatch by themselves.

Aphycus wasps are parasites of scale; tiny *Encarsia* wasps are parasites of whiteflies. And one type of mite (*Phytoseiulus persimilis*) consumes its destructive relatives.

Spiders eat lots of insects, and since some are nocturnal, they can be working in your garden both night and day. The most impressive looking is the enormous garden spider, which spins a large and beautiful web.

Among the small-animal helpers look for amphibians (toads, frogs, and salamanders) and many kinds of lizards. They all do a good job of eating insects and other creatures such as pillbugs. Some people may be lucky enough to have box turtles around to work on their slugs and snails.

You'll find that a great many birds feed on insects, too. You can encourage birds to remain in your garden by setting out suet in cold weather and providing a bath for them when it's warm. But be sure to keep the bath very clean or you may spread disease and kill off your helpers. Hummingbirds like to vary their nectar diet with some bugs. A well-stocked hummingbird feeder will keep them around.

If you don't mind their presence, the real insect-eating champions of any garden are the shrew and the bat. The shrew is an above-ground relative of the mole. You will probably never see one, but you should hope that it's around. The bat is also a nearly invisible bug-gobbler. (You should never touch a bat or try to doctor a sick one, because they are apt to carry rabies.)

Some gardeners like to bring in ducks, bantam chickens, or even geese because they've heard that these birds eat slugs, insects, and weeds. Unfortunately, they also love to eat good plants and dig holes.

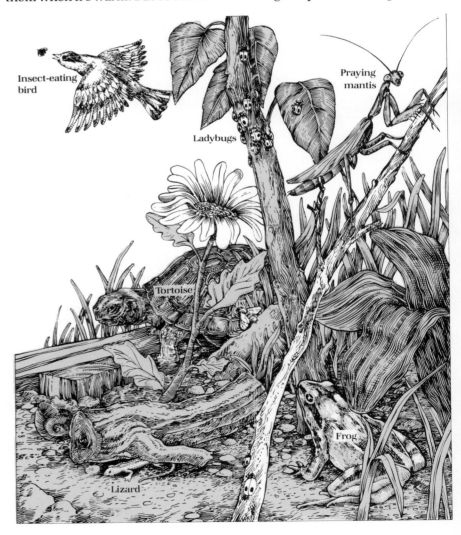

Insect-eating bird

Ladybugs

Praying mantis

Tortoise

Lizard

Frog

Garden Tools &
How to Use Them

- Which tool for
  which job?: page 132
- Making garden chores
  easier: page 134
- Maintaining garden
  equipment: page 136

Which tool for which job?

A new homeowner, about to buy that first set of garden tools, may find the display of tools at garden centers and hardware stores somewhat bewildering. Does gardening require such an array? Which tools are necessary? What should you know about them?

Shovels & spades

Long handle, round point. A versatile tool for digging and scooping. The round-point irrigation shovel (see sketch of two shovels at left) has a straighter shank, which gives it more strength and makes it better for digging holes with vertical sides.

Long handle, square point. For leveling areas for patios and walks, squaring off the bottoms of ditches, and shoveling snow. When shoveling dirt or gravel, this shovel is especially handy when you get toward the bottom.

D-handle shovel. For jobs such as moving soil, sand, gravel, and for picking up litter. Round-point and square-point models are available.

Square-end spade. For edging, digging, and cultivating (see page 8). This tool is easy to use. You have a choice of a long handle or shorter D-handle.

Garden shovel. Somewhat smaller and lighter than the regular round-point shovel. Use it for digging holes, cultivating, and edging. It can be used with a chopping motion to break up earth clods.

Transplanting spade. A favorite with gardeners for transplanting shrubs and moving perennials.

Scoop shovel. For moving sawdust, manure, and other light materials. Serves as a garden dust pan for collecting litter.

Spading forks

Long-handle spading fork. Long handle gives good leverage when you are working hard soil. Breaks up adobe clods better than a spade. Buy the

best-quality fork; otherwise, tines may bend.

Short-handle fork. You have a choice of a number of models. Tines range from 7 to 11 inches long. Weight also varies. Get the model that's right for you. Generally, short-handled spading forks work best for cultivating crowded planting beds or to lift clumps of perennials without damaging the tubers, rhizomes, or a plant's fleshy or thick matted root system.

Barn or manure fork. Not for spading, but for moving garden prunings, long weeds, manure, and other coarse materials. Also good for turning over layers of compost.

Don't buy all your tools at once

If you follow your hunches and buy the most familiar forms—shovel, rake, and hoe—you'll be right.

But how about all the other tools offered? Actually, most of these were originally introduced to do specific agricultural jobs, but sometimes a home gardener found other functions for one or two of them, or the manufacturer altered a tool's design to fit the home gardener's needs.

Hoes

Garden hoe. There is a hoe for just about every job, from a hoe with a 2 1/2-inch-wide blade for light jobs in narrow spots to an 8-inch-wide blade for driveways and walks. The 6-inch-wide hoe is the most commonly used.

A number of hoes have names that suggest their use: planter hoe, cotton hoe, square-top onion hoe. The latter, also called a strawberry hoe, has a blade 7 inches wide and about 1 3/4 inches high; use around shallow-rooted plants.

To be effective, a hoe should be sharpened each time you take it into the garden. On hard cutting jobs, resharpen about every two hours.

Hoes with the conventional design of those sketched at left work best with a chopping action, the flat front edges cutting weeds off at ground level or the sharp edges working like a small pick. Get a hoe that is light enough to be wielded for an hour or two at a time.

Choose tools carefully

Tools are very personal pieces of equipment and all experienced gardeners have their favorites.

In the text accompanying the sketches of tools, no attempt is made to judge whether a tool is good or bad. Your work habits, your plants, your strength, and your stature will determine which tools work most efficiently for you.

The tools shown on these two pages are those most commonly used. You won't find any of the very specialized hand tools, power tools, or lawn clippers and edgers.

It's not likely that a gardener would buy all the tools shown, since many perform the same function. When you buy garden tools, though, get the very best you can afford. A top-quality product, if properly taken care of, will last you through most of your gardening years.

Don't buy any tool until you have checked it over thoroughly. Lift and swing the piece of equipment around to test its weight and proper balance.

How about handle length? You may feel that a long-handled spade or fork is easier to wield—but what about other gardening members of the family? It's a good idea to take them all along when you're out buying garden tools. Try the grip on all small hand tools.

Pruning tools are illustrated on page 112. Some additional hoe styles are shown on page 61. Shovels and spades are also on page 8.

Scuffle hoe. A special hoe for the fast removal of weeds. You don't chop, but push the hoe ahead of you as if you were playing shuffleboard, then pull. Most cut on either stroke. It's a good tool for cutting the tops off annual weeds. (Perennial weeds need to be dug up.) This hoe works best on packed, level ground.

Grape hoe or eye hoe. Wide blade smashes through hard, root-filled soil. Use it to cut bushy weeds, invasive tree roots, spreading ground cover.

Rakes

Level-head rake. Flat top used to level seed beds and make seed furrows. It won't do the heavy work the bow rake will.

Metal bow rake. Good tool for leveling soil or gravel and collecting earth clods. The bow acts as a shock absorber, giving the rake a springy, resilient quality.

Lawn rake. Indispensable for raking lawn clippings, leaves, and other light matter on both paved and natural surfaces. You have a wide selection to choose from. Some are made of metal, others of bamboo; some are fan-shaped, others rectangular. On some models you can adjust the width of the raking face.

Self-cleaning rake. This rake, heavier than the other types, is for clearing out lawn thatch and severing long surface runners of certain lawn grasses. You don't lift it from the ground: the pull stroke gathers debris toward you, the push stroke clears material from the blades.

Special tools

Cultivator. Good for breaking up hard soil around plants. Won't qualify for deep spading, though. For best results, combine chopping and pulling motions.

Weed and grass cutters. Weed cutter is used for rugged weeds and grasses in uncultivated garden areas. It removes top growth but not weed roots, unless you use blade as a chopper. Grass cutter helps in cutting grass along the edge of a lawn. Swing it as you would a golf club. Test various models for correct balance and weight.

Trowel. One of the most personal of all garden tools. Shop around until you get one that fits your hand, is well balanced, and feels light enough to handle easily. A straight shank model is good for bulb planting. Drop shank is most popular.

Dandelion weeder (asparagus knife). For lifting out tap-rooted weeds in the garden and for weeding in such tight places as between steppingstones in a path. These tools are useful, too, for small cultivating jobs. Dandelion weeders with long handles are for standup use.

Small hand cultivator and hoe. For close-up kneeling or sitting jobs or for planting on a hillside. The end of this cultivator is the same shape and design as that of the regular-sized tool, but it's smaller, with palm-sized handle.

Mattock. Wide blade, similar to a grape hoe, breaks through hard-packed soil, cuts tough roots and fibrous weeds. You can use the ax end to trim ivy edges or cut side roots in tree and bush removal. Some types have a pick end instead, will even break up asphalt.

Making garden chores easier

Most gardeners learn through hard experience how to make the occasional difficult and hard-to-manage chores as easy as possible.

So that you, too, won't have to learn the hard way, study the helpful suggestions and illustrations given below and on the following page. Some of the suggestions are just common-sense approaches. Others were carefully thought out and developed by long-time gardeners.

Lift with a straight back

Whatever the weight of the object you are lifting, bend your knees and use your larger leg muscles as you lift. The bent-over, straight-legged position that many inexperienced gardeners use to lift and move plants can strain the lower back muscles and leave you exhausted, if not in pain.

Large objects should never be lifted. Instead, use a cart or dolly, or drag them on a piece of canvas or a wooden plank.

Use wheels where you can

A wheelbarrow is considered to be an essential in most gardens, but there are other wheeled vehicles and devices that can lend a helping hand—some of these you may already have available.

When you're using a wheelbarrow, guard against letting it tip as you go around a curve. If it should tip to one side, let go and back away fast. A loaded wheelbarrow can give a tremendous twist that strains muscles, and the handles may gouge you as they go by. It's much better to reload than to hurt yourself.

A large, four-wheeled child's wagon is perfect for moving masonry blocks and works well for

Try a lever

Wheel power

Lifting heavy objects

The inclined plane

hauling sacks, nursery flats, potted plants, or other heavy objects.

A big, two-wheeled cart can be bought or made of lumber scraps. It has a bit more room than a wheelbarrow can provide, and is ideal for moving big bulky loads like prunings, leaves, or even a collection of odd-shaped spades, shovels, and picks.

A hand truck or dolly is a necessity if you'd like to move heavy containers here and there. It also helps with moving heavy bags of soil amendment. A wheeled platform can be a movable seat for ground-level chores, or it can be just big enough to hold a pot.

Use a lever

A 2 by 4 or a steel fence post becomes a handy lever if you want to move a rock, lift a heavy plant out of a hole, or pry up a stubborn root system. For use at ground level, prop the lever on a rock as illustrated below left, or use a wood block. At the edge of a hole, lay a board or beam under the lever to keep the earth from crumbling.

You can also use a lever to slide heavy objects into position. On soft ground, use boards under the object as runners.

Use the inclined plane

You can use a few smooth boards to form a ramp for hauling plants into and out of a car. The same boards can bridge a short flight of steps or form a gangway from ground level to the rim of a raised bed. Then instead of lifting a heavy bale of peat moss or a bag of sand, you just slide or roll it along the ramp.

The same ramp with a block of wood or log supporting the center makes it easier to wheel a load of compost up onto the compost pile.

Overcoming friction

The illustrations below show three ways to overcome friction when you want to shift heavy objects about. The easiest way is to simply slide a shovel blade under the object, then lift the handle and pull.

A smooth board will act as a runner when you want to pull a load across soil or grass, or move a heavy object across paving.

Another technique is to use several lengths of thick dowel—as you push the plant container onto the last dowel, pick up the first dowel and place it in front. It helps to have a second person shifting dowels as you push.

Reducing friction

Maintaining garden equipment

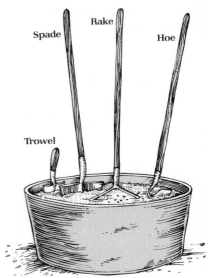

Container of oiled sand (tub, keg, or bucket)

Oiled sand works in two ways: sand is abrasive for cleaning; oil preserves metal.

Garden tools, like any other equipment, will last longer and do a better job for you if they are properly maintained. Not that it is necessary to clean them and check them after each use—only one gardener in a thousand takes that kind of time and trouble.

Just remember these three things: 1) Keep cutting tools sharp; 2) don't let tools rust; and 3) store them sensibly.

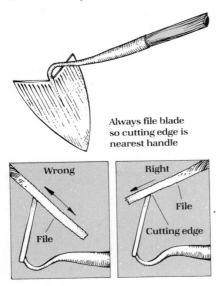

Always file blade so cutting edge is nearest handle

Wrong / Right / File / File / Cutting edge

Right way to file a hoe is shown on triangular-bladed weeding hoe. Hold by handle; file away from you.

Hoes should be sharpened frequently with a file (see sketch above), sharpening stone, or an electric drill with an abrasive disc. This is a simple process that any gardener can accomplish in 5 minutes or less; the results are well worth the little trouble it takes, since the sharpness of the hoe dictates the amount of energy you must expend when you're using it. Sharp, rust-free tools make gardening easier.

Other cutting tools, such as lawn mowers, pruning shears, and saws, should be sharpened about once a year. If you don't have a sharpening wheel or other specialized equipment, check the yellow pages of your telephone book under "Sharpening Service" for the names of shops in your region who can do this task for you. Cost is minimal compared to what you'd spend if you were to throw the tool away and buy a new one.

Before you put your garden tools away for the winter months, clean the rust from them with liquid rust cleaner (for especially stubborn jobs), emery paper, a disc sander, or a wire brush. After cleaning, oil the working parts and put a light coating of grease over surfaces likely to rust. Drain fuel out of gasoline-powered tools. Clean strainers in lawn sprinklers.

Hang sharp tools securely and out of the way—they can be dangerous. Store the lawn mower so the blades are away from foot traffic.

Most garden tools are hung, from one end or the other, in a rather standard fashion by means of nails, cup hooks, lag screws, or spring clips. Real satisfaction, though, comes from devising new and better ways to hang the garden hose. The sketch at right shows three good examples.

Replacing handles

Years of hard use and exposure to the elements may result in the handles of your garden tools deteriorating until they eventually break. If this happens to you, don't automatically throw the tool away. Most likely, the handle can be repaired and replaced for quite a bit less than the price of a new tool. (Broken metal parts usually are too costly to repair.)

Hardware stores or garden centers stock replacement handles for most popular tools. To make sure the handle will fit properly, take the broken tool along when you go shopping. Also, be sure to buy the necessary hardware to keep the new handle in place.

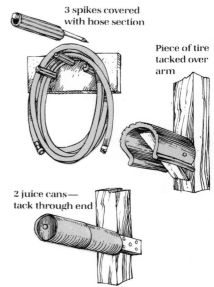

3 spikes covered with hose section

Piece of tire tacked over arm

2 juice cans— tack through end

Methods for hanging hose have one thing in common: they prevent sharp kinks in your hose.

Using Plants Effectively

- Hedges, screens, backgrounds & barriers: page 138

- North, south, east, west... planting for exposures: page 140

- In & around paved areas, parking strips: page 142

- Shady places: page 144

- Dramatic foliage: page 146

- Plants with fragrant flowers & foliage: page 148

- Attracting birds, bees & butterflies: page 150

- Autumn color: page 152

Hedges, screens, backgrounds & barriers

Shared by these shrubs and small trees are generally fast growth, frequently dense foliage, and sturdy permanence.

Whether clipped into formal neatness or allowed to follow natural shapes, hedges provide privacy and create a sense of enclosure.

Those plants best used as backgrounds tend to be taller growing, with inconspicuous flowers and foliage.

Barrier plants, by their appearance and texture, say "keep out." Most are densely branched or thorny. Screens, too, should be thickly branched plants, but more importantly they should be very fast growing and provide effective concealment the year around.

Deciduous/Name	Clipped hedge	Informal hedge	Back-ground	Barrier	Screen	Climate and Comments
Barberry, Japanese *Berberis thunbergii*	X	X		X		Hardy to −20°F/−29°C. Very dense and spiny, growing to 6 ft. Dwarf varieties. See page 34.
Blueberry, Highbush *Vaccinium corymbosum*		X	X		X	Hardy to −30°F/−34°C. Slow-growing to 12 ft., needs acid soil.
Border forsythia *Forsythia intermedia*		X			X	Hardy to −20°F/−29°C. Arching habit to 7–10 ft., well adapted to pollution.
Buckthorn, Tallhedge *Rhamnus frangula* 'Columnaris'	X	X	X	X	X	Hardy to −40°F/−40°C. Narrow hedge to 12–15 ft., can be pruned to 4 ft. high.
Chinese lilac *Syringa chinensis*		X		X		Hardy to −10°F/−23°C. Densely branched to 10 ft. Spring flowers very fragrant.
European cranberry bush *Viburnum opulus* 'Nanum'	X	X				Hardy to −30°F/−34°C. Densely branched, grows 1–2 ft. tall.
European hornbeam *Carpinus betulus*	X		X		X	Hardy to 0°F/−18°C. Small tree to 40 ft. Responds to shearing.
Hawthorn, Cockspur *Crataegus crus-galli*	X	X		X	X	Hardy to −20°F/−23°C. Densely branched to 30 ft., with long thorns. Withstands shearing.
Hedge maple *Acer campestre*	X	X	X	X		Hardy to −20°F/−29°C. Dense, easily sheared. Grows to 25 ft., but compact form available.
Mock orange *Philadelphus* hybrids			X		X	Hardy to −10°F/−23°C. Many varieties ranging from 4 to 9 ft. See page 35.
Nannyberry *Viburnum lentago*	X		X			Hardy to −40°F/−40°C. Vigorous grower to 30 ft. Glossy foliage. Shade or sun.
Privet, Amur *Ligustrum amurense*	X	X			X	Hardy to −30°F/−34°C. Oval shaped. Thickly branched, to 15 ft.
Rose of Sharon *Hibiscus syriacus*		X	X		X	Hardy to −10°F/−23°C. Compactly branched from base, growing to 15 ft. 'Diana' good variety.
Rugosa rose *Rosa rugosa*		X		X		Hardy to −40°F/−40°C. Grows to 3–8 ft. Tolerant of temperature extremes, drought, wind, and salt spray.
Russian olive *Elaeagnus angustifolia*	X	X	X		X	Hardy to −40°F/−40°C. Small tree to 20 ft. Gray foliage makes good background. See page 36.
Sea buckthorn *Hippophae rhamnoides*		X	X	X		Hardy to −30°F/−34°C. Provides gray-green background to 10–15 ft.; thorny.
Sweet briar rose *Rosa eglanteria*		X	X	X	X	Hardy to −30°F/−34°C. Dense, spiny, vigorous growth to 8–12 ft. Prune annually.
Weigela *Weigela* 'Bristol Ruby'			X		X	Hardy to −10°F/−23°C. Fast-growing to 7 ft. Needs occasional pruning. See page 35.
Western sand cherry *Prunus besseyi*		X			X	Hardy to −40°F/−40°C. Low-grower to 3–6 ft. Tolerates wind and drought.
Winged euonymus *Euonymus alata*	X	X			X	Hardy to −30°F/−34°C. Round form to 4–8 ft., with many winged branches.

Evergreen/Name	Clipped hedge	Informal hedge	Background	Barrier	Screen	Climate and Comments
Abelia, Glossy *Abelia grandiflora*		X			X	Hardy to 10°F/−12°C. Arching shrub to 8 ft. or more. Dwarf forms available. See page 34.
Box, English boxwood *Buxus sempervirens*	X	X				Hardy to 0°F/−18°C. Traditional hedge of fine texture. Slow-growing to 18 ft. (dwarfs available). See page 34.
Canada hemlock *Tsuga canadensis*	X	X	X		X	Hardy to −30°F/−28°C. Fast-growing to 90 ft. Likes cool moist areas.
English laurel *Prunus laurocerasus*	X		X	X	X	Hardy to 10°F/−12°C. Large shrub or small tree to 30 ft. Dwarf types. Hardier varieties available.
Evergreen euonymus *Euonymus japonica*	X	X			X	Hardy to 10°F/−12°C. Fast-growing to 8–10 ft., many varieties. See page 34.
Firethorn *Pyracantha* 'Mohave'	X	X		X	X	Hardy to −10°F/−23°C. Large stiff shrub to 12 ft. Can be trained. See page 34.
Fruitland silverberry *Elaeagnus pungens* 'Fruitlandii'			X	X	X	Hardy to 10°F/−12°C. Sprawling growth to 15 ft. high. Dense and twiggy.
Heavenly bamboo *Nandina domestica*		X			X	Hardy to 10°F/−12°C. Airy foliage. Grows to 8 ft. Dwarf types available. See page 35.
Holly, Burford *Ilex cornuta* 'Burfordii'	X	X	X	X	X	Hardy to 10°F/−12°C. Forms rounded shrub to 10 ft. Foliage less spiny than other hollies.
Holly, English *Ilex aquifolium*	X		X	X	X	Hardy to 10°F/−12°C. Pyramidal to 40 ft. Shiny prickly foliage. See page 35.
Holly, Japanese *Ilex crenata*	X	X				Hardy to 0°F/−18°C. Hardier varieties available. Small rounded leaves. Many varieties from 3 to 20 ft.
Juniper, Chinese *Juniperus chinensis*	X	X	X	X	X	Hardy to −20°F/−29°C. Many varieties from 4 to 50 ft. Mostly mounded types. See page 35.
Juniperus scopulorum (varieties)	X	X	X	X	X	Hardy to −10°F/−23°C. Upright to 20 ft. with several forms. Takes heat and drought.
Laurustinus *Viburnum tinus*		X			X	Hardy to 10°F/−12°C. Grows to 6–12 ft. Luxuriant foliage. Retains neat form for years.
Leatherleaf viburnum *Viburnum rhytidophyllum*			X	X	X	Hardy to −10°F/−23°C. Coarse, upright shrub to 6–15 ft. Leaves rough-surfaced.
Lemon bottlebrush *Callistemon citrinus*		X	X		X	Hardy to 20°F/22°C. As shrub, rounded to 15 ft., with open branching. See page 36.
Leyland cypress *Cupressocyparis leylandii*		X	X		X	Hardy to 0°F/−18°C. Very fast-growing to 50 ft. Pyramidal. Blue-green foliage.
Oregon grape *Mahonia aquifolium*		X		X	X	Hardy to −20°F/−2.°C. Upright shrub to 6 ft., with spined leaflets.
Pineapple guava *Feijoa sellowiana*	X	X	X		X	Hardy to 20°F/22°C. Grows 18–25 ft. Easily trained. Edible fruit.
Pittosporum *Pittosporum tobira*		X			X	Hardy to 20°F/−7°C. Slow-growing to 15 ft. Rounded shiny foliage. See page 35.
Sweet bay, Grecian laurel *Laurus nobilis*	X	X	X		X	Hardy to 10°F/−12°C. Dense growth to 30 ft. Often pruned into globes or cones. Use leaves for seasoning.
Sweet olive, tea olive *Osmanthus fragrans*		X	X		X	Hardy to 20°F/−7°C. Slow-growing to 20 ft. Easily trained. Powerfully fragrant.
Waxleaf or Texas privet *Ligustrum japonicum* 'Texanum'	X	X	X		X	Hardy to 10°F/−12°C. Grows to 6–9 ft. Responds to shearing and shaping.
White spruce *Picea glauca*			X		X	Hardy to −40°F/−40°C. Dense. Vigorous growth to 70 ft.
Winter creeper *Euonymus fortunei* 'Sarcoxie'	X	X				Hardy to −20°F/−29°C. Upright growth to 4 ft. Shiny dark green leaves. Sun or shade.
Yew *Taxus baccata, T. cuspidata, T. media*	X	X	X			Hardiness varies. Upright or spreading types from 3 to 60 ft. Many varieties.

North, south, east, west... planting for exposures

Plantings around houses and garages, as well as against garden walls and fences, make the visual transition from the structure to the surrounding garden. Since they tend to be the permanent background or framework for an area, they should be in scale with the structures and offer year-round interest.

You can use plants to provide wind or sun protection and to screen ugly vents and utilities while adding a natural and unified look to the property.

Southern and western exposures call for extremely tough plants—those that can tolerate part to full sun as well as reflected heat. Grapefruit are ideal in a southern exposure because they need much heat for ripening; the same heat brings gardenias to their best bloom. In snowy, cold climates temperate fruits also do well in this exposure—especially apples and pears, which have historically been grown as espaliers on southern walls.

The full shade cast by a northern exposure will vary in size from winter to summer depending on the height of the sun in the sky. The size of the shady area will also depend on the slope of the roof and the height of the wall. A northern exposure tends to stay cool and moist. (Not many needle evergreens like this situation.) Flowering shrubs such as camellias and rhododendrons do well with some shade on a north or east-facing wall.

Morning sun on an eastern wall often provides just enough light without excessive drying; on the other hand, a western wall is a much drier atmosphere.

When you're planting, keep the full-grown size of the plants in

West-facing Wall/Name	Kind	Climate and Comments
California privet *Ligustrum ovalifolium*	Shrub	Hardy to 0°F/−18°C. Rapid grower to 15 ft. Tolerates heat, takes shearing. (E)
Carolina cherry laurel *Prunus caroliniana*	Shrub	Hardy to 10°F/−12°C. Grows 20–40 ft. with thick waxy leaves; tolerates heat. (E)
Cotoneaster horizontalis	Low shrub	Hardy to −10°F/−23°C. Low grower to 2 ft. Prefers hot dry conditions. (E) See page 34.
Firethorn *Pyracantha*	Shrub	Hardiness varies. Stoutly branched, growing to 12–30 ft. Fruits best in full sun. (E) See page 34.
Fraser photinia *Photinia fraseri*	Shrub	Hardy to 10°F/−12°C. Several good types from 3 to 10 ft. Good in heat or drought. (E) See page 35.
Fig, Edible *Ficus carica*	Tree	Hardy to 0°F/−18°C. Many prefer hot dry areas; to 15–30 ft. (E) See page 96.
Pearl bush *Exochorda racemosa*	Shrub	Hardy to −10°F/−23°C. Arching branches to 10–15 ft. Needs warm spot for good bloom. (D)
Rose *Rosa*	Shrub	Hardiness varies with species. Many types from 1 to 10 ft. All take full sun. (D) See pages 100–101.
Shiny xylosma *Xylosma congestum*	Shrub	Hardy to 10°F/−12°C. Moderate growth to 10 ft. Drought tolerant. (E)
Silverberry *Elaeagnus pungens*	Shrub	Hardy to 10°F/−12°C. Spreading mound with rough leaves, growing to 6–15 ft. (E) See page 35.
Washington hawthorn *Crataegus phaenopyrum*	Tree	Hardy to −20°F/−29°C. Small tree to 30 ft. Ornamental year-round with flowers, fruit, and foliage. (D) See page 36.
Wisteria	Vine	Hardy to −20°F/−29°C. Needs support when young. Will grow to 25 ft. (D) See page 48.
North-facing Wall		
Baltic ivy *Hedera helix* 'Baltica'	Vine	Hardiest of English-type ivies, −20°F/−29°C. Small leaves, easily trained. (E)
Camellia	Shrub	Hardy to 10°F/−12°C. Grows to 20 ft. in acid soil. Handsome foliage, roselike flowers. (E) See page 34.
Climbing hydrangea *Hydrangea anomala petiolaris*	Vine	Hardy to −20°F/−29°C. Roundish, heart-shaped leaves. Makes nice espalier. (D)
Fiveleaf akebia *Akebia quinata*	Vine	Hardy to −10°F/−23°C. Dainty with rounded leaflets and purple flowers. Prune yearly. (D)
Fuchsia hybrids	Shrubs	Hardy to 30°F/−1°C. Many types from 3 to 8 ft. Graceful branches may need staking. (D, E) See page 35.
Japanese aralia *Fatsia japonica*	Shrub	Hardy to 10°F/−12°C. Shiny star-shaped leaves. Looks tropical. Grows to 10 ft. in shade. (E)
Rosemary barberry *Berberis stenophylla*	Shrub	Hardy to 0°F/−18°C. Fine-leaved branches to 2 ft., thorny. (E) See page 34.
Virginia creeper *Parthenocissus quinquefolia*	Vine	Hardy to −20°F/−29°C. Leaflets turn red in fall. Makes shapely wall pattern; good ground cover. (D) See page 48.
Winter creeper *Euonymus fortunei*	Vine/ shrub	Hardy to −20°F/−29°C. Dark rich green leaves; use for ground cover or backdrop. (E)

(D) *means deciduous.*
(E) *means evergreen.*

East-facing Wall/Name	Kind	Climate and Comments
Chinese holly-grape *Mahonia lomariifolia*	Shrub	Hardy to 20°F/−7°C. Exotic leaves for outline against a wall. 6–10 ft. (E)
Chinese photinia *Photinia serrulata*	Shrub/ tree	Hardy to 10°F/−12°C. Dense-growing to 35 ft. Flowers and berries. (E)
Delavay osmanthus *Osmanthus delavayi*	Shrub	Hardy to 10°F/−12°C. Broad and graceful, to 6 ft. Good for foundations. (E)
Escallonia	Shrub	Hardy to 20°F/−7°C. Several types from 3 to 25 ft. Dense, glossy foliage on stocky plants. (E)
European cranberry bush *Viburnum opulus*	Shrub	Hardy to −30°F/−34°C. Grows to 10–20 ft. Good background. (D)
Flowering dogwood *Cornus florida*	Tree	Hardy to −20°F/−29°C. Forked branches make interesting appearance on 15–25 ft. trees. Showy flowers, fruit, and foliage. (D) See page 36.
Flowering quince *Chaenomeles*	Shrub	Hardy to −20°F/−29°C. Tough sturdy plant with thorns. Grows to 6 ft. (D)
Japanese maple *Acer palmatum*	Shrub/ tree	Hardy to −10°F/−23°C. Interesting textural leaf patterns and shadows. Many types from 3 to 20 ft. (D) See page 36.
Japanese viburnum *Viburnum japonicum*	Shrub/ tree	Hardy to 10°F/−12°C. Good for shaded background. (E)
Kerria japonica 'Pleniflora'	Shrub	Hardy to −20°F/−29°C. Lacy foliage and yellow flowers make pleasant wall pattern. Grows to 6 ft. (D)
Loquat *Eriobotrya japonica*	Tree	Hardy to 10°F/−23°C. Growth to 15–30 ft., with edible fruit. Needs some sun. (E) See page 36.
Yew, Hybrid *Taxus media*	Shrub	Hardy to −20°F/−29°C. Many types from 2 to 20 ft. All need good drainage. (E)
South-facing Wall		
Apple	Tree	Hardy to −20°F/−29°C. Train as espalier for big harvest in a small space. (D) See page 96.
Boston ivy *Parthenocissus tricuspidata*	Vine	Hardy to −20°F/−29°C. Vigorous grower, can damage woodwork. (E) See page 48.
Chinese hibiscus *Hibiscus rosa-sinensis*	Shrub	Hardy to 30°F/−1°C. Grows to 15 ft., thriving in hot, well-drained areas. (E)
Daylily *Hemerocallis*	Perenn.	Hardy to −30°F/−34°C. Summer blooms and straplike foliage to 2 ft. (D,E) See page 42.
Lantana hybrids	Shrub	Hardy to 30°F/−1°C. Many colors. Some shrubby, others somewhat vinelike. (E)
Leatherleaf viburnum *Viburnum rhytidophyllum*	Shrub	Hardy to −10°F/−23°C. Fully branched to 15 ft., with large coarse leaves. (E)
Maple, Paperbark *Acer griseum*	Tree	Hardy to −10°F/−23°C. Interesting small tree to 25 ft., with red-brown peeling bark. (D)
Pear *Pyrus communis*	Tree	Hardy to −20°F/−29°C. Fruit tree to 30–40 ft. Dwarf varieties make excellent espaliers. (D) See page 96.
Pomegranate *Punica granatum*	Tree/ shrub	Hardy to 20°F/−7°C. Shrubby tree to 10 ft. Needs full sun for ornamental/ edible fruit. (E)

(D) *means deciduous.*
(E) *means evergreen.*

Along a brick wall, plants in this narrow bed thrive in north exposure. Purple lobelia and a bright mix of nemesia and poppies provide seasonal color for row of azalea plants and a dogwood tree. Landscape architect: R. David Adams.

mind. Generally, place taller plants closer to the house and gradually add shrubs and ground cover to create a fluid transition. Remember to allow growing room next to windows and window wells. You could plan a hidden passageway to the utilities meter. Provide wire trelliswork for climbing plants that could damage wooden siding and shingles.

Be sure your gutters and downspouts work properly, and remember to provide for drainage away from the house. Runoff water accumulating in the foundation area often causes dieback of susceptible plants due to root rot, and excess leaching of lime from the foundation can alter the soil pH to the detriment of nearby plants.

In & around paved areas, parking strips

When planted, those narrow areas between the sidewalk and the curb, or the marginal length that separates one suburban driveway from the next, can add an extra dimension to the yard area. When neglected, they become eyesores.

Most often, parking strips are places where even weeds won't grow. The soil is usually poor, and the confines of a curb make it difficult to irrigate or mow.

The plants listed here can tolerate the restrictions of a parking strip environment. They are not overly large growers, so are suited to a confined space. And many of them require little care.

Shrubs/Name	Low care	Informal	Foot traffic	Barrier	Flowers	Fruit	Climate and Comments
Arnold dwarf forsythia *Forsythia intermedia* 'Arnold Dwarf'		X		X			Hardy to −20°F/−29°C. Fast-growing; dense branches to 3 ft. (D) See page 35.
Bearberry, Kinnikinnick *Arctostaphylos uva-ursi*	X	X		X	X		Hardy to −20°F/−29°C. Rugged grower to 1 1/2 ft. Drought tolerant. Bell-like flowers. (E)
Bearberry cotoneaster *Cotoneaster dammeri*	X	X		X	X	X	Hardy to 0°F/−18°C. Low, dense mat to 1 ft. Red fruit on stiff branches. See page 34. (E)
Bush cinquefoil *Potentilla fruticosa*		X		X	X		Hardy to −40°F/−40°C. Low grower to 4 ft. Yellow flowers. (D)
Compact Oregon grape *Mahonia aquifolium* 'Compacta'	X	X		X	X	X	Hardy to −20°F/−29°C. Shiny foliage, yellow flowers, black fruit in clusters. About 2 ft. tall. (E)
Coyote brush *Baccharis pilularis*	X	X					Hardy to 10°F/−12°C. Very tolerant of soil conditions. Two feet high.
Creeping juniper *Juniperus horizontalis* varieties	X	X		X			Does well in all climates, growing 6–12 inches. Must have good drainage. (E) See page 35.
Creeping St. Johnswort *Hypericum calycinum*	X	X			X		Hardy to −10°F/−12°C. Clean foliage. Grows to 1 1/2 ft. Bright yellow flowers. (E) See page 47.
Crimson pygmy barberry *Berberis thunbergii* 'Crimson Pygmy'	X	X		X			Hardy to −20°F/−29°C. Very thorny. Grows to 2 ft. with dark maroon foliage. (D)
Dwarf heavenly bamboo *Nandina domestica* 'Nana Compacta'	X			X			Hardy to 10°F/−12°C. Mounded, to 1 1/2 ft. Red, yellow, and green foliage. (E) See page 35.
Dwarf yaupon *Ilex vomitoria* 'Nana'	X	X		X			Hardy to −10°F/−23°C. Neat, compact to 18 in., with 36-in. spread. (E)
Germander *Teucrium chamaedrys*	X		X				Hardy to −10°F/−12°C. Low, growing to 1 ft. tall. Red-purple or white flowers.
Heath *Erica carnea*		X		X	X		Hardy to −10°F/−23°C. Many color types; most grow to 1 ft. Prefers acid soil. (E)
India hawthorn *Raphiolepis indica*	X	X		X	X	X	Hardy to 20°F/−7°C. Grows 2–8 ft. Several good types with pink or white flowers. (E) See page 35.
Paxistima canbyi	X						Hardy to −20°F/−7°C. Forms mat 9–12 in. tall. Needs moist soil, partial shade.
San Jose juniper *Juniperus chinensis* 'San Jose'	X	X		X			Hardy to −20°F/−29°C. Very flat with sage-green foliage. 2 ft. (E)
Santa Cruz firethorn *Pyracantha* 'Santa Cruz'				X	X	X	Hardy to 10°F/−12°C. Low-growing to 3 ft. Bright orange fruit, thorns. (E) See page 34.
Sargent juniper *Juniperus chinensis* 'Sargentii'	X	X		X			Hardy to −20°F/−29°C. Blue-green or green color. Grows to 1 ft. See page 35. (E)
Scotch heather *Calluna vulgaris*		X		X	X		Hardy to −20°F/−29°C. Much like heaths, growing to 18 in. Many flower and foliage colors. (E)
Warty barberry *Berberis verruculosa*		X		X			Hardy to 0°F/−18°C. Very thorny, low grower to 4 ft. (E) See page 34.

(D) *means deciduous.*
(E) *means evergreen.*

Planter separating driveway and entry is packed with flowers: chrysanthemums are ready to bloom as soon as marigolds, zinnias, and baby's breath are spent. Behind planter, a row of star jasmine softly defines edge of brick expanse. Architect: George Cody.

Vines and Ground Covers	Low care	Informal	Foot traffic	Barrier	Flowers	Fruit	Climate and Comments
Carpet bugle *Ajuga reptans*	X		X		X		Hardy to −30°F/−34°C. Purplish-bronze or green foliage. 4–12 in. tall. Easily rejuvenates. (E) See page 47.
Chamomile *Chamaemelum nobile*			X				Hardy to −20°F/−29°C. Ferny, aromatic foliage; grows 3–12 in. high. Can be mown. (E) See page 98.
Dwarf periwinkle *Vinca minor*	X				X		Hardy to −20°F/−29°C. Freely rooting vine, blue flowers. (E)
English ivy *Hedera helix*	X						Hardy to −10°F/−23°C. Roots itself. Many types. (E) See page 47.
Japanese spurge *Pachysandra terminalis*	X						Hardy to −10°F/−23°C. Deep green tufts of foliage to 12 in. (E) See page 47.
Mother-of-thyme, creeping thyme *Thymus praecox arcticus*	X		X				Hardy to −30°F/−34°C. Low, creeping mat from 3 to 6 in. Fragrant when crushed. (E)
Scotch moss, Irish moss *Sagina subulata*			X				Hardy to −20°F/−29°C. Golden-green mosslike foliage to 4 in. (E)
Star jasmine *Trachelospermum jasminoides*	X	X		X	X		Hardy to 20°F/−7°C. Vigorous grower to 2 ft. Shiny foliage; fragrant white flowers. (E) See page 48.
Winter creeper *Euonymus fortunei*	X	X					Hardy to −20°F/−29°C. Shiny, round leaves. Many types. (E)
Perennials							
Blue fescue *Festuca ovina 'Glauca'*	X						Hardy to −20°F/−29°C. Short-tufted bluish gray mounds of grass to 10 in. (E)
Common aubrieta *Aubrieta deltoidea*		X			X		Hardy to −20°F/−29°C. Mat-forming at 3–6 in. Rose to purple flowers. (E)
Evergreen candytuft *Iberis sempervirens*	X				X		Hardy to −30°F/−34°C. White flower clusters on 12-in. plants in spring. (E) See page 41.
Gazania	X				X		Hardy to 20°F/−7°C. Yellow-orange flowers, green or gray leaves. 6–8 in. (E) See page 42.
Rusty cinquefoil *Potentilla cinerea*		X			X		Hardy to −30°F/−34°C. Yellow flowers on 2–4-in. trailing plants. (E)
Wall rockcress *Arabis caucasica*	X				X		Hardy to −30°F/−34°C. Mat-forming at 4–10 in. Gray foliage topped with white flowers. (E) See page 43.

(D) *means deciduous.*   (E) *means evergreen.*

Shady places

Rare is the yard or garden that is exposed to full sun throughout the year. Most of us put up with some unplanned shade, perhaps from nearby buildings or neighbors' overhanging trees. We also deal with the planned shade created by our own planting schemes and the structures we add to them.

Too often shade and the cooling, moisture-retaining effect it has on the soil are considered drawbacks to gardening, when actually some of the choicest and most beautiful plants perform their best out of direct sun.

Plants, like animals, can tolerate different exposures based on their native habitat and their adaptability.

A brief seasonal analysis of your own situation will determine what type of shade you have. Generally speaking, large-leafed trees and northern exposures cast the deepest shade, or full shade. High trees with small leaves or lacy foliage give filtered shade—that soft, dappled effect on the ground below. A plant that catches some morning or afternoon sun, but not both, is in part shade. Remember, afternoon sun tends to be stronger and has a greater drying effect.

You can achieve a natural-looking layered effect by planting shrubs under trees and facing them with a ground cover. In this situation, be sure to use plants that not only will tolerate the shade, but also will endure the competition from surface tree roots.

With so many different plants available, it's not difficult to create a complete landscape in the shade that offers year-round interest and utility. You can combine spring-blooming plants with late-summer flowers, colorful fall foliage and bright-colored berries. Intense colors like red and orange will draw attention to the shady spot; softer blues will tone it down.

Trees/Name	Climate and Comments
Canada hemlock *Tsuga canadensis*	Hardy to −20°F/−29°C. Young natives sprout in forest shade. Soft foliage. (E)
Eastern redbud *Cercis canadensis*	Hardy to −20°F/−29°C. Happiest at woodland edge. Spring branches clothed in deep pink buds. (D) See page 36.
Flowering dogwood *Cornus florida*	Hardy to −20°F/−29°C. Small trees, like filtered sun. (D) See page 36.
Japanese maple *Acer palmatum*	Hardy to −10°F/−23°C. Lacy foliage. Prefers filtered shade. (D) See page 36.
Vine maple *Acer circinatum*	Hardy to −20°F/−29°C. Low tree or shrub, densely branched, red-gold in fall. (D)
Shrubs	
Camellia	Hardy to 10°F/−12°C. Shiny leaves, large flowers. Many varieties. (E) See page 34.
David viburnum *Viburnum davidii*	Hardy to 0°F/−18°C. Clean, deeply veined foliage. Need both male and female plants for fruiting. (E)
Drooping leucothoe *Leucothoe fontanesiana*	Hardy to −10°F/−23°C. Graceful branches. Takes some drought with age. (E)
Heavenly bamboo *Nandina domestica*	Hardy to 10°F/−12°C. Airy foliage. Needs sun for fall color, but flowers, fruits in shade. (E) See page 35.
Holly grape, mahonia *Mahonia*	Hardiness varies. Year-round ornamental. Yellow flowers, blue fruits. (E)
Japanese aucuba *Aucuba japonica*	Hardy to 10°F/−12°C. Shiny leaves, smooth or toothed; variegated or dark green. (E) See page 34.
Japanese skimmia *Skimmia japonica*	Hardy to 10°F/−12°C. Glossy foliage; pinkish buds, white flowers, red fruits. (E)
Lily-of-the-valley shrub *Pieris japonica*	Hardy to −10°F/−23°C. Colorful buds in autumn; drooping bell-like flowers February–May. Needs moist spot. (E)
Mountain laurel *Kalmia latifolia*	Hardy to −20°F/−29°C. Happiest in filtered shade with acid soil. (E)
Rhododendron and azalea	Hardiness varies. Many varieties and types grown for striking flowers in many colors. Need acid soil. (E, D) See page 35.
St. Johnswort *Hypericum*	Hardiness varies. Have lemon-yellow flowers in summer. Any soil. (E)
Sarcococca *S. hookerana humilis*	Hardy to 0°F/−18°C. Low growing; tolerate deep shade. (E)
Yew *Taxus*	Hardiness varies. A needled evergreen, one of few to tolerate shade; must have moist soil yet good drainage. (E)
Vines	
Climbing hydrangea *Hydrangea anomala petiolaris*	Hardy to −20°F/−29°C. Glossy leaves, flat flower clusters; tolerates some sun in coastal areas. (D)
Fiveleaf akebia *Akebia quinata*	Hardy to −10°F/−23°C. Delicate appearing, yet thrives in sun or shade. (D, E)
Virginia creeper *Parthenocissus quinquefolia*	Hardy to −20°F/−29°C. Vigorous vine; five-part leaves with saw-toothed edges. Superb fall color. (D) See page 48.
Winter creeper *Euonymus fortunei*	Hardy to 0°F/−18°C. Will grow almost anywhere; many fine varieties. (E)

(D) *means deciduous.*

(E) *means evergreen.*

Perennials and Bulbs/Name	Climate and Comments
Bear's breech *Acanthus mollis*	Hardy to 10°F/−12°C. Large, shiny leaves get their deepest green in moderate shade. See page 41.
Bishop's hat *Epimedium grandiflorum*	Hardy to −30°F/−34°C. Will compete with tree roots. Does best in light shade.
Bleeding heart *Dicentra spectabilis*	Hardy to −30°F/−34°C. Large clump with arching branches of heart-shaped flowers. (D) See page 41.
Cineraria *Senecio hybridus*	Hardy to 30°F/−1°C. Perennial or winter-spring annual provides bright flowers.
Columbine *Aquilegia*	Hardy to −30°F/−34°C. Several types, all requiring excellent drainage. (D) See page 42.
Ferns	Hardiness varies with each kind. Most like a cool spot. (D, E)
Forget-me-not *Myosotis*	Hardy to −30°F/−34°C. Perennial or annual. Delicate blue flowers. (D) See page 39.
Japanese anemone *Anemone hybrida*	Hardy to −20°F/−29°C. Best performance in part shade; needs good drainage. (D) See page 42.
Japanese spurge *Pachysandra terminalis*	Hardy to −10°F/−23°C. Common ground cover. Tufted leaves come in green or variegated form. (E)
Kaffir lily *Clivia miniata*	Hardy to 20°F/−6°C. Striking orange flowers in winter. (E)
Lily *Lilium*	Hardiness varies with kind. Best with cool, shaded roots and filtered sun on flowers; many hybrids. (D) See page 45.
Lily-of-the-valley *Convallaria majalis*	Hardy to −30°F/−34°C. Thrives in filtered shade; needs cool spot. (E) See page 42.
Lily turf *Liriope* and *Ophiopogon*	Hardiness varies. Dark grasslike foliage and purple or white spike blooms. (E)
Mondo grass *Ophiopogon japonicus*	Hardy to 10°F/−12°C. Clumps of dark green grasslike foliage. Good as ground cover. See page 47.
Plantain lily *Hosta*	Hardy to −30°F/−34°C. Spear-shaped cool green leaves and late summer flowers. (D) See page 43.
Primrose *Primula*	Hardiness varies—many types and varieties. (D, E)
Violet *Viola*	Hardiness varies. Many types; some may be weedy. (E) See page 43.
Virginia bluebells *Mertensia virginica*	Hardy to −30°F/−34°C. True blue flowers in spring; foliage dies down in summer. (D)
Annuals	
Calceolaria *C. crenatiflora*	Showy, spotted, slipperlike flowers; bedding or container plant.
Foxglove *Digitalis*	Long-blooming spikes of tubular flowers; prefers heavy moist soil and part shade. See page 39.
Impatiens	Several types and hybrids. All require filtered shade and moist cool spot.
Wax begonia, bedding begonia *Semperflorens begonia*	Small, colorful mounds; profuse flowers. Prefers shade in warm summer regions.
Wishbone flower *Torenia fournieri*	Can take sun with cool, short summer; otherwise prefers part shade.

Lath-shaded garden walkway *leads to a round "moon gate." Pink and red impatiens highlight planting of baby's tears, Scotch moss, English ivy, ferns.*

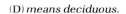

(D) *means deciduous.*

(E) *means evergreen.*

Dramatic foliage

Many of our most-prized ornamental plants are grown for their attractive or interesting foliage. Flowers are often seasonal, but foliage has long-term showiness.

Dramatic foliage catches your eye with its interesting shape, its size, or its unusual color. In our list you'll find a wide variety of trees, shrubs, annuals, and perennials—exotic-looking plants perhaps with big, star-shaped leaves or long, swordlike leaves.

Gray, bronze, yellow, even blue make quite a contrast to the familiar green hues of most foliage. Increasingly popular are the variegated plants. Their leaves display cream, silver, or golden mottling; white stripes; and, in the case of some beeches and dogwoods, pink and white mottling together.

Dramatic foliage enables some plants to stand out as individuals; others go well in a loose or formal grouping. A small group of colorful Japanese maples creates a delicate, natural setting, while a lone blood-leaf Japanese maple outlined only by sky and lawn is outstanding in its beauty.

Combining dramatic foliage is a matter of personal taste, but some compositions have proven better than others. Variegated and yellow-foliaged plants show up best with a solid green background. The gray and bronze plants go well together. Bronze foliage is especially attractive with red and orange-flowered plants, while blue and gray plants go well with pink and white-flowered plants.

Texture, an important facet of landscape design, can be modified by the use of plants with dramatic foliage. We like to see variation in the textures of a garden scheme. A bold-leaved ground cover such as hosta, used with a lighter-textured shrub like golden yew, creates a striking contrast.

Trees/Name	Large	Sword	Gray	Bronze	Yellow	Blue	Variegated	Climate
Chinese angelica *Aralia chinensis*	X							−10°F/−23°C
Colorado spruce *Picea pungens*			X			X		−40°F/−40°C
Common catalpa, Indian bean *Catalpa bignonioides*	X							−20°F/−29°C
Cucumber tree *Magnolia acuminata*	X							−20°F/−29°C
Empress tree *Paulownia tomentosa*	X							−10°F/−23°C
Gum *Eucalyptus*			X			X		Varies
Hercules' club *Aralia spinosa*	X							−10°F/−23°C
Holly *Ilex*							X	Varies
Juniper *Juniperus*			X	X	X	X	X	Varies
Lawson cypress *Chamaecyparis lawsoniana*			X		X	X	X	0°F/−18°C
Palm (many kinds)	X	X						Varies
Purple beech *Fagus sylvatica* 'Atropunicea'				X				−20°F/−29°C
Purple-leaf plum *Prunus cerasifera* 'Atropurpurea'				X				−30°F/−34°C
Red Japanese maple *Acer palmatum* 'Atropurpureum'				X				−10°F/−23°C
Royal purple smoke tree *Cotinus coggygria* 'Royal Purple'				X				−10°F/−23°C
Tricolor beech *Fagus sylvatica* 'Tricolor'							X	−20°F/−29°C
Tricolor dogwood *Cornus florida* 'Welchii'							X	−20°F/−29°C
Shrubs								
Artemisia			X					Varies
Chinese holly grape *Mahonia lomariifolia*	X							20°F/−7°C
David viburnum *Viburnum davidii*	X							0°F/−18°C
Dwarf red-leaf plum *Prunus cistena*				X				−40°F/−40°C
Evergreen euonymus *Euonymus japonica* varieties							X	10°F/−12°C
Fatshedera lizei	X							10°F/−12°C
Golden English yew *Taxus baccata* 'Aurea'					X			0°F/−18°C
Holly (see page 35) *Ilex*							X	Varies
Japanese aralia *Fatsia japonica*	X							10°F/−12°C
Juniper (see page 35) *Juniperus*			X	X	X	X	X	Varies
Kiwi *Actinidia chinensis*	X							10°F/−12°C
Lavender cotton *Santolina chamaecyparissus*			X					−10°F/−23°C

Shrubs (cont'd.)/Name	Large	Sword	Gray	Bronze	Yellow	Blue	Variegated	Climate
Leatherleaf viburnum *Viburnum rhytidophyllum*	X							−10°F/−23°C
Rheingold American arborvitae *Thuja occidentalis* 'Rheingold'					X			−40°F/−40°C
Sage (see page 99) *Salvia officinalis*			X	X	X		X	−20°F/−29°C
Silver buffaloberry *Shepherdia argentea*			X					−40°F/−40°C
Texas ranger *Leucophyllum texanum*			X					10°F/−12°C
Tricolor big-leaf hydrangea *Hydrangea macrophylla* 'Tricolor'	X						X	−10°F/−23°C
Variegated weigela *Weigela florida* 'Variegata'							X	−10°F/−23°C
Vicary golden privet *Ligustrum* 'Vicaryi'					X			−10°F/−23°C
Yucca *Yucca filamentosa*	X	X	X					−20°F/−29°C
Annuals and Perennials								
Bear's breech (see page 41) *Acanthus mollis*	X							Peren.
Bedding begonia, wax begonia *Semperflorens begonia*	X			X				Annual
Blue fescue *Festuca ovina* 'Glauca'						X		Peren.
Canna	X	X		X				Peren.
Carpet bugle *Ajuga reptans*				X			X	Peren.
Castor bean *Ricinus communis*	X			X				Annual
Coleus *Coleus hybridus*				X	X		X	Annual
Dusty miller *Centaurea cineraria*			X					Annual
Fairy wand *Dierama*		X						Peren.
Fountain grass *Pennisetum setaceum* 'Cupreum'		X		X				Peren.
Giant rhubarb *Gunnera chilensis*	X							Peren.
Hellebore *Helleborus*	X		X					Peren.
Lamb's ears *Stachys byzantina*			X					Peren.
Mullein-pink *Lychnis coronaria*			X					Peren./ Bien.
Plantain lily *Hosta*	X		X			X	X	Peren.
Sedum spurium 'Dragon's Blood'				X				Peren.
Shiso *Perilla frutescens*				X				Annual
Snow-in-summer *Cerastium tomentosum*			X					Peren.
Snow-on-the-mountain *Euphorbia marginata*			X				X	Peren.
Yarrow (see page 43) *Achillea*			X					Peren.

Giant, tropical-looking leaves belong to giant rhubarb (Gunnera), a plant that can take some frost and snow. Orange flowers are lilies. Landscape architect: R. David Adams.

Deep red leaves with showy edges, variegated green and white leaves, and pink-toned ones show a few of the variations in coleus.

Plants with fragrant flowers & foliage

Flowers, leaves, stems, bark, and even roots can give off a wide range of fragrances, from the pungent aroma of pines and cedars to the heady scent of gardenias.

Locate your fragrant plants so they can bestow maximum fragrance. Place sweet-scented trees on the windward side of your house so the perfumed breezes blow your way. Plant herbs between paving blocks—each time you walk, the aroma from crushed leaves floats up to you. Some flowers are more fragrant in the evening. Arrange these around bedroom windows and patios or along the path most often used for evening strolls. Train redolent vines over doorways and arbors, and group pots of your choicest blossoms in sitting areas.

Often a crushed leaf or scratched stem releases an even stronger aroma. Sassafras and spice bush can be identified by the tingling scent of their bark. For more fragrant arrangements and spicier potpourri, try crushing some leaves or scraping a few stems. Many plants with pungent foliage are also culinary herbs (see pages 98–99).

Some plants release more scent when their foliage is moistened. After a rain or on a warm, humid day, the air may be permeated with a hundred different scents.

Fragrance in the garden need not be confined to spring and summer. Let each season bring its collection of sweet scents to your garden. In autumn, late-blooming annuals or a second flowering of earlier types can add a cheery note to hazy days. Flowering tobacco (*Nicotiana*) by the patio door will yield its soft evening fragrance well up until the first frost. Plant winter-flowering Chinese witch hazel as a colorful and sweet-smelling companion for fresh green junipers.

Trees/Name	Flowers	Foliage	Climate and Comments
Black locust *Robinia pseudoacacia*	X		Hardy to −30°F/−34°C. Long clusters of fragrant, creamy flowers in late spring. (D)
Crabapple *Malus*	X		Hardiness varies. Spring blossoms are red, pink, and white. Many freshly fragrant varieties. (D) See page 36.
Flowering ash *Fraxinus ornus*	X		Hardy to −10°F/−23°C. Sweetly fragrant greenish white flower clusters in May. (D)
Incense cedar *Calocedrus decurrens*		X	Hardy to −20°F/−29°C. Strong clean scent from foliage and bark. (E)
Linden *Tilia*	X		Hardiness varies. Very sweet flower clusters at branch tips in June–July. (D) See page 37.
Pine *Pinus*		X	Hardiness varies widely according to kind. Pungent/spicy needles and bark. Many selections. (E)
Russian olive *Elaeagnus angustifolia*	X		Hardy to −40°F/−40°C. Tiny, fragrant, yellow flowers at leaf bases in late spring. (D) See page 36.
Shrubs			
Bayberry *Myrica pennsylvanica*		X	Hardy to −40°F/−40°C. All parts are pungently aromatic when crushed. (E)
Carolina allspice *Calycanthus floridus*	X	X	Hardy to −20°F/−29°C. Little maroon flowers with aroma like strawberries. (D)
Chinese witch hazel *Hamamelis mollis*	X		Hardy to −10°F/−23°C. Yellow, spiderlike, sweetly spiced blooms along bare branches in late winter. (D)
English lavender *Lavandula angustifolia*	X	X	Hardy to 0°F/−18°C. Scented lavender flowers on long spikes in summer; used for sachets. (E)
Gardenia *Gardenia jasminoides*	X		Hardy to 20°F/−7°C. Creamy, roselike flowers—strong, heady fragrance. (E)
Lilac *Syringa*	X		Hardy to −10°F/−23°C. Fragrant flower clusters, white to purple, at branch tips in late spring. (D) See page 35.
Mexican orange *Choisya ternata*	X		Hardy to 10°F/−12°C. White spring blossoms are sweetly fragrant. (E)
Mock orange *Philadelphus*	X		Hardy to −10°F/−23°C. White flowers are strongly sweet like orange blossoms. (D) See page 35.
Rose *Rosa*	X		Hardiness varies. Old-fashioned types more fragrant than most modern hybrids. (D) See pages 100–101.
Sarcococca *S. hookerana humilis*	X		Hardy to 0°F/−18°C. Tiny, nose-tickling flowers at leaf bases in early spring. (E)
Summersweet *Clethra alnifolia*	X		Hardy to −30°F/−34°C. Long spikes of very sweet white flowers at branch tips. (D)
Sweet olive *Osmanthus fragrans*	X		Hardy to 20°F/−7°C. Bold yet sweet fragrance from tiny white flowers. (E)
Viburnum, Burkwood *Viburnum burkwoodii*	X		Hardy to −20°F/−29°C. Large, pinkish-white flower clusters in early spring. Strong fragrance resembles lilacs. (D, E)
Winter daphne *Daphne odora*	X		Hardy to 10°F/−12°C. Perfumed pink or white flowers in winter. (E)

(D) *means deciduous.*
(E) *means evergreen.*

Vines/Name	Flowers	Foliage	Climate and Comments
Carolina jessamine *Gelsemium sempervirens*	X		Hardy to 10°F/−12°C. Fragrant, tubular yellow flowers in late winter, early spring. (E)
Evergreen clematis *Clematis armandii*	X		Hardy to 10°F/−12°C. Large, white spring flowers are mildly fragrant. (E)
Hall's honeysuckle *Lonicera japonica* 'Halliana'	X		Hardy to −20°F/−29°C. White to yellow flowers in spring and summer. Clean, sweet fragrance. (E) See page 48.
Japanese wisteria *Wisteria floribunda*	X		Hardy to −20°F/−29°C. Long clusters of sweetly fragrant purple or white flowers. (D)
Star jasmine *Trachelospermum jasminoides*	X		Hardy to 20°F/−7°C. Heady, sweet fragrance from creamy-white flowers in summer. (E) See page 48.
Perennials and Bulbs			
Bee balm *Monarda didyma*	X		Hardy to −30°F/−34°C. Mint-scented, reddish flower clusters atop tall stems.
Belladonna lily *Amaryllis belladonna*	X		Hardy to 10°F/−12°C. Rose-colored, trumpetlike blossoms in August.
Crocus chrysanthus	X		Hardy to −10°F/−23°C. Orange-yellow, sweet-scented spring bulb.
Fernleaf yarrow *Achillea filipendulina*		X	Hardy to −30°F/−34°C. Pungent, gray foliage is good for dried arrangements.
Heliotrope *Heliotropium arborescens*	X		Hardy to 30°F/−1°C. Mildly fragrant, deep purple to white flower heads. See page 42.
Hyacinth *Hyacinthus orientalis*	X		Hardy to 0°F/−18°C. Dense flower spikes in pastel colors. Heavy perfume. See page 45.
Lily-of-the-valley *Convallaria majalis*	X		Hardy to −30°F/−34°C. Spring-blooming, white, bell-shaped flowers have soft fragrance. See page 42.
Narcissus	X		Hardiness and fragrance vary with kind. Yellow and white flowers from bulbs. See page 45.
Plantain lily *Hosta plantaginea*	X		Hardy to −30°F/−34°C. Very sweet, long, white, bell-shaped flowers on 2–3-ft. stalks.
Annuals			
Flowering tobacco *Nicotiana*	X		Sweet scent day and night from rose, pink, or white summer blooms. See page 40.
Nasturtium *Tropaeolum majus*	X	X	Yellow to red flowers with peppery scent. Bright green leaves also peppery. See page 39.
Sweet alyssum *Lobularia maritima*	X		Profuse, tiny, white or purple honey-scented flowers.
Sweet pea *Lathyrus odoratus*	X		Sweet-smelling spring climber in shades of pink, violet, white, or red.
Stock *Matthiola incana*	X		Heavy-scented, good cut flower. Technically a perennial. See page 40.
Wallflower *Cheiranthus cheiri*	X		Orange, yellow, or red flower clusters with mildly sweet fragrance.

Some are noticeably fragrant, others aren't—rhododendrons, like many other plants, have especially fragrant varieties. This sweet-smelling rhododendron is 'Loderi King George'.

Attracting birds, bees & butterflies

Attracting birds, bees, and butterflies to the garden requires more than planting the right plants. You need to cultivate a style of gardening that is harmonious with the habits of wildlife. This may mean leaving some unpruned shrubbery around to provide shelter, and letting flowers go to seed to provide food. It also means creating a welcome year-round environment, especially if you want to enjoy the presence of hummingbirds, who depend on a continuous food supply. Think first of what these creatures need, then incorporate it into your garden, whether it be a shallow pond, a perch, or a posy.

Hummingbirds and butterflies are interested in nectar and will seek out those long, tubular, nectar-producing flowers that accommodate pointed beaks and long

Half-hidden *in a rose bush, mourning dove takes his turn on the nest. Doves may spend the whole year in one spot.*

Trees/Name	Birds	Humming-birds	Bees	Butterflies	Climate and Comments
Chaste tree *Vitex agnus-castus*	✕		✕		Hardy to 10°F/−18°C. Blue flowers in summer. (D)
Flowering dogwood *Cornus florida*	✕				Hardy to −20°F/−29°C. Bright red fruits. Grows to 20 ft. (D) See page 36.
Little-leaf linden *Tilia cordata*			✕		Hardy to −30°F/−34°C. Very fragrant flower clusters in summer. (D) See page 37.
Mountain ash *Sorbus aucuparia*	✕		✕		Hardy to −40°F/−40°C. Creamy flower clusters followed by red berries. (D)
Mulberry, Black or Persian *Morus nigra*	✕				Hardy to 0°F/−18°C. Fast-growing, somewhat messy, prolific fruiter. (D)
Shadblow, service berry *Amelanchier laevis*	✕				Hardy to −20°F/−29°C. Long flower clusters; dark blue, edible fruit. (D) See page 36.
Silk tree *Albizia julibrissin*	✕				Hardy to 0°F/−18°C. Pink, powder-puff-like flowers in summer. (D) See page 37.
Weeping willow *Salix babylonica*	✕			✕	Hardy to 0°F/−18°C. Provides shelter and food; invasive roots. (D)
Shrubs					
Amur privet *Ligustrum amurense*	✕		✕		Hardy to −30°F/−34°C. Flowers attract bees. Blue-black berrylike fruit in fall; thick foliage. (E)
Bottlebrush *Callistemon*		✕		✕	Hardy to 30°F/−1°C. Bright red flowers. Vary kinds for year-round bloom. (E)
Common butterfly bush *Buddleia davidii*			✕	✕	Hardy to −10°F/−23°C. Very fragrant, cone-shaped floral clusters in pink, white, lilac, blue, or purple. (D)
Cotoneaster	✕		✕		Hardiness varies. Many types; small flowers and tiny red berries. (D) See page 34.
Elderberry *Sambucus*	✕				Hardiness varies. Weedy shrubs. Blue-black or red fruit. (D)
English holly *Ilex aquifolium*	✕				Hardy to 10°F/−12°C. Need both sexes to produce fruit. Provides shelter. (E) See page 35.
Firethorn *Pyracantha coccinea*	✕		✕		Hardiness varies. Strong-smelling flowers; red or orange fruit. (E) See page 34.
Fuchsia magellanica	✕	✕			Hardy to 10°F/−12°C. Woody shrub. Single red-violet flowers. (E)
Glossy abelia *Abelia grandifolia*			✕	✕	Hardy to 10°F/−12°C. Pink-white, bell-shaped flowers on large, round shrub. (E) See page 34.
Red chokeberry *Aronia arbutifolia*	✕		✕		Hardy to −10°F/−23°C. White flowers. Red berrylike fruit persists in winter. (D)
Red flowering currant *Ribes sanguineum*	✕	✕			Hardy to 0°F/−18°C. Deep pink to red flower clusters in spring; blue-black berries. (D)
Redtwig dogwood *Cornus stolonifera*	✕				Hardy to −40°F/−40°C. Bluish white fruit, thicketlike growth. (D)
Viburnum	✕				Hardiness varies. Red or blue fruit; shrub provides shelter. (D) See page 35.
Weigela		✕			Hardy to −10°F/−23°C. Tubular red or pink flowers. (D) See page 35.

(D) *means deciduous.*
(E) *means evergreen.*

Annuals and Perennials	Birds	Humming-birds	Bees	Butterflies	Climate and Comments
Anise *Pimpinella anisum*				X	Aromatic, 2-ft. annual herb. White or yellow flower heads. See page 98.
Bee balm *Monarda didyma*		X	X		Red to maroon flower heads on 2 1/2–4-ft. stems. Perennial.
Borage *Borago officinalis*			X		Annual herb with broad leaves, blue flowers. See page 98.
Butterfly weed *Asclepias tuberosa*			X	X	Orange-flowered perennial for dry, sandy soil.
Cardinal climber *Ipomoea quamoclit*		X			Fine-leaved annual vine with scarlet, funnel-shaped flowers.
Cardinal flower *Lobelia cardinalis*	X	X			Perennial. Bright red flowers; grows at water's edge.
Columbine *Aquilegia*		X			Colorful flowers with long, nectar-bearing spurs. Perennial. See page 42.
English lavender *Lavandula angustifolia*			X		Hardy to 0°F/−18°C. Purple flowers and gray foliage. Dwarf varieties.
Flowering tobacco *Nicotiana*		X	X		Tender perennial grown as annual. Very fragrant flowers; to 2 1/2 ft. See page 40.
Hollyhock *Alcea rosea*	X	X			Tall coarse-leaved biennial. Flowers in many colors. See page 39.
Marigold *Tagetes*	X			X	Annual. Flowers provide seeds and nectar; colors are pale yellow through gold to orange and maroon brown. See page 39.
Penstemon	X	X			Mostly perennials or low evergreen shrubs. Tubular flowers in many colors. See page 43.
Sunflower *Helianthus annuus*	X				Annual. Grows to 8–10 ft., produces abundant seed. See page 40.
Thyme *Thymus vulgaris*			X		Common cooking herb. Lilac flowers in summer. See page 99.
Vines					
American bittersweet *Celastrus scandens*	X				Hardy to −40°F/−40°C. Need both sexes to produce orange-yellow fruit capsules with bright red seeds. (D)
Blueberry climber *Ampelopsis brevipedunculata*	X				Hardy to −20°F/−29°C. Attractive blue fruits in fall. Vigorous climber. (D)
Carolina jessamine *Gelsemium sempervirens*	X	X			Hardy to 10°F/−12°C. Fragrant, tubular yellow flowers in late winter, early spring. (E)
Flame vine *Pyrostegia venusta*		X	X		Hardy to 30°F/−1°C. Clusters of orange trumpet flowers in fall, early winter. (E)
Hall's honeysuckle *Lonicera japonica* 'Halliana'	X	X	X		Hardy to −10°F/−23°C. White flowers, black fruits. Rampant grower. (E, D) See page 48.
Star jasmine *Trachelospermum jasminoides*			X	X	Hardy to 20°F/−7°C. Use as ground cover or train on support. Creamy fragrant flowers. (E) See page 48.
Wisteria			X	X	Hardy to −20°F/−29°C. Long clusters of fragrant blooms, in white, pink, blue, violet, or purple. (D) See page 48.

Spectacular Western tiger swallowtail lights on a bright pink zinnia. Butterflies, like bees, feed on flower nectar.

tongues. Hummers are primarily attracted to red flowers but will search in many different flowers for life-giving nectar.

Some other birds are nectar eaters, but most are interested in seeds and insects. Berry-producing plants, such as dogwood, holly, and cotoneaster, provide a good fruit supply. A light hand on the pesticide will keep costs down and allow for integrated pest management: the birds help control the insect population while having their main course. By avoiding pesticides you can also maintain a good bee population.

Butterflies, of course, spend part of their lives as caterpillars. Caterpillars chew on plants, but in most cases the plants can tolerate a few holes in their leaves.

A few plants on our lists have neither showy flowers nor conspicuous fruits, but they do provide a home and shelter for birds and butterflies. Weeping willows, with their rough bark trunks, house a multitude of insects and are usually located near a water source. Many fir trees have dense foliage and provide a sheltered perching and nesting area.

Of the plants listed, most are popular ornamentals along with being attractive to wildlife. Whether it's a wild garden or a very small, formal area you're planning, it will be easy to invite birds, bees, and butterflies to be frequent garden visitors.

Autumn color

Anyone who has driven through New England on a crisp autumn day will hold forever the rich, colorful impressions of scarlet hillsides and golden valleys. No place matches the Northeast for miles of vivid countryside, but fortunately many of its plants and others like them can be grown across the United States.

Look for plants that fit your climate needs and also your garden design, as fall color is available in a variety of sizes and shapes.

Foliage isn't the only color in fall—many plants hold their clumps of red, blue, and black fruits well into winter. Tree bark becomes more obvious an ornamental factor as the leaves begin to fall, often revealing a shiny red (many ornamental cherries) or a lovely curled and shingled appearance (paperbark maple). Branching patterns also stand out.

Shopping for autumn color, they're surrounded by glowing leaves. Clockwise from right of woman's shoulder: yellow is Chinese tallow; tall scarlet trees are Pyrus calleryana; nandinas are in front; ferny tree is pistache; in back is liquidambar.

Trees/Name	Climate and Comments
American sweet gum *Liquidambar styraciflua*	Hardy to −10°F/−23°C. Gold, red, maroon. Selected varieties for mild climates. See page 37.
Chinese pistache *Pistacia chinensis*	Hardy to −10°F/−23°C. Compound leaves turn scarlet or orangish yellow; red fruits turn dark blue. See page 37.
Chinese witch hazel *Hamamelis mollis*	Hardy to 0°F/−18°C. Wavy-edged leaves hang in golden bunches.
European mountain ash *Sorbus aucuparia*	Hardy to −40°F/−40°C. Orange or red berries persist into winter; gold leaves. See page 37.
Flowering dogwood *Cornus florida*	Hardy to −20°F/−29°C. Drooping leaves first turn red, then blend to bronze. See page 36.
Hawthorn *Crataegus*	Hardiness varies. Shades of gold with red fruits. Many hardy types.
Maidenhair tree *Ginkgo biloba*	Hardy to −20°F/−29°C. Fan-shaped leaves turn gold in a few days time and drop just as quickly.
Maple *Acer*	Hardiness varies. Some of the most striking fall specimens in gold, orange, red, and brown.
Oak *Quercus*	Hardiness varies. Shades of yellow, orange, red, and brown.
Poplar, cottonwood, aspen *Populus*	Hardy to −20°F/−29°C. Known for fluttering leaves that turn soft yellow.
Shadblow, serviceberry *Amelanchier laevis*	Hardy to −20°F/−29°C. Leaves turn deep yellow and red. See page 36.
Sour gum, tupelo *Nyssa sylvatica*	Hardy to −20°F/−29°C. Bright red fall color of smooth, shiny leaves contrasts with dark bark. See page 37.
Tulip tree *Liriodendron tulipifera*	Hardy to −20°F/−29°C. Lyre-shaped leaves of golden yellow when in full sun.
Shrubs	
Blueberry *Vaccinium corymbosum*	Hardy to −30°F/−34°C. Handsome scarlet foliage. See page 97.
Common witch hazel *Hamamelis virginiana*	Hardy to −20°F/−29°C. Small, yellow spiderlike flowers along with golden leaves in fall.
Crape myrtle *Lagerstroemia indica*	Hardy to 0°F/−18°C. Blooms of pink, rose, purple, and fuchsia July–Sept. Golden leaves. See page 34.
Red chokeberry *Aronia arbutifolia*	Hardy to −10°F/−23°C. Bright red berries persist after golden red leaves have dropped.
Red twig dogwood *Cornus stolonifera*	Hardy to −40°F/−40°C. White berries on red or yellow-stemmed type; brilliant red leaves.
Red-vein enkianthus *Enkianthus campanulatus*	Hardy to −20°F/−29°C. Shiny, leathery leaves turn bright red; needs acid soil.
Staghorn sumac *Rhus typhina*	Hardy to −30°F/−39°C. Large exotic leaves of deep red and bronze; crimson fruit clusters at branch tips last all winter.
Viburnum	Hardiness varies. Many types with deep wine color, some with red or black fruits. See page 35.
Winged euonymus *Euonymus alata*	Hardy to −30°F/−34°C. Leaves turn fierce red with first cold snap. See page 34.
Vines	
American bittersweet *Celastrus scandens*	Hardy to −40°F/−40°C. Yellow-orange seed capsules pop open to reveal bright red seeds.
Virginia creeper *Parthenocissus quinquefolia*	Hardy to −20°F/−29°C. Much like Boston ivy; turns bright then deep red.

Gardeners' Language:

a concise glossary of words you should know

The listing of gardening terms below is not limited to those terms used in this book. It includes a number of other terms that you should be familiar with in order to talk knowledgeably with nursery personnel or with other amateur gardeners. A few terms that are well defined within the book are followed by a brief definition and a page reference.

Acid soil, Alkaline soil. Acidity and alkalinity describe one aspect of the soil's chemical reaction: the concentration of hydrogen ions (an ion is an electrically charged atom or molecule). The relative concentration of hydrogen ions is represented by the symbol pH followed by a number. A pH of 7 means that the soil is neutral, neither acid nor alkaline. A pH below 7 indicates acidity, above 7 indicates alkalinity.

Many plants will grow well over a range of pH from slightly acid to slightly alkaline. Some garden favorites are more particular; usually they need an acid soil (most rhododendrons, azaleas, heathers, for example). Soils in areas with high rainfall tend to be acid. Areas where rainfall is light tend to have alkaline soils. For more information, see page 5.

Actual (as in actual nitrogen). Sometimes we recommend a certain amount of actual nitrogen; to calculate it, multiply the total weight of fertilizer by the percentage of the particular nutrient. A 25-pound bag of fertilizer that contains 5 percent nitrogen will yield 1 1/4 pounds actual nitrogen (25 pounds × .05 = 1.25 pounds). The same formula will allow you to calculate actual phosphorus or potash. It will also allow you to calculate the real nutritive value of a given fertilizer.

Alkaline soil. See **Acid soil.**

Annual. A plant that completes its life cycle in a year or less. Seed germinates and the plant grows, blooms, sets seed, and dies—all in one growing season. Examples are marigolds and zinnias. The phrase "grow as an annual" or "treat as an annual" means to set out a plant in spring after the last frost, enjoy it from spring through autumn, and pull it out or let the frosts kill it at the end of the year. (Some plants that desert gardeners treat as annuals are planted in autumn, grow and bloom during winter and spring, and then are killed by summer heat.) The plant may normally live through more than one season in a milder climate.

Backfill. Soil that's returned to a planting hole after a plant's roots have been positioned. Sometimes backfill is simply the soil dug out to create the planting hole; more often it is mixed with some organic soil amendments to improve its texture.

Balled and burlapped (sometimes abbreviated B and B). Shrubs and trees with a large *ball* of soil around the roots, wrapped in *burlap* to hold the soil together; sold at nurseries from late autumn to early spring. Usually these are plants that cannot be offered **Bare root.**

Bare root. Deciduous shrubs and trees, as well as some perennials, with all soil removed from their roots; sold in winter and early spring. These are dormant plants dug from growing fields, trimmed and freed of soil, and then protected against drying out.

Biennial. A plant that completes its life cycle in two years. Two familiar biennials are foxglove and Canterbury bells. Typically you plant seeds in spring and set out the seedling plants in summer or fall. The plants bloom the following spring, then set seed and die.

Bolt. To grow too quickly to flowering stage at the expense of developing well otherwise. This happens most often when annual flowers and vegetables are set out too late in the year or when unseasonably hot weather rushes the growth.

Bonsai. A Japanese term for one of the fine arts of gardening: growing carefully trained, dwarfed plants in containers selected to harmonize with the plants. The objective is to create in miniature scale a tree or landscape; often the dwarfed trees take on the appearance of very old, gnarled specimens. To get the desired effect the bonsai craftsman meticulously wires and prunes branches, and trims roots.

Bracts. Modified leaves that may grow just below a flower or flower cluster (not all flowers have bracts). Usually bracts are green, but in some cases they are conspicuous and colorful, constituting what people regard as "flowers" (examples are bougainvillea, dogwood, and poinsettia).

Broadcast. To scatter seed by hand over the soil surface. The ground may be a prepared surface, as for a lawn, or uncultivated, as in scattering wildflower seed.

Broad-leafed The phrase "broad-leafed evergreen" refers to a plant that has green foliage all year but is not an evergreen **Conifer** such as a juniper, with needlelike or scalelike foliage. A broad-leafed weed is any weed that is not a grass.

Bud. This word has several meanings. A flower bud is one that develops into a blossom. A growth bud may be at the tip of a stem (*terminal*) or along the sides of a stem (*lateral*); these buds will produce new leafy growth. Finally, *to bud* a plant is to propagate by a process similar to grafting (see pages 77–78).

Bulb. In everyday conversation, any plant that grows from a thickened underground structure is referred to as a "bulb." But a true bulb is one particular type of underground stem. (Others defined in this glossary are **Corm, Rhizome, Tuber,** and **Tuberous root.**) The true bulb is more or less rounded and composed of fleshy scales (actually modified leaves) that store food and protect the developing plant inside. The outer scales dry to form a papery covering. Slice an onion in half from top to bottom to see a typical example.

Caliche. A deposit of calcium carbonate (lime) beneath the soil surface. A soil condition found in some areas of the arid Southwest. For help in dealing with it, see "Shallow soil" (page 5).

Calyx. See *Sepal* under **Flower parts.**

Cambium layer. The layer just inside a plant's bark or outer "skin" is called the cambium.

Catkin. A slender, spikelike, and often drooping flower cluster. Catkins are either male or female: in some plants the male catkins are borne on one individual plant, the female on another (cottonwoods, willows); in other plants, both male and female catkins may be produced on each individual plant (alders, birches).

Chilling requirements. Many plants require certain amounts of cold weather in order to produce flowers and fruit, or even to leaf out properly. Some examples are cherries, lilacs, and peonies. If your winter climate is warm, ask at your local nursery for advice before planting such plants. Sometimes varieties exist that will grow well in warm areas.

Chlorosis. When a leaf looks yellower than it should (especially between the leaf veins), it often is chlorotic or suffering from *chlorosis*. Frequently chlorosis is caused by a plant's inability to obtain the iron it needs to produce green coloring. For one way to correct this solution, see **Iron chelate.**

Complete fertilizer. Any plant food that contains all three of the primary nutrient elements—nitrogen, phosphorus, potassium. Some complete fertilizers are organic. Chemical fertilizers come in dry, liquid, and tablet form.

Composite family (Compositae). The enormous family of plants that includes all the flowers known as daisies. What appears to be an individual flower actually is many small flowers tightly grouped into a head and surrounded by **Bracts** that form a cup *(involucre)*. A typical daisy is composed of two kinds of flowers: *disk flowers* are the small tubular flowers that usually are tightly packed together to form the round, cushionlike center of a daisy; *ray flowers* are those that appear to be petals (each "petal" is an individual ray flower) surrounding the central disk flowers. Some composites have disk flowers only (chamomile and santolina, for example); others, such as most dahlias, marigolds, and zinnias, have blossoms that consist only of ray flowers.

Composite family — Disk flowers, Ray flower, Disk, Bracts

Conifer. Plants such as juniper, cypress, fir, and pine that are sometimes called evergreens. Several are not green all year round, but all produce seeds in a conelike structure. Leaves on most are narrow and needlelike or tiny and scalelike.

Conservatory. Originally a greenhouse for displaying rather than growing plants; now simply a fancy greenhouse.

Corm. Technically, a thickened underground stem capable of producing roots, leaves, and flowers during the growing season. Gladiolus and crocus are two familiar plants that grow from corms. A corm differs from a bulb in that food is stored in the solid center tissue, whereas in bulbs food is stored in scales. See also **Bulb** and pages 44–45.

Corolla. See *Petal* under **Flower parts.**

Crown. Portion of a plant at the juncture of the root and stem or trunk. Sensitive to rotting if kept too moist.

Cultivate. To break up the soil surface around plants, removing weeds as you go. The resulting rough surface allows air to circulate and helps retain moisture.

Cuttings. Portions of stem or root, sometimes called "slips," that can be induced to form roots and develop into new plants. A more complete description is on pages 70–72.

Daisy flower. See **Composite family.**

Damping off. Plant disease, caused by fungi in the soil, that makes small seedlings rot, wilt, or fall over and die, just before or soon after they break through the soil.

Deciduous. Any plant that sheds all of its leaves at one time each year (usually in autumn). Some desert plants drop their leaves in summer to protect themselves from too much heat.

Defoliation. Unnatural loss of a plant's leaves, usually to the detriment of the plant's health. May result from high winds that strip foliage away, intense heat (especially if accompanied by wind) that critically shrivels or wilts leaves, drought, unusually early or late frosts that strike a plant still in active growth, or insects or disease.

Dieback. Death of a plant's stems, beginning at the tips, for a part of their length. Causes are various: not enough water; nutrient deficiency; plant not adapted to climate in which it is growing; severe insect, mite, or disease injury.

Disk flower. See **Composite family.**

Dividing. Easiest way to increase perennials, bulbs, and shrubs that form clumps of stems with rooted bases. Procedural information is on pages 67–69.

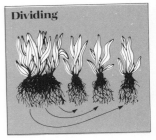

Dividing

Double flower. A flower where the petals are numerous and clustered so that the center is covered by petals. Most hybrid roses are double.

Drainage. Movement of water through the soil in a plant's root area. When this happens quickly, the drainage is "good," "fast," or the soil is "well drained"; when it happens slowly the drainage is said to be "slow," "bad," or soil is "poorly drained." For plants to grow, water must pass through soil. Plant roots need oxygen as well as water, and soil that remains saturated deprives roots of necessary oxygen. Fast drainage (water disappears from a shrub planting hole in 10 minutes or less) is typical of sandy soils; slow drainage (water still remains in planting hole after an hour) is found in clay soils and where hardpan exists. Refer to pages 6–9 for more information.

Drip line. The circle that you would draw on the soil around a plant directly under its outermost branch tips. Rainwater tends to drip from the tree at this point. The term is used in connection with feeding, watering, and grading around existing plants. Roots are concentrated here.

Drip line

Dust (noun or verb). A chemical product in the form of extremely fine powder, used to control insects or disease organisms. You apply by blowing the powder from a special applicator (sometimes the container is the applicator) in windless weather. It forms a cloud that settles on the plant. Since it requires no mixing or water it is convenient to use; however, you never should try to apply it in windy weather.

Epiphyte. Plant that grows on another plant for support but receives no nourishment from the host plant. Familiar examples are cattleya orchids and staghorn ferns. Often mistakenly called *parasites*; true parasites steal nourishment from the host.

Espalier. Tree or shrub trained so that its branches grow in a flat pattern—against a wall or fence, on a trellis, along horizontal wires. Espaliers may be formal and geometric, or informal.

Established. Established plant is one that's firmly rooted and is producing a good growth of leaves. Remember that an established container plant, such as one you buy from a nursery, must have time to reestablish itself after you transplant it.

Evergreen. A plant that never loses all of its leaves at the same time. Examples are pines, citrus, rhododendrons, and agapanthus. The term is often used as if it meant only **Conifers.**

Everlastings. Flowers that hold their shape and color when dried.

Eye. Usually, an undeveloped bud on a tuber, which will sprout after the tuber is planted. Common potatoes have eyes in slight depressions over their surfaces. The word may also refer to any leaf bud that is completely undeveloped, such as those at the joints of a new hardwood cutting.

Fertilize. In popular usage, this word has two definitions: to fertilize a flower is to apply pollen (the male element) to a flower's pistil (the female element) for the purpose of setting seed. See **Pollination.** To fertilize a plant is to apply nutrients (plant food, usually referred to as fertilizer).

Flower parts. Parts are listed from the outermost cover to the center of the flower.

Bract. Modified leaflike structure that grows below a flower cluster or encircles a flower. Can be more striking than the flower. The white cone of a calla is a bract. Not all flowers have bracts.

Sepal. The outer circle of flower parts; for example, the green covering of a rosebud. Sepals may be colored as well as green. If they are united, the structure is called a calyx.

Petal. The second circle of flower parts. If petals are joined, the structure is called a corolla. The corolla may flare, as with petunias; or it may be bell or tube-shaped, as with various campanulas.

Segments. Lilies and tulips show no difference between sepals and petals, so both are called segments.

Spurs. Projections from the rear of the flowers, arising from either sepals or petals. Columbine has spurs.

Stamens. Parts of the central flower that produce pollen. Stamens are usually fragile stalks with pollen-covered swellings at the top. The stalks are filaments, the swellings anthers.

Pistil. The central part of the flower. It is often visible as a stalklike tube with a moist or sticky end. The tube is the style and the end is the stigma. At the stem end of the style is the ovary, the part that may produce seed and fruit.

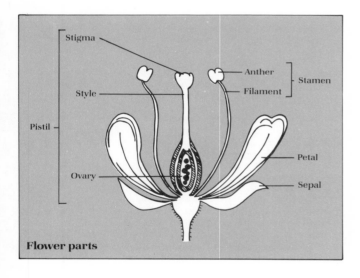

Flower parts

Forcing. Causing a plant to grow or bloom more rapidly or earlier than normal. Forcing may require extra heat, controlled light, or other special techniques.

Formal. A term meaning regular, rigid, and geometric. In gardening, it is variously applied to flowers, methods of training, and styles of garden design. A formal double flower, as in some camellias, consists of layers of regularly overlapping petals. Examples of formal plant training are rigidly and geometrically structured espaliers and evenly clipped hedges. Formal gardens are those laid out in precise geometric patterns, often containing formal hedges and espaliers.

Foundation plant. Originally a plant used to hide the foundation of a house. Since many of today's homes lack high or even visible foundations, the term has come to mean any shrub you plant near the house walls.

Friable soil. Easily crumbed soil that's ready for planting. To test for friability, ball up a fistful of soil. If compressed soil stays balled, it's too wet to dig and probably too heavy. If it's just dry enough to crumble, the soil is friable.

Frond. In the strictest sense, refers to the foliage of ferns, but the word is sometimes used to designate any foliage that looks fernlike, as well as the featherlike leaves of many palms.

Genus. See **Plant classification.**

Girdling. The choking of a branch by a wire, rope, or other inflexible material. It occurs most often in woody plants that have been tightly tied to a stake or support. As the tied limb increases in girth, the tie fails to expand in diameter and cuts off supplies of nutrients and water to the part of the plant above the tie; if girdling goes unnoticed, the part of the plant above the constriction will die.

Grafting. Method of plant propagation in which a section of one plant (called the *scion*) is inserted into a branch of another plant (the *stock*). Procedural information is on pages 74–76.

Ground bark. The bark of trees that's been ground up or shredded for use as a mulch or soil amendment. It may have other names in some areas.

Harden off. To adapt a plant that's been grown in a greenhouse, indoors, or under protective shelter to full outdoor exposure. Expose the plant, over a week or more, to increasing intervals of time outdoors, so that when you plant it out in the garden it can make the transition with a minimum of shock.

Hardy. A term describing a plant's resistance to, or tolerance of, frost or freezing temperatures (as in "hardy to −20°F"). The word does not mean tough, pest resistant, or disease resistant. A half-hardy plant is hardy in a given situation in normal years, but subject to freezing in coldest winters.

Heading back. A pruning term for cutting a branch back to a bud or side branch to change the direction of growth or force bushiness.

Heavy soil. Dense soil made up of extremely fine particles packed closely together. The term is used interchangeably with clay and adobe. See pages 6–7.

Heeling in. Temporary storage of certain plants by burying the roots in soil or sawdust. You might heel in bare root trees for a few days while waiting to plant; or you might lift bulbs while leaves are still green, then heel them in until the leaves die and you can store the bulbs.

Heeling in

Herbaceous. A term describing a plant with soft (nonwoody) tissues. In the strictest sense it refers to plants that die to the ground each year and regrow stems the following growing season. In the broadest sense it refers to any nonwoody plant—annual, perennial, or bulb.

Honeydew. A sticky, sweet substance produced by aphids and related insects. It may drip from trees, leaving sticky dirt on paving or cars underneath, and it sometimes supports the growth of a black fungus that spoils the looks of a plant.

Humus. Soft brown or black substance formed by vegetable matter in the last stages of decomposition.

Hybrid. See **Plant classification.**

Iron chelate (pronounced *key-late*). A compound containing iron in a form that plants can easily use. (See Chlorosis, page 5.)

Lath. In gardening, any overhead plant-protecting structure (originally a roof of spaced laths) that reduces the amount of sunlight that shines on plants beneath or protects them from frost.

Layering. A method of propagating plants by which you root a branch while it's still attached to the plant. See page 73.

Leaching. Pouring water through soil to dissolve and carry away soluble minerals that might otherwise damage plants. To leach, water slowly for a long time, or set containers in water and let soak. Leaching will also wash away nitrogen compounds that plants need, so fertilize after leaching, not before.

Leader. In a single-trunked shrub or tree, the central, upward-growing stem.

Leaflet. A completely separated division of a leaf. Leaflets may be arranged like the fingers of a hand (palmate) or like the divisions of a feather (pinnate).

Leaf mold. Partially decomposed leaves that can be dug into the soil as an organic amendment. Most familiar is oak leaf mold.

Leaf scar. Rounded or crescent-shaped mark on a branch, indicating where a leaf stalk once was attached.

Light soil. An imprecise term referring to soil composed of relatively large particles loosely packed together. Opposite of **Heavy soil;** synonymous with sandy (see pages 6–7).

Loam. Soil (often dark colored) that is rich in organic material, does not compact easily, and drains well after watering.

Mulch. Any loose, usually organic material placed over the soil, such as ground bark, sawdust, straw, or leaves. The process of applying such materials is called *mulching*. A mulch can do any of these tasks: reduce evaporation of moisture from soil; reduce or prevent weed growth; insulate soil from extreme or rapid changes of temperature; prevent mud from splashing onto foliage and other surfaces; protect falling fruit from injury; or make a garden bed look tidy.

Naturalize. To plant out randomly, without precise pattern, and leave in place to spread at will. Some plants have the capability to naturalize, meaning they can spread or reseed themselves, growing as wildflowers.

Node. A joint along a plant stem where a leaf or branch may grow. The part between joints is the internode.

Node

Node

Internode

Nodes

Offset. A small new plant growing at the end of a short stem sent out from the base of a mature perennial. Familiar examples are hen and chicks and strawberry. Also see **Stolon.**

Organic. In gardening, a term referring to any material that was once alive or that comes from a living creature. Sawdust, compost, bone meal, and guano are organic; perlite and ammonium sulfate are inorganic. In the term "organic gardening," organic refers to gardening without chemical sprays or manufactured fertilizers.

Parasite. See **Epiphyte.**

Peat moss. Highly water-retentive, spongy organic soil amendment—the partially decomposed remains of any of several mosses. It is somewhat acid in reaction, adding to soil acidity.

Perennial. A nonwoody plant that lives for more than two years. Frequently the word is used to mean a plant in which the top growth dies down each winter and regrows the following spring, but some perennials keep their leaves all year.

Perlite. A mineral expanded by heating to form white, very light-weight, porous granules useful in container soil mixes for retaining moisture and air.

Petal. See **Flower parts.**

Pinching. Removing the tips of twigs and branches to force bushiness (see page 113). Called pinching because you use your thumb and forefinger rather than a tool.

Pistil. See **Flower parts.**

Plant classification. Botanists (and other scientists) use a standard system for grouping and naming living creatures. This system of names can be useful to an amateur gardener, since a single common name often refers to a number of different plants. The terms below are those most useful to a gardener.

Family. Every member of a family shares some characteristics, although individual plants may look quite different. In the rose family are such plants as cherries, pyracantha, roses, and strawberries. The lily family includes onions, tiger lilies, and yucca plants. Sometimes many members of the same family are prone to the same disease.

Genus. The plural is *genera.* The first word in a botanical name is the genus to which the plant belongs, for example *Rosa, Prunus, Viola.* Occasionally this name is also the common name, as with anemone or zinnia.

Species. A genus often contains many close relatives, or species. A species is a single kind of plant, although there may be differences in appearance within a species. For example, *Viola odorata* is only the sweet violet, although it has a number of flower colors and forms. *Viola cornuta* is the viola, while *Viola tricolor* is the Johnny-jump-up.

Variety, subspecies. A variety is some special form of a species. It is almost like other plants of its species, but may have a different flower or plant shape.

Strain. Many popular annuals and some perennials are sold as strains, such as State Fair zinnias. Plants in a strain usually share similar growth characteristics but are variable in some way—usually in flower color.

Hybrid. A result of a cross between two species or varieties or strains—or even between two plants belonging to different genera.

Pleaching. A method of training plant growth so that branches are interwoven and plaited together to form a hedge or arbor. Subsequent pruning merely keeps a neat, rather formal pattern.

Pollarding. A pruning style in which the main limbs of a young tree are drastically cut back to short lengths. Each dormant season following, the growth from these branch stubs is cut back to one or two buds. In time, branch ends become large and knobby. The result is a compact, leafy dome during the growing season and a somewhat grotesque branch structure during the dormant months. London plane tree (*Platanus acerifolia*) is most often pollarded.

Pollination. Transfer of pollen from flower stamens to pistils for development of fruit and seeds. This straightforward process is complicated for a home gardener by the fact that some plants have male and female flowers on separate individuals (holly), or separate male and female flowers on the same plant (cucumber), or mixed flowers with pollen that is useless on plants of the same variety (sweet cherries). Usually pollination is accomplished by natural means— wind, insects, self-pollination—though the gardener can do it.

Potbound. See **Rootbound.**

Pseudobulb. A thickened, above-ground modified stem, found in some orchids such as *Cymbidium*, that serves as a storage organ for nutrients.

Ray flower. See **Composite family.**

Rhizome. A thickened, modified stem that grows horizontally along or under the soil surface. It may be long and slender, as in some lawn grasses, or thick and fleshy, as in many irises.

Pseudobulb

Pseudobulb

Rock garden. Usually a manmade landscape, often on sloping ground, that contains natural-appearing rock outcrops and rocky soil surfaces. Plants grown in a rock garden are generally low-growing, spreading or mat-forming types that conform to the rocky terrain. A special type of rock garden is the alpine garden, in which plants from high altitudes are grown in a replica of their native setting. Many favorite rock garden plants require fast drainage and full sun, and are somewhat drought-tolerant plants.

Rootbound. A term used to describe a plant that has remained in a container for so long that the roots grow around it in a circle. Seriously rootbound plants are useless for planting in the garden since their roots will not grow normally. They may die or fail to grow, or they may blow over in the first good wind. Frequent repotting (see pages 22–23) will keep plants from becoming rootbound.

Rooting hormone. A powder containing growth hormones and sometimes certain vitamins. You dip the end of a cutting in rooting hormone before setting it in soil. The hormone stimulates root growth.

Rootstock. The part of a budded or grafted plant that furnishes the root system and sometimes part of the branch structure. **Understock** has the same meaning.

Runner. In common usage, an imprecise term referring to either **Offsets** or **Stolons.** A runner is actually a slender stem sent out from the bases of certain perennials, at the end of which an offset develops and a new plant grows.

Salinity. Gardeners use this word when speaking of an excess of salts in the soil. Frequently a buildup of salts occurs in semiarid regions, resulting from continued light watering with low-quality water containing sodium. In such regions, gardeners must periodically wash (leach) accumulated salts out of the plant root zone. High salinity can do great harm to many plants, causing leaves to scorch and turn yellow, and stunting plant growth.

Scree. Fragmented rocks and pebbles found in nature at the base of a cliff or around large rocks in a rocky landscape. Some gardeners create their own artificial scree as a place for growing choice alpine plants. Also see **Rock garden.**

Self-branching. A term describing certain annuals that produce numerous side growths and grow compactly without having to be pinched back.

Semidouble flower. A flower form having a few more than the basic minimum number of petals for its kind (see **Single flower**), but not so many petals that the stamens and pistils are obscured. (*Petal, stamen, and pistil* are defined under **Flower parts.**)

Sepal. See **Flower parts.**

Single flower. A flower with just a few petals (depending on the family the number varies). A single rose has five petals, a single poppy has four.

Species. See **Plant classification.**

Sphagnum. A moss with long fibers sold dry for various garden uses. Use it for lining wire fern baskets, for air layering, or in chopped form as a soil conditioner. Much of the peat moss sold by nurseries contains sphagnum moss.

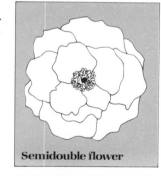

Semidouble flower

Single flower

Spike. A flowering stem on which flowers are directly attached (without any short stem to each flower) along the upper portion of its length. The flowers open in sequence, usually beginning at the bottom of the spike. Familiar examples are gladiolus and red-hot poker.

Spore. A simple type of reproductive cell capable of producing a new plant. Certain kinds of plants (such as algae, fungi, mosses, and ferns) reproduce by spores.

Spur. A specialized short twig on which blossoms and fruit grow on some fruit trees, particularly apples and cherries. Spurs are pruned selectively.

Spurs. Short and saclike or long and tubular projections from a flower (the columbine, *Aquilegia*, is a familiar example). Spurs can arise from either sepals or petals (see **Flower parts** for *sepal* and *petal* definitions).

Stamen. See **Flower parts.**

Standard. A plant that does not naturally grow as a tree but that is trained into a small treelike form, with a single, upright trunk topped by a rounded crown of foliage. The "tree rose" is the most familiar example of a standard.

Stolon. A stem that creeps along the surface of the ground, taking root at intervals and forming new plants where it roots (as opposed to **Offsets**, which may form at the ends of **Runners**). Bermuda and St. Augustine grasses spread by stolons.

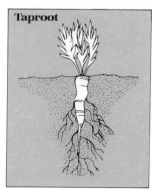

Stolon

Strain. See **Plant classification.**

Stress. Stress refers to the condition or conditions under which a plant is growing with danger to its health. Stress may result from lack of water, from too much heat, wind, or moisture, or from low temperatures. The stressful condition varies according to the particular plant and its needs.

Subshrub. A type of plant, usually under 3 feet high and with more or less woody stems, that's sometimes grown and used as a perennial, sometimes grown and used as a shrub. Examples of subshrubs are dusty miller and cushion bush.

Sucker. In a grafted or budded plant, sucker growth originates from the **Rootstock** rather than from the desired grafted or budded part of the plant. In trees, any strong vertical shoot growing from the main framework of trunk and branches is sometimes called a sucker, though the more proper term for such growth is *watersprout*.

Systemic. Any chemical that's absorbed into a plant's system, either to kill organisms that feed on the plant or to kill the plant itself. There are systemic insecticides, fungicides, and weed killers.

Taproot. Root resembling a carrot. Some plants that produce a taproot are dandelions and oak trees. It often grows very deeply into the soil if there is a lack of water near the surface

Tender. The opposite of hardy. That is, sensitive to cold weather, with low tolerance of freezing temperatures.

Thinning out. In pruning, the term means removing entire

Taproot

branches, either large or small ones, to make a plant or tree less dense. In speaking of seedlings or young plants, thinning out means removing enough plants so that those remaining have room to spread leaves and roots.

Topdress. To apply on the surface, usually referring to the spreading of an organic material such as ground bark or manure on the soil as a mulch. Sometimes to topdress means to apply manure or sewage sludge on a lawn as a low-grade fertilizer.

Topiary. The technique of pruning shrubs and trees into formalized shapes resembling such things as animals and geometrical figures. Sometimes inaccurately called "poodle pruning," which really describes only the sort of topiary work that produces puffs of growth.

Truss. A cluster of flowers, usually rather compact, at the end of a stem, branch, or stalk. The most familiar rhododendrons carry their flowers in trusses.

Tuber. Fat underground stem, from which a plant grows, that is similar to a **Rhizome** but is usually shorter and thicker, and doesn't lengthen greatly as it grows. The world's most famous tuber is the potato.

Tuberous root. Thickened underground food storage structure that's actually a root rather than a true tuber, which is a modified stem. Growth buds are in the old stems at the upper end of the root. The dahlia is a familiar example.

Underplanting. Planting one plant beneath another, such as a ground cover under a tree.

Understock. See **Rootstock.**

Variety. See **Plant classification.**

Vermiculite. A mineral (mica) that's heated and puffed up to form spongelike, lightweight granules useful in conditioning container soils. Vermiculite granules hold both water and air.

Watersprout. See **Sucker.**

Wettable powder. Finely ground pesticide that can be mixed in water and sprayed onto plants. Some kinds also can be dusted on, as described under **Dust**.

Whorls. Three or more leaves, branches, or flowers growing in a circle from a joint (node) on a stem or trunk.

Index

Boldface numbers indicate color illustrations.

A

Abelia, **34**
Acanthus, **41**
Acer palmatum, **36**
Achillea, **43**
Aeonium, **102**
Aesculus carnea, **37**
African daisy, **38**
African violet, **104**
Agapanthus, **41**
Agathaea, **41**
Agave, **103**
Ageratum, **38**
Air layering, 73
Ajuga, **47**
Albizia julibrissin, **37**
Alcea rosea, **39**
Aloe, **103**
Alyssum, **41**
Amelanchier laevis, **36**
Amendments, 6–7
Andromeda, **34**
Anemone, 26, **42**, **45**
Anethum graveolens, **99**
Anise, **98**
Annuals, **38–40**, 153
Anthriscus cerefolium, **98**
Antirrhinum majus, **40**
Ants, 122
Aphids, 123
Aphycus wasps, 130
Apple, **96**, 117
Apricot, **96**, 117
Aquatic plants, 27
Aquilegia, **42**
Arabis, **43**
Arbutus unedo, **36**
Artemisia dracunculus, **99**
Artichokes, **91**

Ash, 7
Asparagus, **91**
Asparagus fern, **105**
Aspidistra, **105**
Asplenium nidus, **105**
Aster, **38**, **41**
Astilbe, **41**
Aucuba, **34**
Aurinia saxatilis, **41**
Autumn color, 152
Autumn planting, 88
Azalea, 27, **34**, 70–71, **141**

B

Baby's breath, **38**, **41**, **143**
Baby's tears, **145**
Bachelor's button, **38**
Bacillus thuringiensis, 124
Background plants, 138–139
Balled and burlapped plants, 16, 18, 153
Balloon flower, **41**
Balsam, **38**
Barberry, **34**
Bare-root plants, 16, 17, 153
Bark, 153
Barrier plants, 138–139
Basil, **98**
Bats, 130
Beans, **91**
Bedding plants, 16
Bees, 150–151
Beetles, 123
Beets, **91**
Begonia, 26, **42**, **45**, 67, **105**
Bellis perennis, **42**
Beneficial animals, 130
Berberis, **34**
Bergenia, **41**
Bermuda grass, 63

Berries, 96–97
Betula pendula, **37**, **44**
Biennials, **38–40**, 153
Birch, **37**, **44**
Birds, 128–129, 130, 150–151
Bird's-nest fern, **105**
Blackberries, **97**
Bleeding heart, **41**
Blueberries, **97**
Bolt, 153
Borage, **98**
Borers, 123
Boston fern, **104**
Boston ivy, **48**, 114
Bottlebrush, **36**
Boxwood, **34**
Bradford pear, **37**
Broadcast, 64, 153
Broccoli, **91**
Brussels sprouts, **91**
Budding, 77–78
Buds, 110–111, 153
Bulbs, 16, **44–45**, 153
  dividing, 67
  planting, 26
Burnet, **98**
Butterflies, 150–151
Buxus, **34**

C

Cabbage, **91**
Cactus, 102–103
Calendula, **38**
California poppy, **38**
Calla, 26, **45**
Calliopsis, **38**
Callistemon citrinus, **36**
Callistephus chinensis, **38**
Camellia, 27, **34**, 127
Campanula, **41**

Campanula medium, **38**
Campsis, **48**
Candytuft, **38**, **41**
Canna, 26, **45**
Canterbury bells, **38**
Caraway, **98**
Carnation, **42**
Carrots, **91**
Carum carvi, **98**
Caterpillars, 123
Catharanthus roseus, **39**
Catnip, **98**
Cauliflower, **92**
Celery, **90**, **92**
Cell packs, 20–21
Celosia argentea, **39**
Centaurea cyanus, **38**
Cerastium tomentosum, **47**
Ceratostigma plumbaginoides, **43**, **47**
Cercidiphyllum japonicum, **37**
Cercis canadensis, **36**
Cereus, **103**
Chaenomeles, **35**
Chamaemelum nobile, **98**
Chamomile, **98**
Chard, **90**
Cherry, **96**, 117, 127
Cherry tomatoes, **92**
Chervil, **98**
Chickens, 130
Chilling requirement, 153
Chinese forget-me-not, **38**
Chinese pink, **39**
Chinese pistache, **37**
Chinese tallow, **152**
Chionanthus retusus, **36**
Chives, **90**, **99**
Chlorophytum comosum, **106**
Chlorosis, 5, 154

Chrysanthemum, **42**, **143**
Chrysanthemum coccineum, **43**
Chrysanthemum frutescens, **43**
Chrysanthemum maximum, **43**
Cineraria, **39**
Cissus rhombifolia, **105**
Citrus, 27, **96**
Clarkia, **39**
Cleome spinosa, **40**
Climbing rose, 115
Clytostoma, **48**
Cockscomb, **39**
Codiaeum variegatum, **105**
Codling moths, 122
Coldframes, 86–87
Coleus, **105**, **147**
Columbine, **42**, 69
Columnea, **105**
Compacted soil, 5, 51
Compost, 10, 12–13
Conifers, 111, 154
Consolida ambigua, **39**
Contact poisons, 124
Container plants
    bulbs as, 26
    in the house, 104–106
    vines as, 115
    watering, 57
Convallaria majalis, **42**
Coral bells, **42**, 69
Coreopsis, **42**
Coreopsis tinctoria, **38**
Coriander, **99**
Coriandrum sativum, **99**
Corm, 44, 154
Corn, **92**
Cornus florida, **36**
Cosmos, **38**, **39**
Cotoneaster, **34**, **47**
Cotyledon, **103**
Crabgrass, 63
Crape myrtle, **34**
Crassula, **102**
Crataegus phaenopyrum, **36**
Creeping Charlie, **104**, **105**
Creeping fig, **48**
Creeping St. Johnswort, **47**
Crocus, 26, **45**
Croton, **105**
Cucumbers, **92**
Cultivating, 8–9, 154
Cultivator, 133
Cutting back, 113
Cuttings, 70–72, 154
Cutworms, 123
Cynoglossum amabile, **38**

D
Daffodil, 26, **44**, **45**, 67
Dahlia, **45**, 67, 108
Damping off, 127, 154
Daylily, **42**, 68
Deer, 128–129
Defoliation, 154
Delphinium, **42**, 108
Diabrotica, 123
Dianthus, **42**
Dianthus barbatus, **40**
Dianthus caryophyllus, **42**
Dianthus chinensis, **39**
Dicentra spectabilis, **41**
Dichondra, 24, 46
Dieback, 154
Dieffenbachia, **104**
Digitalis purpurea, **39**
Dill, **99**
Dimorphotheca, **38**
Diospyros kaki, **37**
Disbudding, 113
Diseases, 126–127
Distictis, **48**
Dividing, 67, 68–69, 154
Dizygotheca elegantissima, **106**
Dogwood, **36**, **141**
Double-digging, 9

Dracaena, **105**
Drainage, 6–7, 154
Dramatic foliage, 146–147
Drip irrigation, 56
Drip line, 32, 51, 154
Ducks, 130
Dudleya, **102**
Dust pesticides, 124, 154
Dwarf periwinkle, **47**

E
Earwigs, 123, 130
Eastern redbud, **36**
Echeveria, **102**, **103**
Echinocactus, **103**
Echinopsis, **103**
Eggplant, **93**
Elaeagnus angustifolia, **36**
Elaeagnus pungens, **35**
English daisy, **42**
English ivy, **47**, **145**
English laurel, **34**
Eriobotrya japonica, **36**
Eschscholzia californica, **38**
Espalier, 118, 154
Eucalyptus polyanthemos, **37**
Euonymus, **34**, **47**
Euphorbia, **103**
Euphorbia lathyrus, 130
Exposures, planting for, 140–141

F
Fairy primrose, **39**
False dragonhead, **42**
Felicia amelloides, **41**
Fennel, **99**
Ferns, **145**
Fertilizer, 7, 29–32, 155
Fertilizing, 31, 32, 155
Ficus benjamina, **105**
Ficus pumila, **48**
Fiddleleaf fig, **105**
Fig, **96**
Firethorn, **34**
Flats, 20–21
Flats, heated, 70–71
Flies, 122
Flowering cherry, **37**
Flowering crabapple, **36**
Flowering plum, **36**
Flowering quince, **35**
Flowers, removing, 113
Foeniculum vulgare, **99**
Foliage plants, 146–147
Forget-me-not, **39**
Forsythia, **35**
Foxglove, **39**
Fragrant plants, 148–149
Freesia, 26, **45**
Fringe tree, **36**
Frogs, 130
Frost damage, 111
Frost protection, 82–83, 84, 86–87
Fruit, 96–97
Fruit trees, **96**, 113, 117
Fuchsia, **35**

G
Gaillardia, **39**, **42**
Galium odoratum, **99**
Gardenia, **35**
Garlic, **93**
Gazania, **42**, **47**
Geese, 130
Geranium, **42**
Gerbera jamesonii, **43**
Geum, **42**
Gladiolus, 26, **45**, 67, 108
Gloriosa daisy, **42**
Glossary, 153–157
Glossy privet, **37**
Godetia, **39**
Goldenrain, **37**
Gophers, 128, 129, 130

Grafting, 74–76, 155
Grape, **97**
Grape hyacinth, 26, **45**
Grape ivy, **105**
Grass cutter, 133
Grasses, 46
Grasshoppers, 123
Ground bark, 10, 155
Ground covers, **47**, 109
Ground squirrels, 128
Grubs, 122
Gunnera, **147**
Gymnocalycium, **102**
Gymnocladus dioica, **37**
Gypsophila elegans, **38**
Gypsophila paniculata, **41**

H
Halesia carolina, **36**
Hall's honeysuckle, **48**, 114
Hand casting, 31
Hand tools, 133
Hardwood cuttings, 72
Hardy, 44, 155
Haworthia, **103**
Heading back, 111, 155
Heat and cold, 79–88
Heat protection, 80, 85
Heavenly bamboo, **35**
Heavy loads, lifting, 134–135
Hedera helix, **47**
Hedges, 27, 111, 138–139
Hedge shears, 112
Helianthus annuus, **40**
Helichrysum bracteatum, **40**
Heliotrope, **42**
Hemerocallis, **42**
Herbs, 98–99
Heuchera sanguinea, **42**
Hoeing, 60
Hoes, 61, 132–133
Holly, **35**
Hollyhock, **39**
Hopper spreader, 31
Hoses, 54–55, 136
Hosta, **43**
Hotbeds, 86–87
Hot-weather planting, 85
Houseflies, 122
House plants, **104–106**
Howea palm, **106**
Hummingbirds, 130
Hyacinth, 26, **45**
Hydrangea, **35**
Hypericum calycinum, **47**

I
Iberis amara, **38**
Iberis sempervirens, **41**
Iberis umbellata, **38**
Iceland poppy, **39**
Ice plant, **47**
Ilex, **35**
Impatiens, **39**, **145**
Impatiens balsamina, **38**
India hawthorn, **35**
Insects, 120–125, 130
Iris, 26, **45**, 67
Iron chelate, 5, 155
Italian parsley, **98**
Ivy, 115
Ivy geranium, **104**

J
Jacaranda, **37**
Japanese anemone, **42**
Japanese maple, **36**
Japanese privet, **35**
Japanese snowdrop, **37**
Japanese spurge, **47**
Japanese tree lilac, **36**
Jasmine, 115
Juniper, **35**, **47**

K
Kalanchoe, **102**, **103**
Kale, **93**
Katsura, **37**
Kentucky coffee tree, **37**
Kniphofia, **42**
Koelreuteria paniculata, **37**
Kohlrabi, **93**

L
Lacewings, 130
Ladybugs, 130
Lagerstroemia indica, **34**
Lampranthus, **47**
Larkspur, **39**
Lath, 80–81, 155
Laurus nobilis, **99**
Lawn
    fertilizing, 31
    planting, 24–25
    sprinkler system, 53
    weeds, 63
Lawn grasses, 46
Lawn moths, 122
Layering, 73, 156
Leaf cuttings, 72
Leafhoppers, 123
Leaf miners, 122
Leeks, **93**
Lemaireocereus, **103**
Lemon balm, **99**
Lemon thyme, **98**
Lettuce, **90**, **93**
Leucojum, **45**
Ligustrum japonicum, **35**
Ligustrum lucidum, **37**
Lilac, **35**
Lily, 26, **45**, **147**
Lily-of-the-valley, **42**
Lime sulfur, 124
Limonium, **43**, **46**
Linum grandiflorum 'Rubrum', **40**
Liquidambar, **37**, **152**
Liquid fertilizing, 31
Lithops, **103**
Little-leaf linden, **37**
Lizards, 130
Lobelia, **39**, **141**
Lobularia maritima, **40**
Lonicera japonica 'Halliana', **48**
Loppers, 112
Loquat, **36**
Lupine, **43**
Lycoris, **45**

M
Madagascar periwinkle, **39**
Magnolia, **36**
Malus 'Katherine', **36**
Mantids, 130
Manure, 10
Maranta leuconeura, **106**
Marguerite, **43**
Marigold, **39**, **46**, **98**, **143**
Marjoram, **98**, **99**
Matthiola incana, **40**
Mattock, 133
Mealybugs, 123
Melissa officinalis, **99**
Melons, **93**
Metaldehyde, 124
Mexican sunflower, **39**
Mice, 128
Mimulus, **39**
Mites, 123, 130
Mock orange, **35**
Moles, 128–129
Mondo grass, **47**
Monstera deliciosa, **106**
Morning glory, 114
Mountain ash, **37**
Mulch, 52, 60–61. 156
Muscari, **45**
Myosotis sylvatica, **39**

N

Nandina, **35**, **152**
Narcissus, 26, **44**, **45**
Nasturtium, **39**
Nectarine, **96**, 117
Nemesia, **40**, **141**
Nepeta cataria, **98**
Nephrolepis exaltata 'Bostoniensis', **104**
Nerium oleander, **35**
Nicotiana, **38**, **40**
Nitrogen, 7, 153
Nursery shopping, 16
Nyssa sylvatica, **37**

O

Oak moths, 123
Ocimum, **98**
Oleander, **35**
Onions, **93**
Opuntia, **102**
Organic, 6–7, 156
    fertilizers, 30
    mulches, 52
    soil amendments, 6–7
Origanum majorana, **98**, **99**

P

Pachysandra terminalis, **47**
Paeonia, **43**
Pagoda tree, **37**
Pansy, **40**
Papaver nudicaule, **39**
Papaver rhoeas, **40**
Parking strips, 142–143
Parrotia persica, **37**
Parsley, **90**, **99**
Parsnips, **94**
Parthenocissus quinquefolia, **48**
Parthenocissus tricuspidata, **48**
Passiflora, **48**
Passion vine, **48**, 114
Peach, **96**, 117, 127
Pear, **96**, 117
Peas, **94**
Peat moss, 10, 156
Peat pots, 20
Pelargonium, **42**, **43**
Penstemon, **43**
Peony, **43**
Peperomia, **106**
Peppers, **94**
Perennials, **41–43**, 68–69, 156
Perlite, 6, 156
Persian parrotia, **37**
Persimmon, **37**
Pest control, 119–125, 128–130
Petunia, **40**, **101**
Philadelphus, **35**
Philodendron, **106**
Phlox, **38**, **40**, **43**
Photinia, **35**
Physostegia virginiana, **42**
Phytoseiulus persimilis, 130
Pieris japonica, **34**
Piggy-back plant, **106**
Pillbugs, 130
Pimpinella anisum, **98**
Pinching, 113, 156
Pincushion flower, **40**
Pistache, **152**
Pistacia chinensis, **37**
Pittosporum, **35**
Plantain lily, **43**
Planting, 15–28
    in autumn, 88
    in hot weather, 85
    seeds, 65, 66
Plant selection, 16
Platycodon grandiflorus, **41**
Plectranthus, **105**
Plugs, 24
Plum, **96**, 117
Plumbago, **43**

Poppies, **141**
Portulaca, **40**
Potatoes, **94**
Poterium sanguisorba, **98**
Pothos, **106**
Power tiller, 8, 9
Prayer plant, **106**
Praying mantis, 130
Primula malacoides, **39**
Propagating plants, 64–78
Prune, **96**
Pruning, 110–111, 112, 116, 117
Prunus blireiana, **36**
Prunus laurocerasus, **34**
Prunus serrulata 'Kanzan', **37**
Pumpkins, **94**
Pyracantha, **34**
Pyrus calleryana, **152**
Pyrus calleryana 'Bradford', **37**

Q

Quack grass, 63

R

Rabbits, 128
Radishes, **94**
Raised beds, 14
Rakes, 133
Ranunculus, 26, **45**
Raphidophora aurea, **106**
Raphiolepis indica, **35**
Raspberries, **97**
Red horsechestnut, **37**
Repotting, 22–23
Retaining walls, 14
Rhizome, 44, 156
Rhododendrons, 27, **34**, **35**, **149**
Rhubarb, **94**
Rockcress, **43**
Rock garden, 157
Rodents, 128–129
Rootbound, 19, 22–23, 157
Root cuttings, 72
Rooting hormone, 70, 157
Root-pruning, 22–23
Roots, 51
Rootstock, 74, 157
Rosemary, **99**
Roses, 17, 84, **100–101**, 116, **150**
Rototiller, 8, 9
Rudbeckia hirta, **42**
Russian olive, **36**
Rutabagas, **95**

S

Sage, **99**
St. Johnswort, **47**
Saintpaulia ionantha, **104**
Salamanders, 130
Saline soil, 5, 7, 157
Salpiglossis, **40**
Salvia, **38**
Salvia officinalis, **99**
Salvia splendens, **40**
Satureja, **99**
Savory, **99**
Sawdust, 10
Scabiosa atropurpurea, **40**
Scale, 122
Scarlet flax, **40**
Scarlet sage, **40**
Schefflera, **106**
Scotch moss, **47**, **145**
Sea lavender, **43**
Sedum, **43**, **102**, **103**
Seeds, 16, 64–66
Sempervivum, **103**
Senecio hybridus, **39**
Shadblow, **36**
Shade, 51, 60, 61, 80–81, 85, 144–145
Shade-tolerant plants, 144–145
Shasta daisy, **43**
Shears, 112

Shirley poppy, **40**
Shovel, 8, 132
Shrews, 130
Shrubs, 28, **34–35**
Silk tree, **37**
Silver bell, **36**
Silver dollar gum, **37**
Silverberry, **35**
Slugs, 122, 130
Snails, 122
Snapdragon, **40**
Snowdrop, 26, **45**
Snowflake, 26, **45**
Snow-in-summer, **47**
Softwood cuttings, 70–71
Soil, 4–14, 50, 51
Soil mealybugs, 122
Sophora japonica, **37**
Sorbus aucuparia, **37**
Sour gum, **37**
Spade, 8, 132
Spading forks, 132
Spathiphyllum, **106**
Spider flower, **40**
Spider lily, 26, **45**
Spider plant, **104**, **106**
Spiders, 130
Spinach, **94**
Spiraea, **35**
Spittle bugs, 122
Split-leaf philodendron, **104**, **106**
Sprigs, 24
Sprinklers, 53, 54–55
Spur, 117, 157
Squash, **90**, **95**
Squirrels, 128
Staking, 108–109
Standard, 101, 157
Stapelia, **103**
Star jasmine, **48**, **143**
Statice, **46**
Stink beetles, 130
Stock, **40**
Stolons, 24, 157
Strawberries, **97**
Strawberry tree, **36**
Strawflower, **40**
Styrax japonicus, **37**
Subsoil irrigator, 55
Succulents, **102–103**
Suckers, 113, 157
Sunflower, **40**
Sunshades, 80–81
Sweet alyssum, **38**, **40**
Sweet bay, **99**
Sweet gum, **37**
Sweet pea, 114
Sweet William, **40**
Sweet woodruff, **99**
Swiss chard, **95**
Syringa, **35**
Syringa reticulata, **36**

T

Tagetes, **39**, **46**, **98**
Taproot, 69, 157
Tarragon, **99**
Tender, 44, 157
Thinning fruit, 113
Thinning out, 111, 157
Threadleaf false aralia, **106**
Thrips, 123
Thyme, **98**, **99**
Tilia cordata, **37**
Tilling soil, 8, 9
Tithonia rotundifolia, **39**
Toads, 130
Tolmiea menziesii, **106**
Tomatoes, **92**, **95**, 109
Tools, 112, 131–136
Tortoise, 130
Trachelospermum jasminoides, **48**
Tradescantia, **43**, **106**

Tradescantia, **43**, **106**
Transplanting, 20–23, 28
Transvaal daisy, **43**
Trees, **36–37**
    anchoring, 109
    fertilizing, 32
    staking, 109
    transplanting, 28
Trellis, 114, 115
Tropaeolum majus, **39**
Trowel, 133
Trumpet vine, **48**
Tuber, 44, 158
Tuberous begonia, 26, **45**, 67
Tulip, 26, **45**
Turnips, **95**
Turtle, 130
Tying plants, 108–109

V

Vegetables, 58, **90–95**
Verbena, **40**
Vermiculite, 6, 158
Viburnum, **35**
Vinca minor, **47**
Vines, **48**, 114–115
Viola, **40**
Viola odorata, **43**
Violet, **43**
Virginia creeper, **48**, 114
Voles, 128

W

Wandering Jew, **104**, **106**
Washington thorn, **36**
Water, Conserving, 50–51
Watering, 49–58
Water plants, 27
Watsonia, 26, **45**
Weed cutter, 133
Weeding, 52, 59–63
Weeding tools, 61, 133
Weed killers, 62
Weeds, 63, 130
Weevils, 123
Weigela, **35**
White birch, **37**
Whiteflies, 123, 130
Wind, 51
Windflower, **45**
Winter protection, 82–83, 84, 86–87
Wireworms, 123
Wisteria, **48**

Y

Yarrow, **43**
Yucca, **103**

Z

Zantedeschia, **45**
Zephyr flower, 26, **45**
Zinnia, **40**, **143**, **151**
Zucchini, **90**

Photographers

William Aplin: 90 left, 152. **James Carey:** 151. **Glenn Christiansen:** 44, 48, 150. **Ells Marugg:** 38, 46, 92, 98, 101, 102, 141, 143, 147 top. **Stephen W. Marley:** 97, 100. **Jack McDowell:** 47. **Don Normark:** 149. **Norman A. Plate:** 95, 104. **Bill Ross:** 145, 147 bottom. **Darrow M. Watt:** 90 right.